To my parents and parents-in-law

献给

我的父亲母亲、公公婆婆

深圳大学学术著作出版基金资助
Subsidized by the Shenzhen University Foundation for the Production of Scholarly Monographs

功能语言学论丛

Code-switching as Social Practice: A Systemic Functional Approach to the Chinese/English Code-switching in Chinese Newspapers

作为社会实践的语码转换

——中文报章汉英语码转换的系统功能语言学研究

王　瑾◎著

中山大学出版社
·广州·

图书在版编目(CIP)数据

作为社会实践的语码转换:中文报章汉英语码转换的系统功能语言学研究 = Code-switching as Social Practice: A Systemic Functional Approach to the Chinese/English Code-switching in Chinese Newspapers:英文/王瑾著.—广州:中山大学出版社,2013.9
(功能语言学论丛)
ISBN 978-7-306-04074-9

Ⅰ.①作…　Ⅱ.①王…　Ⅲ.①英语—汉语—转换(语言学)—研究—英文　Ⅳ.①H314②H14

中国版本图书馆 CIP 数据核字 (2011) 第 237892 号

出 版 人: **徐　劲**
策划编辑: 熊锡源
责任编辑: 熊锡源
封面设计: 林绵华
责任校对: 刘学谦
责任技编: 何雅涛
出版发行: 中山大学出版社
电　　话: 编辑部 020-84111996, 84111997, 84113349, 84110779
　　　　　发行部 020-84111998, 84111981, 84111160
地　　址: 广州市新港西路 135 号
邮　　编: 510275　　传　真: 020-84036565
网　　址: http://www.zsup.com.cn
　　　　　E-mail: zdcbs@mail.sysu.edu.cn
印 刷 者: 广州中大印刷有限公司
规　　格: 880mm×1230mm　1/32　7.25 印张　248 千字
版次印次: 2013 年 9 月第 1 版　2013 年 9 月第 1 次印刷
定　　价: 24.00 元

序

王瑾是我招收的博士生中第一个获得“硕博连读”资格的。事实上，王瑾进入中山大学外国语学院读大学时我就认得她，后来她在我的指导下完成了本科论文，免试推荐读硕士时我也是她的导师。在读博期间，她学习优秀，表现突出，获得2005年广东省南粤优秀研究生称号。知道她的《作为社会实践的语码转换——中文报章汉英语码转换的系统功能语言学研究》专著即将出版，我感到非常欣慰。对于王瑾这样优秀的学者，我可以说是看着她慢慢成长、渐渐成熟起来的。读书时，王瑾属于那种“根红苗正”、“优生优培”的学生；工作上，她属于“勤勤恳恳”、“踏踏实实”的老师；生活上，她“诚实待人”、“不卑不亢”。她既有信念，又有能力，同时还内心淡定，处理事情游刃有余。王瑾的这些优点也充分体现在她这本新著中。

这些年我一直关注王瑾的学术研究，这是因为，她的研究方向与我自己的研究属于一个领域，理论框架都主要是系统功能语言学，研究重点主要是“作为适用语言学的系统功能语言学”。她发表的多篇很有影响的文章都是把语言学理论应用于解决各种与语言有关的问题。我多次说过，从系统功能语言学视角看，语言研究离不开社会现实和社会实践，语言研究要为识解经验和社会实践服务；系统功能语言学者认为，理论是解决问题的资源，这就是为什么系统功能语言学也是“适用语言学”。正如系统功能语言学创始人 M. A. K. Halliday 所多次强调的，系统功能语言学可以看作是“以（解决）问题为导向”（problem-oriented）的理论；因此，这个理论的设计与发现问题和解决问题紧密联系在一起；这里所说的问题，除了语言本身的问题外，还指语言理论以外的问题，包括人们在社会实践中所碰到的与语言和语言使用有关的问题。

王瑾的这本新著把“语码转换”看作是社会实践的表现。语码转换涉及双语与语言接触，是典型的社会语言学问题，这是众所周知的；但是她在这个研究中却独辟蹊径，根据自己的学术背景，从系统功能语言学的角度对其进行研究，分析材料来自广州三份中文报纸《羊城晚报》、《广州日报》、《南方都市报》的中英语码转换实例。不难想象，她研究所涉及的例子是鲜活的，贴紧生活的。

王瑾首先对中国大陆的中英语言接触作大致勾勒，指出与国外大多研究关注的殖民、后殖民、移民的语码转换情况不同，中国社会出现的中英语码转换是英语在第三世界国家作为外语广泛传播和“学习性语言接触”的结果。接着她回顾相关文献并指出存在问题，介绍系统功能语言学社会的、功能的理论取向，并讨论采用系统功能语言学作为理论框架的理据。后面的具体分析，则从语言、即时语境、文化语境三个层面来组织分析和讨论。她的分析表明，语码转换的形式与功能是“汉英学习型语言接触”这一社会语境在语言层面的投射，情景类型变量既解释语码转换的语域变异，又解释语码转换所表达的纯理功能意义；西方优越话语与双语精英话语作为文化语境中自然化的意义表达，通过中英语码转换在语篇中得到体现，语码转换则籍由英语作为世界通用语的权力以“全球化”的名义，帮助将相关的价值论话语强化为中国社会的意识形态。

对于语码转换、双语与语言接触这些学术界原本是社会语言学家研究的问题，我也有一些这方面的知识和研究经历。我曾两次与两位学者做过这些方面的研究。第一次是 1992 ～ 1994 年，我在英国纽卡斯尔大学言语系师从著名社会语言学家 Lesley Milroy 从事研究，第二次是 2000 年和 2003 年在香港理工大学双语系跟 Doreen Wu（吴东英）教授做研究项目；从这两位学者我获得了很多社会语言学观点和非常有益的研究方法。借此机会感谢这两位社会语言学研究者当年所给予我的多方面的指导、支持和帮助。有了一些语码转换、双语与语言接触的基本知识，就更容易明白王瑾的研究的新意所在。在阅读这本新著时，我发现该书有一些明显的闪光点，读后令人激动不已。这里试举三点：

第一，该书首次提出从语域变异和纯理功能角度分析语码转换的语义；前者是对以句内转换和嵌入型转换为主的语料自然和必要的分析视角；后者是目前文献中唯一既确认语码转换多功能性又具有连贯理论支持和可操作性的语码转换功能分析框架。

第二，该书从民族背景、双语能力以及语言态度三个方面指出与国外大多数研究关注的殖民、后殖民、移民的语言接触及语码转换情况不同，当前中国的中英语码转换是英语在第三世界国家作为外语广泛传播和“学习型语言接触”的结果，并首次系统地将中英语码转换置于该语境下进行考察。

第三，该书第一次将系统功能语言学的应用从单语扩展到双语研究领域，证明该理论中系统、纯理功能、体现和建构、潜势与实例等理论范畴在双语语料分析中是有效和适切的，并能够为社会语言学和语码转换研究带来启示。

书中还有很多亮点，我相信细心的读者在阅读此书过程中一定会获得很多意想不到的收获。

在阅读王瑾的这本书稿过程中，我很意外地读到了《雅虎学堂》第一期（http://news.cn.yahoo.com/yahooschool/）：“重拾那些最简单的做人道理。”这一期介绍了 1933 年问世的“模范公民”，这是一本民国年间印行的巴掌大的小册子。阅读该小册子，仿佛就可以看见一位知书达理、温文尔雅的先生在提醒读者做人的最简单最起码的道理。例如，第一条（“我看见新事物要常常留心研究”）不是谈论宏大的理想、主义、爱国或追求，而是谆谆告诫读者，要留心研究新事物：“意大利少年伽利略看见教堂里灯的摆动，遂注意研究发现摆的等时性，于是发明钟表的制造法；牛顿看到苹果落地，遂研究出宇宙引力的原理；瓦特看见蒸汽有掀动壶盖的力量，遂尽力研究而创造出蒸汽机，使世界的工业发生大进步…… 这些很寻常的事情，在科学家的眼光中，无一不可以做研究的资料，做发明的动机。”

“模范公民”所说的其他“最简单最起码的道理”包括：“我发生了疑问，就想法去解决”、“我要仔细地观察事物”、“我不盲从，不随声附和”、“我说话要轻而和气”、“我对人要和颜悦色”等。通过“重拾那些最简单的做人道理”，我们可以重拾那些已经被人们遗忘多年但同时又是做人最起码的道理。今天的物质生活七十八年前丰富多了，但比可悲的是，以前七八岁孩子都知晓的道理，现如今的人们大多要么不知道要么做不到。中国目前处在一个特殊的“转型期”，充满喧嚣和竞争，社区多元化、生活多样化，人们追求时尚化，生活方式快餐化。在这样的特殊时期，回顾“模范公民”所说的最简单最起码的道理，意义更加重大。

王瑾在这本书稿中，处处表现了这些简单的道理。她通过认真观察、留心研究语码转换现象，找到了研究的突破口和新的研究视角；她通过“研究问题”去寻找解决问题的路径和办法；她的分析合理得体，自圆其说，既不盲从也不随声附和；作为一个女性学者，她一直保持着理智，理性地进行学术探索；和风细雨，有利沟通和表明自己的学术观点；义正词缓、理直气和，充分展示了一位富有素养的女学者的风范；书中所展现的和颜悦色，是成功者的气质，是作者心中的善的流露。

子曰：“知之者不如好之者，好之者不如乐之者。”我们学习知识和理论，这是非常重要的，但是，只是学习，就不如喜爱知识和理论，然而，喜爱还不够，还要以它为乐，乐在其中。这是学习的三个层次：知之、好之、乐之；也是从“苦”到“甜”的过渡。如果我们在从事语言教学与研究的过程中能够做到从知之到好之再到乐之，那就会活得开心、活得潇洒、活得美丽！在这里引用孔子的名言，与王瑾和她的新著的读者共勉。

黄国文

2011 年 10 月 29 日于约旦首都安曼

Preface

This book originates as a further and serious exploration of something that was frequently practiced by myself when I was a child, code-switching, the alternating use of two languages or dialects in one discourse. I clearly remember, when I was a child, how I switched between the two dialects at my proposal to demonstrate my language competence, to achieve solidarity with my friends, and later on, with more awareness, to establish my identity. This experience led me to assume that no code-switching practice can be merely understood as a random and personal choice of wording without regard to the environment and social motivations. I was lucky enough to have the opportunity to pick up the issue of code-switching again more seriously, and even more luckily with the help of the principles and methods of Systemic Functional Linguistics, I was able to look into code-switching as social practice and then produce a book on it.

In wiring this book I am indebted to a number of people from whom I have learned a great deal and gained great support overt the years. First and foremost, this book owes a tremendous debt of gratitude to Professor Huang Guowen, the scale of whose support is too great to be merely acknowledged. I need to record my long-standing professional debt to Professor Huang for his enthusiasm for Systemic Functional Linguistics and for the example of his own insightful scholarship, which is a source of inspiration and encouragement.

An earlier version of the present book was accepted as a doctorial thesis at Sun Yat-sen University and I am very grateful to the professors who acted as examiners: Professor Hu Zhuanglin, chair, Professor Qin Xiubai, Professor Chen Jianping, Professor Ou Hong, and Professor Wang Bin. I should also like to acknowledge my profound debt to professors who have given me guidance and support during my study at Sun Yat-sen University. A warm thank-you to Professor Martha Cheung Pui Yiu, field supervisor of my research at Hong Kong Baptist University, both for her academic guidance and for her personal thoughts. I am also grateful to Professor Ruqaiya Hasan for encouraging me to utilize Systemic Functional Linguistics to look at typical sociolinguistic issues such as code-switching and offering me both useful materials and insightful suggestions.

A big thank-you to Dr. Chen Jing, Mr. Robert Hemphill, Dr. Maggie Ma, and Dr. Yang Rufu, who had the unenviable task of suggesting detailed modifications for the earlier version of the book with painstaking care. I must mention Dr Lu Dairong, who gave me her generous help and smart advice in several aspects. Thanks for the help and support are also due to Dr. Xiong Xiyuan, who was a patient source of assistance and advice over publishing the book.

The book would not have been completed without the love from my husband Pan Donghui and my daughter Pan Leyan, who have been guiding me to the abundance and profoundness of life. I should also like to acknowledge my debt to my parents and parents-in-law in that with different dialects they speak and different accents they carry, they have been playing a significant role in promoting my awareness of the complexity of language and of code-switching as social practice. It is to them that this book is dedicated.

Wang Jin

Contents

List of Figures

List of Tables

Abbreviations

Newspaper materials

GZD *Guangzhou Daily*（《广州日报》）
NCN *Nanfang City News*（《南方都市报》）
YEN *Yangcheng Evening News*（《羊城晚报》）

Linguistic terms

CA Conversation Analysis
CC Contextual configuration
CMC Computer mediated communication
EFL English as a foreign language
ESL English as a second language
GSP Generic structure potential
RO Rights and obligations
SFL Systemic Functional Linguistics

1 Introduction

1.1 Code-switching and bilingualism

According to estimations, the majority of the world is bilingual (Myers-Scotton 2000: 290), and bilingualism is considered to be the norm rather than the exception (Thomason 2001: 10). In the last half century, the enhancive mobility and globalization of modern society have resulted in many bilingualism situations and language contact phenomena. There are reasons for studying language contact both from social concerns and from developments of language studies. On the one hand, systematic studies on bilingual language behaviour can provide insight into language problems of groups and individuals and thus support language planning and educational policies. On the other hand, as far as language studies are concerned, language contact and bilingualism provide a site for us to look at the diversity in language use more clearly because the 'major issues in sociolinguistic study of the so-called monolingual speech communities reappear in enlarged form in the study of language contact' (Appel & Muysken 1987: 5). Jakobson (1953, cited in Romaine 1989: 1) views bilingualism as the fundamental problem of linguistics, and for Myers-Scotton (2000: 291), the studies of how two languages come together can lead to important insight into the very object of the investigations by researchers focusing on monolingual issues.

It seems that language contact phenomena are nowhere as obvious as in the case of code-switching, whereby two or more languages are used in one and the same text or utterance. Milroy & Muysken (1995b: 7) view code-switching as the central issue in bilingualism research. Aspects and dimensions of code-switching have been attracting the attention of researchers from different approaches such as linguistics, sociology of language, psycholinguistics, sociolinguistics, Conversation Analysis (henceforth CA) (Auer 1984, 1998a; Blom & Gumperz 1972; Clyne 1991; DiSciullo, Muysken, & Singh 1986; Gumperz 1982; Heller 1988a; Joshi 1985; Milroy & Muysken 1995a; Muysken 2000; Myers-Scotton 1993a, b, 2002; Pfaff 1979; Poplack 1980; Sankoff & Poplack 1981; Sridhar & Sridhar 1980; Timm 1975; Woolford 1983, among numerous others; also see Kamwang-amalu 1999, Li & Chen 2004). It is no exaggeration to say that code-switching is now a subfield of linguistics that has come into its own.

In the last two decades, with the Reform and Opening-up policy, the frequent contact between Chinese and English has resulted in a large number of Chinese-English bilinguals in China. This situation makes English called a Chinese language by some researchers (e. g. McArthur 2002, Jiang 2003). Code-switching as the alternative use between Chinese and English is frequently observed among native Chinese speakers in both spoken and written texts.

This book aims to give an integrated account of Chinese-English code-switching as social practice in the China situation. The focus will be on the code-switching instances in several Chinese newspapers published in Guangzhou. In so doing, analyses will be grounded on Systemic Functional Linguistics (henceforth SFL), which offers useful theoretical and analytical support.

According to Benson (2001), the term 'code-switching' was coined by H. Vogt in his review of Weinreich's (1953) pioneer work *Languages in Contact* in 1954 although before the term was first used, as early as in the 1930s, some scholars were already identifying and discussing this phenomenon. Unfo-rtunately, we do not now have a homogeneous understanding of the term 'code-switching'. It can be used to mean different things by different scholars. In its broad sense, the 'code' in 'code-switching' is used to include languages, language varieties, and even styles of language use. For example, Hudson (1980: 52) holds that 'code-switching' is preferred to 'language-switching' in order to accommodate other kinds of varieties: dialects and registers. In its narrow sense, it can only refer to the switching between languages or geographical dialects and indeed it is on this narrow sense that the main part of code-switching literature focuses. Recently, some conversation analysts (e. g. Alvarez-Cáccamo 1998, Auer 1999, Meeuwis & Blommaert 1998) have claimed another way of understanding 'code' and 'code-switching', believing that the term 'code-switching' should be used where the code and the switching are emblematic of meanings and discourse functions (see Section 2. 3. 1 below). In the present study, 'code-switching' is used to refer to the switching between languages only, viz. between Chinese and English. For the moment, I shall not go into details about the terminologies and taxonomies concerning code-switching as discussed in the literature. They will be introduced in Chapter 2.

Closely related to the term under discussion is the term used at the beginning of this chapter, i. e. bilingualism[1], since code-switching is believed to be only where bilingualism is found. There are many ideas about what can be called bilingual or bilingualism. Appel and Muysken (1987: 2) document two extreme but well-known viewpoints concerning the definition of bilingual. Bloomfield (1933: 56) sees bilinguals as possessing 'native-like control of two or more languages', while Macnamara (1969, cited in Appel and Muysken 1987) on the other hand regards somebody as bilingual if he or she has some second-language skills in one of the four modalities (speaking, listening, writing, and reading) in addition to his first-language skills. Although theories and methods are developed as how to evaluate people's language abilities (see Romaine 1989: 12 – 19 for a summary), it is no easy task for researchers to arrive at an agreement on what can be called bilingual or bilingualism. For Halliday, McIntosh, & Strevens (1964), bilingualism is a cline, ranging in terms of the individual speaker, from the completely monolingual person, through bilingual speakers, who make use in varying degree of a second language or 'L2', to the endpoint of an ambilingual who has complete mastery of two languages.

Similarly, Mackey (1962) argues that in order to study bilingualism, we are forced to consider it as something entirely relative because the point at which the speaker of a second language becomes bilingual is either arbitrary or impossible to determine. Following this argument, Makey (1962) regards the term 'bilingualism' as the alternate use of two or more languages.

Mackey's point parallels Weinreich's (1953) understanding of bilingualism in the sense that the use of two langaugees rather than the competence is highlighted. Weinreich (1953: 7) holds that bilingualism begins 'at the point where the speaker of one language can produce complete meaningful utterances in the other language' and this definition is based more on language use than on language competence. In Auer's (1984: 7) study, 'bilingualism is no longer regarded as mental ability, but as a displayed feature of participants' everyday linguistic behavior' and he argues that 'there is no one definition of bilingualism: being bilingual becomes an achieved status' and that 'how this status is achieved, in different ways by different speakers, is what needs to be investigated' (Auer 1984: 7). More explicitly, Clyne (1997: 301) articulates that 'the term "multilingualism" can refer to either the language use or the competence of an individual or to the language situation in an entire nation or society.' Baetens Beardsmor (1982: 4) sharply points out that 'rather than attempting to provide a definition of bilingualism, which, in the present state of our knowledge in language in general, is likely to be unsatisfactory, most specialists prefer to work within the framework of a typology of bilingualism which allows for a clear delimitation of the particular area of investigation within a larger field'.

In the present study, bilingualism is treated as language performance or language use rather than language competence. This view theoretically echoes the theoretical framework adopted in this book, whereby language is studied from an inter-organism perspective (see Chapter 3 below) and hence the psycholinguistic or neurolinguistic subject has no status in such a framework. This means that subjects are examined as social beings and the focus consequently will be on the use of code-switching in social context. This view is also required by my data, since when code-switching instances in print media are discussed, involved is a huge population of readers; thus it is empirically impossible to measure the language abilities of such a huge number of subjects. Typologies of bilingualism will be discussed in the next section with reference to the Chinese/ English language contact situation in the present-day China.

1.2 A profile of the Chinese/English contact in China

Let me first of all give a brief introduction to the Chinese/ English contact situation in China, which has a long history to tell. The real frequent contact between the two languages did not happen until the 18th century, when Guangzhou (Canton) was made the sole port for foreign trade by a court decree in 1759. At that time foreigners residing in the cantonments in Guangzhou were restricted to a small area of Shamian Island and were forbidden to buy Chinese books or to learn Chinese. The contact between foreigners and Chinese was in effect via the compradors, who used a pidgin variety of English, acting as translators. These compradors were supposed to be the first Chinese to learn English in this native land, usually by private study (Adamson 2004: 23). These compradors, however, were not at all admired by other Chinese due to their foreign associations, with foreigners usually held in contempt as 'foreign devils' and English as an 'evil language' (Cheng 1982: 126). The Opium War during 1839 to1842 had great impact on China in that more trade ports were forced open for foreign trade, which resulted in more language contact. More importantly, the war helped to bring about the emergence of the Self-Strengthening Movement whereby some scholars proposed to set up official colleges to learn foreign languages as a way to strengthen this country through technology transfer. In 1861, Tongwen Guan, the first official institute of translation in China, was established in Beijing. From then on until the end of the Republican era (1911 –1949), the English language was accepted as a communicative vehicle for learning Western advanced technologies and exploring Western philosophies, with an increasingly higher official status. After the founding of the People's Republic of China in 1949, the use of English declined for ideological reasons. While English was no longer considered as an 'evil language', it was deemed as an imperialistic one. The teaching of English in Chinese schools was then replaced by the teaching of Russian and by 1957, there were only 850 secondary teachers of English in the whole country (Bolton 2003: 48). After that, the Cultural Revolution during 1966 to 1976 devastated many aspects of Chinese life, including English education.

Great changes have taken place since the Reform and Opening-up policy was inaugurated in the late 1970s, including an increasing popularity of learning and using English. Realizing the importance of the English language for the modernization drive, the Chinese government has been trying to promote English education in China. For many years, English has been a compulsory course in secondary and tertiary schools and now it is beginning to be offered to many third-year primary school pupils and even to the first-year pupils (Jiang 2003). Apart from the government' promotion, there is an increasing craze for English learning in China. For example, there are now many bilingual kindergartens in big cities and all kinds of English learning programs are offered for people of different ages, with different levels of English proficiency, from different trades, and for different purposes. Indeed English teaching has been a big industry in the Chinese market; the New Oriental School and Li Yang's Crazy English are the most famous brands. Hence it is not so surprising when we are told of such statistics: there are more people learning to speak English in China than there are native English speakers in the whole of the United States (Taylor 2002); it is estimated that there are some 500, 000 teachers of secondary English, and the total number of speakers of English in China has been estimated at over 200 million, even rising fast (Bolton 2003: 48). Consequently, it is sensible to describe the Chinese/English contact situation as one type of bilingualism.

One important reason for the English push in China is the wide spread of English as a global language, i. e. 'a language — *the* language — on which the sun does not set, whose users never sleep' (Quirk 1985: 1; emphasis in the original). With regard to the spread of the English language in the world, China is an EFL (English as a foreign language) country or Expanding Circle country (Kachru 1985, Quirk 1985; also see Chapter 7 below) whereby English is used for communication with other countries rather than for administration purposes. The main contact between Chinese and English is through education. According to Thomason's (2001: 16ff.) classification concerning how languages come into contact, apart from colonialism and migration, language contact can come about solely through education, which is called 'learned contacts'. The present-day China has witnessed, as the aforementioned situation shows, such learned contact between Chinese and English.

When describing societal bilingualism, Appel & Muysken (1987: 1 – 2) identify three theoretical types (Figure 1 – 1).

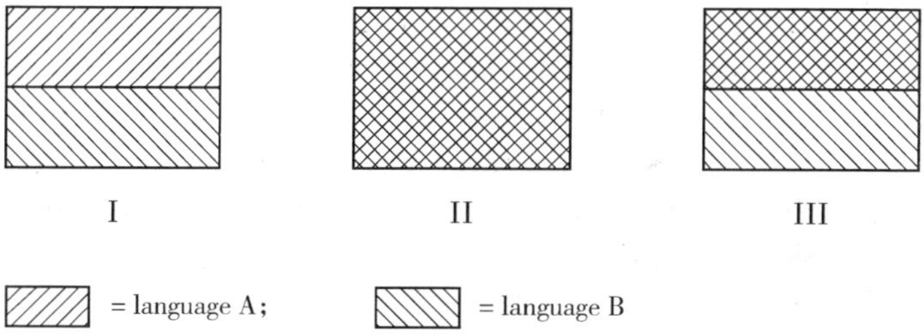

Figure 1 – 1 Three types of societal bilingualism (from Appel & Muysken 1987: 2)

The Chinese/English bilingualism in China under discussion belongs to Type III, but is different from Appel & Muysken's (1987: 2) description of Type III. According to Appel & Muysken, in most cases in Type III, the bilingual group 'will form a minority, perhaps not in the numerical or statistical, but in the sociological sense: it is a non-dominant or oppressed group'. In the present bilingual situation, however, probably we should argue for the opposite: the Chinese/English bilingual group may not be statistically dominant, but it is probably sociologically dominant due to its material and cultural advantages; while Language A is an extra language at their proposal for such material and cultural advantages, Language B is the indigenous language serving administrative functions. This is a possible feature of the 'learned contacts'.

Although the learned contact bilingualism in the present case is still in its infancy, it deserves our attention for two main reasons. One is that it is a newly found language phenomenon in China and calls for thorough and systematic analyses (also see Section 1.3 below). The other reason is that 'learned contacts' situation is much less attended to than bilingualism in colonial, post-colonial, and migration situations and hence also needs more studies. The present study is such an endeavor which explores the learned contact between Chinese and English in the present-day China and focuses on code-switching as one outcome of it.

To look at Chinese/English code-switching in China, I choose to focus on the code-switching examples in several Chinese newspapers published in Guangzhou. Guangzhou is the capital of the Guangdong Province in South China. It is located on the coast of the South China Sea and is an important seaport for foreign trade. It therefore is considered a window to connect China with the outside world. Like Beijing and Shanghai, there are more Chinese/English bilinguals here than in other places in China. Consequently it is little wonder to see that English elements have found their ways into both oral and written texts in Guangzhou.

1.3 The data

The idea of collecting code-switching examples from the Chinese newspapers is motivated by two considerations. The study is first of all sparked by D. C. S. Li's (1996) study on code-switching in the Hong Kong Chinese print media and Huang's (2001: 274–308) discussion of the code-switching in newspapers published in the mainland of China. These two studies show that code-switching not only occurs in daily conversations, but also can be found in written texts. In the literature on code-switching, there is an obvious inclination to use spoken data. Some of the approaches such as the CA approach are intended exactly for analyzing conversational code-switching. Although written code-switching data are by no means outside the arena of the existing studies (e. g. Huang 2001, D. C. S. Li 1996, Yang 1992, Yau 1993), they are far less explored compared to their oral counterparts. Methodologically, one advantage of written data over spoken ones is avoiding Labov's (1972: 209) 'observer's paradox' where analysts want to observe and record speakers talking the way they do when they are not being observed and recorded.

The second consideration is that choosing code-switching instances in newspapers as the data for analysis is more relevant to the present discussions in China on language standardization by reference to language contact and language change. There are usually two types of voices concerning the practice of code-switching, i. e. descriptive point of view and prescriptive point of view (Chen 2000). While some researchers are trying to characterize the Chinese/English code-switching in China (e. g. Huang 2001, Yu 2001), quite a few linguists frown upon code-switching and rule it out as non-standard use of language and as a threat against the pureness of the Chinese language (e. g. Chen 1994, Ge & Ge 1996, Li & Bai 2001). Usually language use in print media is taken up as a target of criticism. Producing and consuming media texts are major social activities in which people engage so as to participate in social life; hence the media is believed to have the power to set examples concerning language use for community members to follow. The present study is a descriptive one in nature. It is so because even in language standardization and language planning where prescriptive stances are taken, much descriptive and explanative work is needed, especially in the China situation which is less explored than other typical language contact situations. Highlighting the language use in written mode, I would assume the language in the print media to be 'well prepared'. This means that code-switches in the newspapers are intended or at least more so compared with some code-switches in spoken data and hence are more confirmed to be serving certain functions rather than merely being non-standard use of language. I shall return to the discussions of descriptive and prescriptive studies in the closing chapter of this book.

The main source of the data comes from my own collection of code-switching instances in three Chinese newspapers in more than two years (September, 2002 – January, 2005): *Guangzhou Daily* (《广州日报》, GZD), *Nanfang City News* (《南方都市报》, NCN), and *Yangcheng Evening News* (《羊城晚报》, YEN). Over four hundred clippings are collected. These three newspapers are chosen because all are local and the most popular newspapers with the citizens according to both statistics (World Association of Newspapers 2003) and newspaper vendors' reports. Since these three are all Chinese newspapers, Chinese will be called the matrix language while English the embedded language. In determining whether an English item should be treated as borrowing or as code-switching, I resort to the *Dictionary of Modern Chinese* (《现代汉语词典》2002): those items that have been included in the dictionary will be considered as having been accepted by the Chinese language system and hence will be treated as borrowing rather than as code-switching. These terminologies will be taken up again with more details in the following chapter.

In the rest of this book, when examples containing code-switches are presented, English translations will be provided. In doing so, free translations are offered since the purpose of translation is to provide readers with a general idea about the environments into which the embedded items are put rather than to highlight the syntactic constructions concerning code-switching. The embedded elements will be italicized in the translations. During the analysis, when a specific Chinese expression is needed to be discussed, it will be transliterated into pinyin according to the *Basic Rules for Hanyu Pinyin Orthography* (1996); in one or two places whereby the Chinese expressions are to be read and understood in Cantonese, they will be transliterated using *The LSHK* (*Linguistic Society of Hong Kong*) *Cantonese Romanization Scheme* (Fan *et al*. 1993).

1.4 Aims and objectives

The long-term aim of this study is to work towards an analytical model for code-switching within the Systemic Functional framework. The objective of this book is to use such a framework to examine the practice of code-switching in several Chinese newspapers published in Guangzhou and the constructivist relations between it and its social context. The results of the study, it is hoped, would help to obtain a more comprehensive understanding of the Chinese/English code-switching in the newspapers and the Chinese/English language contact in the present-day China. The discussions of the book will be centred on the following research questions:

(1) What are the features of the Chinese/English code-switching in the newspapers?
(2) What functions do the code-switches play in the newspapers?
(3) In what way is the practice of code-switching conditioned by, as well as construing, the immediate and wider contexts in which it is embedded?

In the following chapters, I shall undertake detailed analyses of the code-switching instances in the data, and so answer these three research questions. It is also hoped that this study will provide implications for the discussions of language standardization and language planning in China.

While focusing on one particular language contact situation and analyzing empirical data, the present study is also meant to have its theoretical contributions. The study is one of the initial attempts to base on SFL as the theoretical framework to analyze code-switching and bilingual data (see Section 1.5). On the one hand, with regard to such typical sociolinguistic topic as code-switching, utilizing a new perspective can possibly throw new light on it. On the other hand, the theoretical categories and principles of SFL as mainly formulated from monolingual research will be testified with bilingual data. To this end, this study is a descriptive, explanative, and qualitative one in nature with its speculative and theoretical orientation.

1.5 Theoretical framework

To answer the three research questions, the present study will base the investigation of code-switching on SFL (Halliday 1973, 1978, 1994/2000) as a theoretical framework, while obtaining a great deal of inspiration from the diversity of approaches in the literature. Given the rapid developments that have been made in SFL during the past several decades, it is surprising that few, if any, attempts have been made to address questions of bilingual texts. It becomes even more surprising when it is remembered that SFL, developed from the Malinowski-Firth tradition, has the obvious ethnographic intellectual roots as it encourages the study of language in its social and cultural context and therefore is a natural schema to frame analyses on code-switching with its sociological orientation.

The adoption of the proposed framework in the present study involves three interrelated perspectives to look at the practice of code-switching. The first one is the register analysis, which is intended to capture the functional variation dimension of the code-switching. The second one is to examine the functional diversification of code-switching. The third one is to relate the semantics of code-switching to their context including situation types and the wider context of culture. These three aspects in general correspond to the three research questions I set out to explore. More details about this theoretical framework will be discussed in Chapter 3.

1.6 Book structure

This book is divided into eight chapters. This introductory chapter has considered some basic issues of the study. Chapter 2 clears up the terminologies and taxonomies of the language phenomenon which I term generally as 'code-switching' and reviews previous studies in the field. Several drawbacks of and gaps in the existing code-switching studies are also discussed. Chapter 3 provides the theoretical foundations for the present study. It introduces the theoretical assumptions and the basic principles of SFL as the theoretical framework, presents the rationale of a SFL approach to the code-switching in the present case, and discusses briefly how the analyses are modelled in such an approach.

Chapters 4 to 7 are concerned with detailed analyses of the collected code-switching data. Chapter 4 provides a general description of the code-switching in the Chinese newspapers collected in Guangzhou, basically from a registerial variation perspective. Chapter 5 attempts to explore the semantics of code-switching from a multifunctional perspective. While Chapter 4 and Chapter 5 are basically linguistic descriptions of the code-switching in the newspapers, Chapter 6 and Chapter 7 aim to explore the social context in which the practice of code-switching is embedded. Chapter 6 focuses on the immediate context and discusses the practice of code-switching in relation to three contextual variables (i. e. field, tenor, and mode). Chapter 7 on the other hand locates code-switching in the wider social context and examines the practice of code-switching by reference to social discourses and ideologies in this particular culture.

Chapter 8 is the concluding chapter, whereby main findings and basic arguments of the book are presented and its contribution and significance are summed up. I shall also relate the present descriptive study to related prescriptive studies and consider its implications for language standardization. Suggestions for future studies will also be proposed.

Note

1. In this book, the term 'bilingualism' is used to include multilingualism.

2 Code-switching as a Multifaceted Research Topic

2.1 Introduction

The last half century has witnessed an ever increasing body of literature on code-switching involving different language pairs and different language contact situations. These studies represent a broad and multiplex set of perspectives, including sociology of language, sociolinguistics, pragmatics, linguistics, psycholinguistics, CA, etc. Although this study will base on SFL as a theoretical framework, it is useful to review the previous studies on code-switching so as to get inspirations, to identify gaps, and to locate the present study. I shall in this chapter clear up the definitions, terminologies and taxonomies of code-switching and provide an overview of previous studies.

While code-switching has been approached from many different perspectives, it is generally accepted that these studies fall into three categories, viz. the functional and social dimensions of code-switching, the structural and grammatical dimensions of code-switching, and the psycholinguistic dimensions of code-switching. Due to the focus and starting point of this book (see Section 3.4.1 below), I shall mainly concentrate my discussions on the studies of the first category while only introducing the other two very briefly.

2.2 Code-switching: Definitions, terminologies, and taxonomies

Code-switching refers to 'the juxtaposition within the same speech exchange of passages of speech belonging to two different grammatical systems or subsystems' (Gumperz 1982: 59).

Texts or utterances with code-switching are usually called bilingual speech or bilingual texts. In bilingual speech, the two languages often have different statuses, with one more primary than the other. We hence have concepts such as matrix language and embedded language, host language and guest language.

Since code-switching is a kind of language phenomenon involving the operation of two language systems, it needs to be distinguished from borrowing or loans. Usually for such a distinction, researchers will consider the degree to which the foreign item has been adapted to the host language phonologically and morphosyntactically, whether it has served to fill certain lexical gap, whether it has come into the repertoire of the monolinguals, etc. (see Huang 1999: 62 – 77, D. C. S. Li 1996, Myers-Scotton 1992, Poplack & Sankoff 1984, Poplack, Sankoff, & Miller 1988). Sometimes, terminologies such as nonce borrowing also make things more complicated. Believing that singly-occurring code-switching forms and established borrowing or loans are on a continuum, Myers-Scotton (1992) suggests using frequency count as a criterion. Poplack *et al.* (1988) use a similar way to distinguish their nonce borrowing from established loans. Appel & Muysken (1987: 173) hold that it is impossible to distinguish individual cases of code-switching from not-yet-integrated borrowings on the basis of simple diagnostic criteria. As indicated in Chapter 1, to distinguish code-switching from borrowing, the present study relies on the *Dictionary of Modern Chinese* (2002) for deciding whether an item has been accepted into the Chinese language system and the monolinguals' repertoire.

Still, it needs to be noted that while the term 'code-switching' gains more popularity, many researchers are using other terminologies such as 'code-mixing', 'mix', 'alternation', and so forth. The terminologies used are closely related to the taxonomies of code-switching distinguished by different researchers.

Researchers such as Nishimura (1989, 1995a, b), Myers-Scotton (e. g. 1992, 1993a, b), Poplack and her associates (e. g. Poplack 1980, Poplack & Sankoff 1984, 1988, Sankoff & Poplack

1981) are using 'code-switching' as an umbrella term. Poplack (1980) distinguishes among three types of code-switching (i. e. intra-sentential code-switching, inter-sentential code-switching, and tag code-switching). Myers-Scotton (1993b: 23 – 24) holds that both inter-sentential and intra-sentential code-switching can be part of a text and might have similar social motivations; she states clearly that the use of both 'code-switching' and 'code-mixing' only creates unnecessary confusion. I follow these researchers in using 'code-switching' as a covering term in this book.

However, for many other researchers, the term 'code-switching' is reserved for inter-sentential code-switching only while intra-sentential code-switching is referred to as 'code-mixing' (e. g. Bokamba 1989, Kachru 1978, 1983; Kamwangamalu 1989, 1992; Sridhar & Sridhar 1980). Gibbons (1987), whose study focuses on the Cantonese/English bilingual Hong Kong, notices that there is a tendency for English elements to be integrated into Cantonese and thus calls the phenomenon 'MIX'. Bhatia (1989) tends to use 'code-mixing' to refer to what I call generally as code-switching.

Other terms are usually associated with more specific categories of intra-sentential code-switching although some inter-sentential examples might also be included. Auer (1984) uses 'alternation' as the covering term to include both insertion[1] and code-switching, with the former focusing on the grammatical unit of the embedded language and the latter on the location of the alternation in the conversation (see Section 2. 3. 2 below).

Poplack and her associates try to look at more code-switching data from different bilingual communities, on the basis of which they recognize four mechanisms of code-switching, viz. smooth switching, flagged switching, nonce loan and constituent insertion (Poplack & Sankoff 1988; Poplack *et al*. 1988; Poplack, Wheeler, & Westwood 1989; Poplack & Meechan 1995). Smooth code-switching is usually found between two closely related languages such as English and Spanish. Speakers involved in smooth code-switching do not necessarily switch back to the original language but need to observe certain grammatical constraints (see Section 2.4 below). Flagged code-switching is often accompanied with pause, repetition, metalanguage elements, and other discourse markers calling for attention. Because of its rhetoric functions, flagged switching between language pairs such as Finnish/English and French/English is not subjected to grammatical constraints. Nonce loans are frequently found in language pairs where there are relatively big differences between the two languages such as Finnish/English, Tamil/English, and Wolof/French. While nonce loans and established loanwords are different in terms of frequency of use, they are alike in that they are integrated into the base language and thus are also not subjected to the constraints. Constituent insertion refers to the insertion of a constituent of a language into the other language; that means that speakers need to switch back to form this type of code-switching. Constituent insertion can be found in language pairs such as Arabic/French and Fongbe/French. The inner structure of the inserted constituent can be from the grammatical rules of the language insofar the switching point does not offend the grammar of the base language.

Muysken (1995, 2000) also establishes a typology of code-mixing, which is meant to be more comprehensive and have wider relevance. His framework identifies three types of code-mixing, viz. insertion, alternation, and congruent lexicalization. Insertion means insertion of materials (lexical items or entire constituents) from one language into a structure of the other language. Alternation is the real-sense code-switching; it is switching between structures from different languages, with switching between turns or utterances as one type of alternation. Congruent lexicalization refers to the lexicalization of materials from different lexical inventories into a shared grammatical structure. This type of mixing pertains closely to Clyne's (1987, 1991) notion of triggering. Take the following switching between Dutch and English for example:

(1) [between English and Dutch, from Crama & van Gelderen 1984, cited in Muysken 2000: 5]
Weet jij [whaar] Jenne is?
Do you know where Jenny is?

[whaar] in the example can be regarded either as *waar* in Dutch or *where* in English since the pronunciations of the two are very similar. While [whaar] would be considered as a trigger mechanism by Clyne, Muysken (2000: 5) further points out that the sequence *where Jenny is* could as easily be English in structure as Dutch, given that *Jenny* is a name in both languages and *is* is homophonous. Hence congruent lexicalization, albeit involving two languages, is concerned with shared structures of the languages, both of which contribute lexical items.

2.3 The social and functional aspects of code-switching

The alternative use of two or more languages in one interaction was once regarded as defective language acquisition. For example, Weinreich (1953: 73) believed that the ideal bilingual only 'switches from one language to the other according to appropriate changes in the speech situation (interlocutors, topics, etc.), but not in an unchanged speech situation, and certainly not within a single sentence'. Even nowadays, many lay people have the impression that a speaker code-switches simply because he or she has some difficulties in articulating certain items or concepts in a certain language. By contrast, one basic assumption of the studies on the social and functional dimensions of code-switching is that with two languages at their proposal, bilinguals can make use of two codes for different communicative purposes.

Starting from this assumption, researchers set out to explore the functions and motivations of code-switching: why do people code-switch? what are the functions of code-switching? and how does code-switching fulfil these functions? Many researchers have gone into the social context for explanations, with Blom & Gumperz' (1972) study and Myers-Scotton's

Markedness Model (1993a) representing the most typical of such an approach. More specifically, the social 'values' of the languages are highlighted in such studies. By contrast, some other studies, while also discussing functions of code-switching, do no depend on such social values of the languages involved. Some researchers (e. g. Auer 1984, 1988, 1995; Li & Milroy 1995; W. Li 2002) with such a stance take CA as their theoretical support and argue that the meanings of code-switches are associated with their locations in the conversational sequences and only emerge with the unfolding of conversation sequences. In other words, there is a focus on the contributions of code-switching to the organization of conversation. Similarly, some other researchers find that the switched items can be discourse markers (Maschler 1994, Nishimura 1995a), with code-switching serving as discourse strategies.

Roughly corresponding to my distinction between these two approaches here, Stround (1998) calls those researchers who focus on macrosociolinguistic context as universalists and the code-switching CA practitioners as localists. Backus (2000) further points out that Myers-Scotton is a typical universalist while Auer is a localist. Nishimura's (1995a: 12 – 19) distinction of the studies into those on symbolic functions and those on instrumental functions is more in line with my dichotomy here, although I am not happy with the word 'instrumental' because it can be very misleading by implying that code-switching is in some cases employed as an instrument rather than as meaning making practice. These two approaches will be termed respectively as macro approach and micro approach in the present study.

In the rest of this section, I shall first introduce the studies on language choice, which are believed to be relevant for code-switching studies. Then the macro approach and the micro approach will be considered respectively. I shall then discuss and summarize the studies, which can help to locate the present study in Chapter 3.

2.3.1 Language choice

The studies on language choice are often from the perspective of sociology of language. Sometimes language choice is a rather different issue from code-switching because in one given situation only one language is involved rather than two. However, it has important implications for studies on code-switching from the macro approach in that links between language choice and situation are established. Ferguson's (1959) and Fishman's (1965) studies have been very influential in this field.

Ferguson's (1959) work is developed from bilingual settings whereby 'two varieties of a language exist side by side through the community, with each having a definite role to play'. The term 'diglossia', a modified form of the French 'diglossie', is introduced to epitomize such functional differentiation of languages in one community. Diglossia can only be found in a relatively stable language situation. The superposed variety is called the H ('high') variety and the regional dialect, the L ('low') variety. H and L differ in aspects of prestige, acquisition, stability, grammar, lexicon, etc., while the most essential distinction is the specialization of function for H and L: H is only appropriate for some situations and L for others, with overlapping only very slightly.

Fishman (1965) sets out to examine language choice by putting forward the questions: who speaks what language to whom and when? To answer these questions, Fishman proposes an important notion, i. e. domain. Domain is a high order of abstraction or summarization which is arrived at from a consideration of the socio-cultural patterning which surrounds language choice. Factors such as topic and role-relations contribute to the designation of the major clusters of interaction situations that occur in particular bilingual settings. Typical domains include family, friends, acquaintances, mass media, occupations, and the like. For every domain, there is a typical language associated with it.

Both Ferguson's diglossia and Fishman's domain require a very large and general perspective and they only locate on stable bilingual societies whereby the functions of the languages involved are sharply set apart. The normative and conventional aspect of language choice is very much highlighted in situations described by the ideas of diglossia or domain. In Li's (2000b: 59) terms, there is a general agreement that 'language choice is an "orderly" social behaviour, rather than a random matter of momentary inclination'. Fishman's domain theory is in nature a more specific and more accurate version of Ferguson's diglossia theory in that it aims to spell out the correspondence between language choices and more specifically established situations. Although these studies involve no code-switching, they are important for code-switching studies in that it provides the prototypical correlation between language and situation which can serve as social background knowledge in particular bilingual interactions. This is the aspect highlighted in Blom & Gumperz' (1972) situational code-switching and Myers-Scotton's (1993a) sequential unmarked switching (see Section 2. 3. 2 below).

In other places, the issue of language choice is pertinent to code-switching when the mode of code-switching *per se* rather than one or the other language is such a choice. This is what some researchers term as the strategies of neutrality (Appel & Muysken 1987: 129 – 137, Heller 1988b, Myers-Scotton 1993a, Scotton 1976).

When code-switching *per se* can also be counted as a language choice, some researchers raise the question of whether the concept of language is a useful one in accounting for language choices for bilingual speakers and hence there are some suggested terminologies aiming to replace the term code-switching *per se* as a language choice: medium, mixed code, fused lect, bilingual lect, etc. (Alvarez-Cáccamo 1998, Auer 1999, Franceschini 1998, Gafaranga 2000, Gafaranga & Torras 2001, Maschler 1998, Meeuwis & Blommaert 1998). The common thread of these studies is that code-switching *per se* is in fact the basic code of the bilingual communities they are investigating and should not be described in opposition to supposedly more basic monolingual language use. This type of code-switching usually involves intra-sentential code-switching and draws much attention of grammatical analysis; however, social and functional dimensions of such code-switching are rarely explored. For example, Myers-Scotton (1993b) holds that it is the overall pattern of code-switching ('unmarked code-switching' in her terms, see Section 2. 3. 2 below) that indexes social meaning while a single switch does not carry any specific social message. Franceschini (1998) proposes a framework in which code-switching is one manifestation of the inherent variability that characterizes language; speakers use it as one of their codes, but it displays different patterns between subgroups. Similarly, relating the code-switching patterns, or the code patterns to social categories is also found in other studies, although not all of the studies explicitly recognize the code-switching mode as a code (see Section 2. 4 below). Auer (1998b, 1999) and Maschler (1998) on the other hand argue that we need to see code-switching, language mixing, and a fused lect as forming a continuum with code-switching and fused lect representing the polar extremes.

2. 3. 2 The macro approach

Since the language choice theories are not in a position to account for why people's choices do not always correspond to their conventionalized situations, researchers need to take a departure from the theories to account for more dynamic bilingual speech. The focus then needs to be shifted from the sociology of language to a sociolinguistic one, concentrating on bilingual interactions. A common theme of the studies from a macro approach to code-switching is that they seek to interpret meanings, functions, and motivations of code-switching in reference to macrosociolinguistic factors although different studies vary in the ways social factors are inactivated to explain code-witching. Among studies from a macro approach, Gumperz' (Blom & Gumperz 1972, Gumperz 1982) and Myers-Scotton's (1993a) studies are the widely applied analytical models.

One of the basic contributions by Blom & Gumperz (1972)

is the dichotomy of situational code-switching and metaphorical code-switching, which has now been widely applied and frequently cited by studies on code-switching. Blom & Gumperz (1972) is basically a case study on the code-switching between Ranamål and Bokmål, two dialects in the Hemnesberget bilingual community, North Norway. Similar to Fishman's study (1965), contextual constraints on speech events are explored, namely, the participants, the ecological surroundings, and the topic or range of topics. When within the same setting the participants' definition of the social event changes, this change may be signalled among others by linguistic clues and then code-switching may happen. For example, teachers will use Bokmål in delivering formal lectures where interruptions are not encouraged and they will switch to Ranamål to redefine the social event when they want to encourage open and free discussions with students. Such code-switching is termed as situational code-switching which assumes a direct relationship between language and social situation. In contrast to such code-switching, some other code-switches happen in situations where there is no significant change in definition of participants' mutual rights and obligations. For instance, officials often interject casual statements in the dialect into their formal discussions. Blom & Gumperz argue that the choice of Bokmål or Ranamål to which people switch alludes to these relationships and thus generates certain meanings. This type of code-switching is called metaphorical code-switching.

There are several points with Blom & Gumperz' study that call for our attention and here I would like to mention two important ones. The first is that it synthesizes components of the sociology of language (e. g. Ferguson 1959, Fishman 1965) and linguistics (e. g. Weinreich 1953) and is sociolinguistic research in its real sense. Its way of doing so is by focusing on individual and specific interaction events. In other words, on the one hand, it deals with linguistic rules and on the other hand, the explanation of code-switching can only be achieved by reference to the social and cultural context (cf. the CA approach in Section 2. 3. 3 below). The other important implication is that, rather than content themselves with finding out which language is conventionally used in which situation, Blom & Gumperz (1972) shift to explore code-switching as a strategy of meaning making. In other words, code-switching is analyzed as communicative strategies to convey certain pragmatic meanings. In his later work (Gumperz 1982: 59ff.), Gumperz continues his research on metaphorical code-switching and argues more explicitly for code-switching to be viewed as a kind of contextualization cue. This means that speakers can use code-switching to redefine the context, which can be a cue for listeners to contextualize the speakers' intention; if the listeners fail to do so, the communication might break down or respected communicative results will not achieved.

Another well-known distinction articulated by Gumperz is between 'we code' and 'they code' (Gumperz 1982: 66). 'We code' is usually the ethnically specific, minority language associated with in-group and informal activities; 'they code' is on the other hand the majority language associated with the more formal, stiffer, and less personal out-group relations. What is really important here is that the association between code and group identity is a symbolic one.

Myers-Scotton's (Scotton1988; Myers-Scotton 1993a, 1999) Markedness Model, which owns its name from the works by R. Jakobson and N. Trubetzkoy, is developed largely from her studies on code-switching between English and Swahili in Nairobi, Kenya. Aiming to provide explanations for motivations of code-switching, the Markedness Model integrates spirit of a variety of disciplines such as sociology of language (language choice), pragmatics (implicatures and intentional meanings), social anthropology (transactions/negotiation), and linguistic anthropology (communicative competence). The model assumes that speakers have a sense of markedness regarding available linguistic codes for any interaction, but choose their codes based on the persona and/or relation with others which they wish to have in place. The focus of the present study only allows me to sketch this model, unfortunately, without providing specific code-switching examples.

Central to the Markedness Model are the negotiation principle and several maxims[2]. The negotiation principle, which underlies all code choices, states:

> *Choose the form of your conversation contribution such that it indexes the set of rights and obligations (RO set) which you wish to be in force between speaker and addressee for the current exchange.*

There are then three maxims. The first one, the unmarked-choice maxim directs a speaker to:

> *Make your code choice the unmarked index of the unmarked RO set in talk exchanges when you wish to establish or affirm that RO set.*

Following this maxim will lead to two outcomes, either sequential unmarked code-switching or code-switching itself as an unmarked choice, termed as unmarked code-switching. The former refers to the switching which happens when one or more of the situational factors change in the course of a conversation, and hence the unmarked RO set may change as a result of the switching. It is similar to Blom & Gumperz' (1972) situational code-switching. Unmarked code-switching involves several conditions. First, the speakers must be bilingual peers without many significant socio-economic differences. Second, both speakers wish to symbolize duel memberships that the code-switching can index. Third, the speakers positively evaluate their own identities in this type of interaction and the indexical values of the varieties used in the switching. Fourth, the speakers must be proficient enough in the two languages; but engaging in such switching is more associated with familiarity with using the languages together than it is necessarily associated with high proficiency or with any social-identity factors, such as education or age. Regarding structural features, sequential unmarked code-switching usually involves inter-sentential switching while code-switching as the unmarked choice may include alternating sentences, but may more typically include a good deal of intra-sentential code-switching.

The second maxim, the marked choice maxim, would direct a speaker to:

> *Make a marked code choice which is not the unmarked index of the unmarked RO set in an interaction when you wish to establish a new RO set as unmarked for the current exchange.*

In making a marked choice, the speaker is in effect saying 'Put aside any presumptions you have based on social norms for these circumstances. I want your view of me, or of our relationship, to be otherwise.' There are several possible specific effects of using marked code-switching: to increase the social distance via authority or anger; to be an ethnically-based exclusion strategy; to have aesthetic effect; or to encode irony. For marked code-switching, the message is the medium itself and such code-switching usually involves structural flagging such as repetition, being phonologically flagged since marked choice is one strategy that used to call attention.

While in many situations, a speaker is capable of recognizing what is an unmarked code choice for his interaction with other speakers, Myers-Scotton (1993a) also mentions that there are a few situations whereby an unmarked code choice is not clear. In such cases, the speakers will follow the exploratory maxim:

> *When an unmarked choice is not clear, use code-switching to make alternate exploratory choices as candidates for an unmarked choice and thereby as an index of an RO set which you favor.*

Both unmarked code-switching and exploratory code-switching serve as strategies of neutrality because by using code-switching, speakers can avoid committing themselves to one single RO set. While the former is used for intra-group communication, the latter is for inter-group communication (also see Appel & Muysken 1987: 129 –137).

The Markedness Model is a successful one in accounting for social motivations of code-switching, insofar the word 'social' is understood narrowly as only involving negotiation of interpersonal relations and identities. The model is welcomed by some researchers (e. g. Gross 2000, J. W. Li 2002), while it also meets challenges (see Section 2. 3. 3).

2. 3. 3 The micro approach

In contrast to the studies from the macro approach, studies from a micro approach, albeit also aiming to explore the functional aspects of code-switching, concentrate their attention on the embeddedness and sequentiality of the code-switches in conversation rather than resort to the macro social factors.

Focusing on Hebrew/English code-switching in conversation, Maschler (1994) argues that the switched discourse markers are employed to metalanguage the frame of the discourse. Similarly, Nishimura (1995a: 132 – 134) finds one of her subjects used English discourse markers such as *I think so*, *I think*, *Yes*, and *OK* frequently when he spoke Japanese in the interview. Nishimura (1995a: 144 – 153) also notes the organizational functions of code-switching, including frame-marking, topic-introduction, and reintroduction. I would see the code-switching with discourse markers as serving the function of organizing texts. Although neither Maschler (1994) nor Nishimura (1995a) explicitly states which approach their discussions have been following, the important point here is that the functions of code-switching are discussed without referring to the macrosociolinguistic factors as studies from a macro approach will do.

Some other scholars adopt a CA approach to focus on the micro context. Auer (1984) holds that functions of the code-switching only emerge with the sequential development instead of being generalized (see Section 2. 3. 4 below). Auer (1984, 1988) also believes that the meanings of code-switching are closely associated with the locations of the code-switches in the conversational sequences, that the interpretation of code-switching involves the preceding and succeeding sequences of the code-switches, and that the interpretation of code-switching should be undertaken from the perspective of the interactants rather than be related to the macro social contexts which determine the 'value' of languages. In his studies on code-switching, Auer (1984: 5) treats the sequentiality and the embeddedness of code-switching in the sequential organization as the starting point of his analysis. Since the meanings and functions of code-switching cannot be analyzed if divorced from the environment of the sequences, the analysis of code-switching then needs a methodology which has a special attention on the development of sequences. CA provides these researchers with a perfect methodology, with its more emphasis on the contribution of language *per se* to the organization of texts, compared with other sociolinguistic paradigms. As Li points out,

> At the heart of the difference between CA and other sociological perspectives is a tension between language as a medium for the expression of intentions, motives, or interests, and language as a topic for uncovering the methods through which ordered activity is generated—the latter being the CA position. (W. Li 2002: 163)

Although trying to refrain from macrosociolinguistic factors, the CA advocates of code-switching studies think highly of Gumperz' (1982) conception of contextualization cue. In accordance with Gumperz, code-switching is viewed as a similar strategy as intonation and posture which provide certain cues for contextualization.

Below I will introduce the work by two representative conversation analysts of code-switching, viz. P. Auer and W. Li, but very briefly, due to the focus of this chapter.

Auer's analytical framework is his classification of the four procedures as summed up diagrammatically in Table 2-1. Note that what we call code-switching here is termed by Auer as alternation, which in one dimension includes insertion and code-switching.

Table 2 - 1 The four-procedure analytical framework for alternation (according to Auer 1984)

	discourse-related	participant-related
insertion	discourse-related insertion	participant-related insertion
code-switching	discourse-related code-switching	participant-related code-switching

In very simple terms, while insertion concerns with the grammatical unit of the embedded language (e. g. noun or noun phrase, noun or verb, etc.), code-switching concerns with the location of the alternation in the conversation. Alternation in the other dimension can be either discourse-related or participant-related.

Participant-related alternation usually involves code-switching due to the language abilities or language preferences of the participants[3]. More relevant to our discussion in the present section is the discourse-related ones. Discourse-related alternations are those alternations which are associated with the organization of the texts, such as alternation caused by the shift of topic or the participation of new speakers as the instances. Side-sequences can be coded in a different language, resulting in obvious sequential subordination. Most discourse-related insertions (i. e. alternations on the lexical level) are used as anaphoric or the juxtaposition of a lexical item in two languages.

While participant-related code-switching usually occurs between the turns of different speakers, it is noted, however, that one speaker will usually accept the language choice of the other speaker after a stretch of conversation because people tend to use only one language in one interaction:

$$A_i,\ B_g,\ A_i,\ B_g,\ \ldots\ //\ A_i,\ B_i,\ A_i,\ B_i,\ \ldots\ \text{or}\ //\ A_g,\ B_g,\ A_g,\ B_g,\ \ldots$$

A and B denote participants while i and g denote languages.

Figure 2 - 1 Negotiation of a language for interaction (from Auer 1984: 23)

The process as illustrated in Figure 2 - 1 is in effect the

negotiation of the language for interaction. Consequently, the site of the acceptance by one speaker of the other's language also has its discourse meanings. This is what Auer means by saying that the four procedures are actually not categories of functions or structures; rather, they are meaning making procedures which are also interrelated.

Auer's analytical framework with the four sequences is utilized by Shin & Milroy (2000) in their study on the conversation between Korean migrated children in America. They find Auer's framework useful in revealing that the children employ code-switching to negotiate the language for the interaction as well as to organize conversational tasks such as turn-taking, preference marking, repair, and bracketing of side-sequences (Shin & Milroy 2000: 351).

Li & Milroy (1995) attempt to apply CA to their study on the Cantonese/English conversational code-switching in a northeast Britain bilingual Chinese community. The focus is again on the contribution of code-switching to the organization of conversation. Specifically, they discuss two types of structures, i. e. preference organization in adjacency pair and repair sequence. For example[4],

(2) [Between Cantonese and English, from Li & Milroy 1995: 288]
(Dinner table talk between mother A and daughter B)
A: Oy-m-oy faan a? Ah Ying a?
(Want some rice?)
B: (no response)
A: Chaaufaan a. Oy-m-oy?
(Fried rice. Want or not?)
B: (2.0) *I'll have some shrimps.*
A: Mut-ye? (.) Chaaufaan a.
(What?) (Fried rice.)
B: Hai a.
(OK.)

Li's argument is that a switch of language in a piece of

conversation can be indexical of dispreferred responses and such a strategy is by essence the same with the use of markers of dispreferred responses in monolingual situations. Code-switching can also be utilized to contextualize the 'repair':

(3) [Between Cantonese and English, from Li & Milroy 1995: 291]
(A and B are both female speakers in their early forties.)
A: ... koei hai yisaang.
(He's a doctor.)
B: *Is he?*
A: Yichin (.) hai Hong Kong.
(Before) (In Hong Kong.)

In the above example, Speaker B switches to English from Speaker A's Cantonese to initiate a repair sequence. Such repairs can be found both inside a turn and between different turns.

As Auer (1984: 6) remarks, researchers who examine code-switching from a CA approach refrain from 'background knowledge', which is often drawn upon by investigations of code-switching from a macro approach, instead, with a focus on the location of code-switching in the conversation processing. One consequence of the CA approach's divorce from the macro social context is the highlight of the contrast between two languages involved, which is however ignored in the macro approach. In some bilingual communities, the significance of code-switching merely lies in the contrast between the two codes instead of the values that have been attached to specific languages in the macro social context. In such cases, the influence of the macro social context has been most reduced and a stylistic interpretation of the code-switches under discussion is needed. Alfonzetti (1998) finds that in her code-switching data between the Sicilin dialect and standard Italian, a woman switched from standard Italian to the Sicilin dialect to index a new topic in speech. It is not that the Sicilin dialect is a more appropriate language for the new topic because after using code-switching to signify the shift of topic, the woman then switched back to standard Italian. Alfonzetti (1998) illustrates with many similar examples that the functions of the code-switches lie in the contrast between the two languages, independent from the social meanings or social values of the two languages. She argues that there is no clear line between the 'we code' and the 'they code' (Gumperz 1982) in such code-switching examples and the directions of the switches are free to a large extent.

Although the CA approach draws researchers' attention to areas that the macro approach fails to account for, this approach to code-switching has been most criticized on its divorce from the macro social context, which is impossible to be totally suspended in descriptions of code-switching functions. While the CA approach claims that context plays an important role in its analysis, it is obvious enough that not all levels and aspects of context are intended by conversation analysts. Albeit CA is a methodology of discourse analysis which emphasizes context, its attention on context lies in the conversation itself (Schiffrin 1994: 236). This is another way of saying that the 'context' as understood and practised in CA is in effect co-text, i. e. the embeddedness and sequentiality of a stretch of language.

Most CA advocates have now become less radical and begun to consider how synthesis can be made to integrate both macro and micro factors (Auer 1995, 1998b; Li & Milroy 1995; Moyer 1998; Stroud 1998). A strategy of synthesis is setting up layered models. For example, Li and his colleagues (Li & Milroy 1995, Li, Milroy, & Pong 1992) propose a two-step approach whereby social network is used to describe different preferences of subgroups in the community (also see Milroy & Li 1995) before a detailed conversation analysis is conducted. In Moyer's (1998) study, on the highest layer, English, Spanish, and the mixing of English and Spanish as code choices are influenced by the macro sociolinguistic factors; on the intermediate layer, the CA approach is most suitable for case studies on code-switching to find out the specific functions of code-switching; on the lowest layer, speakers can choose to use more or less English with Spanish as the base language, and to use inserted or alternational code-switching. However, while the adoption of such layered models is useful in analyzing practice, it is also true that it takes a departure from CA in theory, on which research of the approach has been based for theoretical support, and the researchers are actually facing a theoretical dilemma (Wang, Huang, & Lü 2004).

2.3.4 Discussion

In the previous sections I attempted to make a distinction of the studies focusing on the social and functional dimensions of code-switching between two types of approaches, the macro approach and the micro approach. The former, as closely related to language choice, which seeks to establish correlation between language and social factors, highlights the symbolic function of language. The latter, on the other hand, limits the influence of the macro context in their analysis of code-switching with a focus on 'message-intrinsic' functions.

We have seen that either approach has its limitations. As far as the macro approach is concerned, Alfonzetti (1998) has found situations where Gumperz' 'we code' and the 'they code' seem to have no status. Also, Shin & Milroy (2000: 352) comment on Myers-Scotton's Markedness Model that although the idea of a particular language being the marked or unmarked choice in one situation is useful, sometimes the model presents difficulties in determining which language(s) become(s) marked or unmarked in a given bilingual interaction. On the other hand, the total divorce from macro social context will lead studies from the micro approach to a blind alley; as was mentioned, many researchers from this approach have begun to consider integrating macro context as a level of analysis (Auer 1995: 116, Li 1998, Li & Milroy 1995, Li, Milroy, & Pong 1992, Moyer 1998, Stroud 1998).

There are other discussions on the functions of code-switching which cannot be simply assigned to a macro approach or a micro approach, because macro and micro contextual factors and even some other factors are considered in the research. Most of these studies make use of a checklist to present the functions of code-switching, and are thus referred to by Myers-Scotton (1993a: 62 – 74) as the 'better-taxonomy' approach[5].

Some case studies attempt to summarize functions of code-switching in particular bilingual communities. For example, Nishimura (1995b) classifies the functions of the patterns of code-switching between Japanese and English among Canadian second generation Japanese into four categories: (1) those which are related to the international processes between the speaker and the interlocutor(s), (2) those concerning the organization of discourse, (3) those which give stylistic effects, and (4) those whose motivations are not clear. More relevant to the present study in terms of language pair, Gibbons (1987) and D. C. S. Li (1996, 2001, 2003) identify the following motivations for the Cantonese/English switching in Hong Kong: availability and specificity, semantic features, discourse markers, exclamations, principle of economy, etc.

Some other studies aim at generalizing functions or motivations of code-switching with wider relevance. The best-known study is Gumperz' (1982: 75 – 83) checklist of conversational functions of code-switching. The functions include quotations, addressee specification, interjections, reiteration, message qualification, and finally personalization versus objectivization. Ritchie and Bhatia's (2004) summary of similar functions includes quotations, reiteration, message qualification, topic-comment/relative clauses, hedging, interjection, and idioms and deep-rooted cultural wisdom. Grosjean (1982: 152) suggests a more comprehensive list of reasons of code-switching:

- Fill a linguistic need for lexical items, set phrase, discourse marker, or sentence filler
- Continue the last language used (triggering)
- Quote someone
- Specify addressee
- Qualify message: amplify or emphasize ('topper' in argument)
- Specify speaker involvement (personalize message)

- Mark and emphasize group identity (solidarity)
- Convey confidentiality, anger, annoyance
- Exclude someone from conversation
- Change role of speaker: raise status, add authority, show expertise

In such lists, headings such as 'addressee specification', 'hedging', 'mark and emphasize group identity' are concerned with macro contextual factors while 'discourse markers', 'topic-comment/relative clauses' are from a micro approach. There are also headings such as 'availability and specificity', 'semantic features', and 'fill a linguistic need for lexical items' that are kept outside both the Markedness Model and the CA approach to code-switching.

Appel & Muysken (1987: 29–31) believe that language use involves various functions of the language system and hence make use of R. Jakobson's typology of language functions to address the issues of language choice in bilingual conversations. They argue that 'different languages may fulfil different functions in the lives of bilingual speakers, and in bilingual conversations a choice for one particular language may signal the primary functions appealed to at that moment'. They then follow Jakobson to distinguish six functions to which a language may be put: the referential function, the directive and integrative function, the expressive function, the phatic function, the metalinguistic function, and the poetic function.

Although presenting functions of code-switching as checklists is straightforward and practical, the methodology of setting up checklists of functions as adopted by Gumperz (1982: 75–83), Grosjean (1982: 152), Appel & Muysken (1987: 29–31) and many other researchers have received many criticisms from theorists such as Auer and Myers-Scotton. For example, Auer (1995) argues strongly against generalizing functions of code-switching as a checklist as in Gumperz' (1982: 75–83) work and points out that there are at least three problems with such a checklist, with some of them also recognized by Gumperz himself (1982: 82–83). First, there are no clear definitions of such functions and a single label of function might involve different code-switching structures. Second, the categories of functions lack specific criteria; some labels refer to functions while some others refer to structures. Third, and perhaps the most importantly, such a checklist is not able to provide interpretations about how exactly code-switching is used to serve the specified functions. The main criticism from Myers-Scotton (1993a: 63) is that the studies stop short of organizing any listings or insights into a coherent and comprehensive theoretical framework. Also, she challenges Appel & Muysken's (1987: 29–31) classification of the functions of code-switching by raising several questions:

> While no one would deny code-switching has these five [sic.] functions, Appel and Muysken's 'linear' presentation generates a number of unanswered questions. Are not such functions as 'expressive' and 'phatic' so vague as to be vacuous? How are the two of them to be distinguished? Is the listing intended to be exhaustive? Are all functions equally important? (For example, surely the 'referential' and 'metalinguistic' functions of CS [code-switching] are not as important as the others.) Are they related to each other? Finally, how are they arrived at (i. e. what is their motivation)? (Myers-Scotton 1993a: 64)

While indeed Auer and Myers-Scotton have pointed out sharply the problems with these studies, there is also something very important in these studies which both Myers-Scotton's and Auer's analytical models fail to capture. Although methodologically not so favourable and in need for abstract constructs to enhance their explanative power, these 'checklist' studies provide us with a more complete picture of why people code-switch, and it permits assigning several functions to one specific switch simultaneously. By contrast, the Markedness Model only sees the negotiation of the RO set between interlocutors via code-switching as its calling and the CA approach to code-switching mainly deals with language intrinsic functions (i. e. the function of organizing texts and discourses).

There is little wonder that some researchers have found that both the macrosociolinguistic analysis and the detailed interaction analysis as focused on by CA should be combined, since the Markedness Model and the CA approach only concentrate on one segment of the whole picture. There are still bilingual situations whereby the referential function should never be neglected in explaining code-switching (e. g. Li 2001). Hence if more empirical data are at hand and to the extent that researchers aim at a more comprehensive picture with wider relevance, some of Myers-Scotton's challenges (e. g. the 'referential' functions of code-switching are not as important as the others) are badly-grounded cheap shot. All this seems to boil down to mean that we still need a theoretical model which not only has the capacity of bringing out a more complete picture but has abstract construct to allow explanative analysis as well. This is what the present study aims to explore. I shall return to this and venture to suggest a multifunctional approach to code-switching in Chapter 3 (see Section 3. 4. 2 below) after the theoretical framework is introduced.

2.4 Other studies on code-switching

In the previous section, I reviewed the studies which explore the functions, meanings, and motivations of code-switching. Some other studies on the other hand focus on the structural and psycholinguistic aspects of code-switching. I shall now introduce these studies very briefly and discuss some studies which have implications for exploring the social and functional aspects of code-switching.[6]

The 1970s witnessed an extension of interest from the social and functional dimensions of code-switching to include the grammatical and structural dimensions. Researchers believe that code-switching is not only constrained by contextual factors, but is subjected to grammatical rules as well. This means that code-switching is believed to be only possible on certain points in a sentence rather than on others. Poplack (1980: 585) might be the first to state explicitly that 'incorporation of both functional and linguistic factors into a single model is necessary to account for code-switching behaviour'. Then there have been efforts to find out universal or non-universal grammatical constraints on code-switching. The most famous constraints and models include Poplack and Sankoff's (Poplack 1980, Sankoff & Poplack 1981) Free Morpheme Constraint and Equivalence Constraint, DiSciullo *et al.*'s (1986) Government Constraint, and Myers-Scotton's (Azuma 1993, Myers-Scotton 1992, 1993b) Matrix Language Frame Model.

While some researchers have been trying to test, prove, and modify these constraints or to articulate new constraints, other scholars point out some problems of such a constraint paradigm. These challenges include that studies such as DiSciullo *et al.* (1986) follow Chomsky's theory and totally ignore contextual factors whereas code-switching is essentially a social phenomenon influenced by many types and aspects of social context (see Clyne 1987, 1991: 200; Poplack 2001). Bokamba (1989: 277) argues that the postulation of universal syntactic constraints on code-switching is premature. Huang (1999: 77) holds that the constraint-oriented exploration will not be the mainstream of code-switching studies that focus on its structures.

Some other studies attempt to consider the structural aspects of code-switching in relation to social factors or psycholinguistic studies. While postulating two grammatical constraints on code-switching, Poplack's (1980) study on the Spanish/English Puerto Rican community in New York is also a variationist one in that she relates types of code-switching (i. e. inter-sentential switching, intra-sentential switching, and tag switching) to social categories such as Spanish-dominant/balanced speakers, male/female speakers, speakers with different ages of L2 acquisition and migration, and other social factors such as education, ethnic identity, social network membership, and work place. The most elaborate correlation articulated by Poplack (1980) is the one between code-switching types and speaker types with regard to their English proficiency. While the reported Spanish-dominant speakers tend to switch to English by means of tag-like switching, the reported balanced bilingual speakers tend to use more intra-sentential code-switching and tag-like switching seldom occurs. Poplack explains that this is because tag-like switching allows the Spanish-dominated speakers to participate in the code-switching mode, without fear of violating a grammatical rule of either of the languages involved.

Poplack's findings, however, are not well confirmed by some studies focusing on other bilingual communities. Huang & Milroy (1994a, b, 1995) further identify two categories of intra-sentential code-switching, i. e. insertional and alternational code-switching in their studies on the Cantonese-English bilingual community in Tyneside, England. It is found that the first and second generations of the community, who are Cantonese-dominated, primarily employ insertional code-switching while the third generation which mainly grow up in Britain use both intra-clausal and inter-clausal code-switching and both insertional and alternational code-switching. Huang & Milroy's conclusion is contradictory to Poplack (1980) but highly confirmed by Bentahila & Davies' (1995) study on the Arabic/French bilingual Moroccan community. Bentahila & Davies's finding is that the most favoured code-switching type of the Arabic/French balanced bilinguals is sentential code-switching, which is least favoured by Arabic-dominated speakers who usually use switches of nouns and noun phrases. Although different correlations in different bilingual communities are illustrated, these studies combine to reveal that patterns or categories of code-switching can be used to index social groups. Partly due to the fact that these studies are usually recognized as research on the structural and grammatical dimensions of code-switching, their social orientation has been neglected and their contributions are not treated seriously by scholars who look at the social and functional dimensions of code-switching (see Section 3. 4. 1 below).

Myers-Scotton and Jake's research is undertaken with a psycholinguistic oreientation. Myers-Scotton's Matrix Language Frame Model and later the Abstract Level Model and the 4-M

Model (Jake 1994; Jake & Myers-Scotton 1997, Myers-Scotton 1993b, 2002; Myers-Scotton & Jake 1995, 2000) are based on W. J. M. Levelt's study, which assumes that a lexicon, in addition to word forms and word meanings, also specifies syntactic and morphological information. Although beginning with an attempt to account for the intra-sentential code-switching, these models are intended also for explaining other language contact phenomena such as attrition and convergence. There are some other studies which are also based on Levelt's study with adaptation (de Bot 1992, Wei 2002; see de Groot & Kroll 1997b). Other researchers such as Green (1986) and Grosjean (1997, 1998) focus on language activation in bilingual speech production. On the level of bilingual speech perception, studies are relatively few and there is a focus on word recognition (also called lexical access) (e. g. Grosjean 1997, P. Li 1996). Although these studies have provided important insight into the understanding of code-switching, they are from an intra-organism perspective (see Section 3. 2), which is less relevant to the present study which looks at code-switching as meaning making practice and therefore will not be introduced in detail here.

Some other linguists, albeit labelled as from a psychological or sociopsychological perspective, are actually interested in functions of code-switching in bilingual context. For example, Clyne's triggering theory, whereby there are words ' at the intersection of the two language systems which can cause speakers to lose their linguistic bearings and continue the sentence in the other language' (Clyne 1991: 193, also see Section 2. 4. 2 above), usually pertains to cohesive device and the organizing function of code-switching. Starting from social psychology and more specifically the accommodation theory (Giles & Smith 1979), which explains convergence and divergence in interactions, Bourhis, Giles, Leyens, & Tajfel (1979) discuss code-switching as a way of psycholinguistic distinctiveness and Sachdev & Bourhis (1990) analyze code-switching as a strategy of convergence.

2.5 Summary

In this chapter, I have begun a review of previous studies on code-switching by offering definitions, terminologies, and taxonomies of what I call generally as code-switching here. It is noted that the definitions of the key term ' code-switching' and the other related terminologies are closely associated with types of code-switching distinguished by researchers in the field.

I then continued to introduce studies on code-switching, with a focus on research which attempts to explore the social and functional dimensions of code-switching. In particular, I summarized the macro approach and the micro approach to the functions of code-switching, arguing that there should be some synthesis.

The review shows that while the studies have been offering important insight into code-switching, there are still areas which call for further exploration. These areas are concerned with a number of issues and here are four important ones: first, most of the previous studies including the widely-accepted theoretical models are intended for code-switching in spoken language while code-switching in written texts is neglected to a large extent; second, research such as Poplack's (1980) variationist study is usually recognized as focusing on the structural dimensions of code-switching and the important implication of aiming at variation of code-switching patterns is thus unfortunately neglected; third, the micro approach and the macro approach have been divorced from each other for a long time and there should be some synthesis; fourth, while macrosociolinguistic research relates code-switching to the social context for the explanation of the phenomenon, very few studies, however, actually attempt to consider code-switching with reference to the wider context of culture and certain ideologies. I explained why I chose to focus on written data with regard to the first gap in the introductory chapter; the other three points will be picked up again in Chapter 3 when I locate my study and suggest possible methods of exploration.

Notes

1. An earlier version of 'insertion' is 'transfer' (Auer 1984). Auer (1998b) uses 'insertion' to replace 'transfer', which has the disadvantage of being used in the field of second language acquisition in a different sense. I follow Auer (1998b) to use 'Insertion' here.
2. Myers-Scotton models after H. P. Grice's co-operative principle to articulate her Markedness Model, using principle and maxims and also borrowing Grice's notion of 'implicature'.
3. Although Auer integrates speaker's language ability and language competence into his analytical framework, he does not mention how we can determine whether one specific code-switch is uttered because of speaker's language ability; nor does he mention how to measure such language ability. In my discussion here, what is important is Auer's (1984) insistence that analysis of code-switching should refrain from 'background knowledge' or macrosociolinguistic factors. It is this aspect of his model that makes me treat it as from a micro approach.
4. In Li & Milroy's (1995) examples, pauses are marked by (.) or transcribed by indications in seconds, given in round brackets.
5. As regards studies on the social and functional dimensions on code-switching, Myers-Scotton (1993a: 62 – 74) identifies three approaches, i. e. the accidental/idiosyncratic approach, the 'better-taxonomy' approach and the 'better-theory' approach. The accidental/idiosyncratic approach refers to the viewpoint whereby code-switching is seen as whichever one happens to be on the tip of the tongue or whereby when code-switching occurs is so much a function of individual preferences that its social motivations are not amenable to study. This approach has been rarely found in recent studies. According to this classification, both Auer's and Myers-Scotton's analytical models are from a 'better-theory' approach.
6. For a more detailed review of the studies on the structural dimensions of code-switching, see Wang & Huang (2004a).

3 Theoretical Foundations

3.1 Introduction

As was stated in the introductory chapter, the theoretical framework of the present study will basically be SFL. Essentially formulated by M. A. K. Halliday, SFL is also called Hallidayan linguistics. As a linguistic theory focusing on language in use, SFL, which has been widely applied to many linguistic fields of studies, however, has not yet been utilized to analyze code-switching. The concern of this chapter is two-fold. One is to introduce the theoretical assumptions and basic principles of SFL, and the other is to provide rationale of a SFL approach to the present code-switching data. To introduce the theoretical preliminaries of SFL, I mainly base on Halliday's work (Halliday 1973, 1978, 1985a, 1994/2000; Halliday *et al*. 1964) while at the same time also adopting interpretations of and developments on the theory by other systemicists (e. g. Eggins 1994; Hasan 1973, 1977, 1985; Hu, Zhu, & Zhang 1989; Lemke 1995, 2002a; Martin 1992, 1997, 1999; Martin & Rose 2003; Matthiessen 1993; Thompson 1996).

3.2 Theoretical assumptions of SFL

SFL, which centres around language function, is essentially a linguistic theory from an inter-organism perspective. When discussing language in relation to social context and the conception of social man, Halliday (1978) details the location of his SFL approach with relation to other language studies. On the whole, according to the relation with other disciplines, Halliday identifies three headings to capture three types of language studies, viz. language as knowledge, language as behaviour, and language as art (Halliday 1978: 11). 'Language as art' refers to literary studies. With regard to 'language as knowledge' and 'language as behaviour', the contrast is of psychophysiological versus social, or in Halliday's terms, of intra-organism versus inter-organism. As Halliday points out,

> The distinction we are drawing here is that between the behaviour of that individual, his actions and interactions with his environment (especially that part of his environment which consists of other individuals), on the one hand, and on the other hand his biological nature, and in particular the internal structure of his brain. In the first of these perspectives we are regarding the individual as an integral whole, and looking at him from the outside; in the second we are focusing our attention on the parts, and looking on the inside, into the works. (Halliday 1978: 12–13)

The intra-organism perspective, broadly speaking, 'reflects the philosophical-logical strand in the history of thinking about language with its sharp distinction between the ideal and the real (which Chomsky calls "competence" and "performance")' (Halliday 1978: 17). The inter-organism perspective on the other hand rejects the distinction of the ideal and the real and sees language as a resource for creating meanings. These two perspectives are also loosely termed as the formal approach and the functional approach. More explicitly, Martin (1992: 3) summarizes the differences of the fundamental assumptions between these two perspectives:

Language as a resource

(i) Language is a network of relationships.

(ii) Description shows how these relationships are inter-related.

(iii) Explanation reviews the connection between these relationships and the use to which language is put.

Language as a system of rules

(i) Language is a set of sentences.

(ii) Description shows which sentences are in the set and which are out.
(iii) Explanation reveals why the line between in and out falls where it does in terms of an innate neurological speech organism.

It needs to be noted that these two perspectives are complementary orientations and indeed Halliday (1978) points out that it is possible to embed one perspective inside the other, as the psycho-sociolinguistics studies do. SFL is a linguistic theory that starts from an inter-organism perspective. Again to quote Halliday,

> We accept a much lower level of formalization; instead of rejecting what is messy, we accept the mess and build it into the theory (as Labov does with variation). To put it another way, we don't try to draw a distinction between what is grammatical and what is acceptable. So in an inter-organism perspective there is no place for the dichotomy of competence and performance, opposing what the speaker knows to what he does. There is no need to bring in the question of what the speaker knows; the background to what he does is what he could do — a potential, which is objective, not a competence, which is subjective. (Halliday 1978: 38)

Language is not an autonomous system of social practice. This view reminds us that fascinating as the work of pure, formal linguistics may be, we are not likely to understand the role of language in our culture and society if we divorce it from its integration into larger systems of resources for making meanings. For a functionalist, although the formal approach to the description of language leads towards psychology and genetics and there are fascinating and worthwhile areas, 'they do involve giving up any idea of looking at language in use' (Thompson 1996: 5). Instead of discussing meaning-making as something that is done by minds, the present study chooses a stance where meaning-making is discussed as a social practice in a community.

I have insofar considered 'functional' in its broad sense; what is specific about the term 'functional' in SFL? The term 'functional' in SFL has special implications. According to Halliday (1973), 'functional' first of all indicates both that SFL is a theory that sets out to explain language functions and that the theory believes that language is structured according to its functions. This functional view upwardly has accorded great significance to the social context of language use, and downwardly has served to be a principle in organizing syntactic analysis. Hence, 'function' is a central conception in SFL.

As was indicated, the functional view on language by SFL requires that it attach significance to the context in which communication is embedded. It is in this sense that Halliday (1978) articulates 'language as social semiotic'. As explained by Lemke (2002a), social semiotics as a whole seeks to connect the meaning making practice deployed in particular situation to the processes by which social and cultural systems are made and changed. Malinowski (1923) and Firth (1957) have been the most influential in the development of the contextual view of SFL.

As regards the relation of language to its context, or more generally, to reality, SFL assumes a constructivist relation rather than an essentialist one. According to such a view, 'the relation of language to the social system is not simply one of expression, but a more complex natural dialectic in which language actively symbolizes the social system, thus creating as well as being created by it' (Halliday 1978: 183). Closely related to this constructivist view is the conception of 'subject' in SFL. In effect, Halliday uses 'social man' or 'social being' instead, viewing 'subject' as constructed in and through language and social communication (Threadgold 1986: 117). A 'social man' is understood as a member of certain groups or categories which are socially significant. It is totally socially constructed and SFL focuses on how it is constructed by verbal communication with other members of the community. In other words, those speaking subjects that are outside of and not displayed by texts as social activities cannot be assumed into the social semiotic framework of SFL. This again leads us back to SFL's starting point i. e. an inter-organism perspective.

Described with a functional orientation, language is regarded as meaning making resources. For Halliday (1985a: 7), 'a language is a semiotic system; not in the sense of signs, but a systematic resource for meaning — what I have often called "meaning potential"'. This is made possible in SFL by modelling language as system network. Halliday (1994/2000: F52) states explicitly that the organizing principle of his theory is that of the 'system', 'which is used essentially in Firth's sense of a functional paradigm but developed into the formal construct of a "system network"'. SFL is hence a paradigmatic rather than syntagmatic theory. Not only are the choices paradigmatically interrelated, but the environments are also defined paradigmatically in that 'the environment of any option is the set of options that are related to it, including those that define its condition of entry' (Halliday 1978: 128). Each system in the network is represented as a choice from a set of potential alternatives. The outcome of a choice leads to another system as a choice until finally we get the realization, i. e. the structural consequences of each of the options. Every actual choice is put in the foreground by contrasting with other alternatives which are possible to be chosen but are not. A system is described by using network of subsystems which can be further described in the same way. Hence the principle of delicacy has made it possible for the description to be open-ended. It is always possible for further subcategorization and there is no point in theory where we should stop.

To sum up, SFL is a linguistic theory that starts from an inter-organism perspective and looks at language as meaning making potential. It is a theory dealing with language functions and believing that language is structured according to their functions. The functional view of language leads SFL to attach great importance to social context and to regard language as social semiotic. SFL is basically a constructivist theory whereby there is a dialectical relationship between text and context. In modelling language as meaning making potential, SFL has chosen to give priority to paradigmatic relation over syntagmatic relation, which makes it a choice grammar.

3.3 Some basic principles of SFL

Starting from the aforementioned underlying assumptions, systemicists have established their particular ways of analyzing language and some basic principles, which will be introduced in this section. In so doing, I shall basically follow Halliday (1978: 183–192) in distinguishing between 'language as system' and 'language as institution' as an underlying conceptual framework. According to Halliday (1978: 183), 'the salient facts about language as *system* are (a) that it is *stratified* (it is a three-level coding system consisting of a semantics, a lexicogrammar and a phonology) and (b) that its semantic system is organized into *functional* components (ideational, including experiential and logical; interpersonal; textual). The salient fact about language as *institution* is that it is *variable*; there are two kinds of variation, (a) *dialect* (variation according to the *user*), and (b) *register* (variation according to the *use*)' (emphasis in the original). Other important principles relevant to the present study, viz. instantiality/potentiality and semogenesis (see Halliday 1999, 1989/2003; Halliday & Matthiessen 1999; Matthiessen 1993), will also be discussed.

3.3.1 Language as system

The particular way that SFL treats language as system is to look at language as stratified and containing diversified functional components. The best known key terms with SFL such as semantics, lexicogrammar, and metafunction, are developed from the conceptions of stratification and metafunctional diversification.

3.3.1.1 Stratification

Influenced by Hjelmslev's (1961) idea concerning linguistic planes, SFL interprets language as a system of systems ordered in symbolic abstraction. This is made possible by the principle of stratification and the realization relationship between a higher stratum and a lower stratum. First of all a basic stratal line can be drawn between context and the semiotic system that is embedded in the former. In linguistic studies, this embedded system is language. Inside the language system, several strata (i. e. semantics, lexicogrammar, and graphology/phonology) can be identified. This stratified view of language system in context can be modelled in Figure 3 – 1 below:

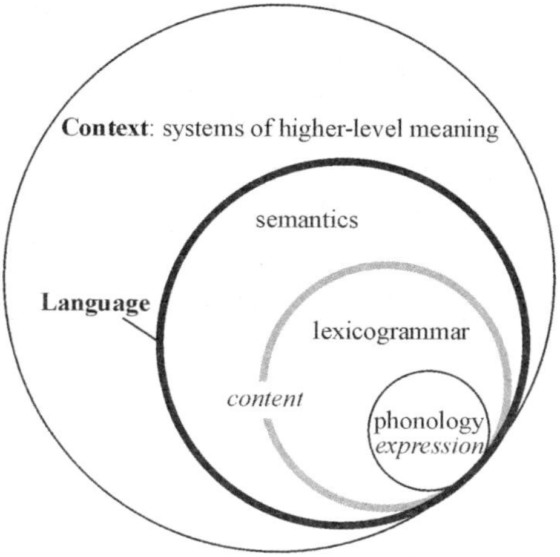

Figure 3 – 1 Stratification of language in context (from Matthiessen 1993: 227)

One basic assumption of SFL is that people do not interact in a vacuum; rather, they communicate within context. Consequently the language system, similar to other symbolic systems, is embedded in context. SFL distinguishes two orders of context, context of situation and context of culture. In Figure 3 – 1 the darkest circle indicates the boundary of language as a semiotic system.

Language as a stratified semiotic system consists of the strata of semantics, lexicogrammar, and phonology/graphology. Although a realization relationship is captured between every two neighbouring strata, semantics and lexicogrammar combine to form the content plane of the language system, with a natural relation between them. In Figure 3 – 1, the natural relation between the semantics stratum and the lexicogrammar stratum is indicated by a lighter circle. This highlights SFL's assumption that language is structured with regard to their functions. As opposed to this content plane, phonology/graphology is the expression plane. The relation between the content plane and the expression plane is essentially an arbitrary and conventional one in Saussure's sense. With regard to the focus of the present study, I shall concentrate on the semantics and lexicogrammar strata and also have a brief discussion on context as a stratum in the model.

(i) **SEMANTICS** Semantics is the highest stratum in the language system and therefore the linguistic inter-level to context. It is the linguistic stratum which has the primary responsibility for accommodating varying contextual demands on language. Registerial and codal variations are essentially semantic variations although they differ in whether there are higher-level constants (see Section 3. 4 below). The stratum of semantics is sometimes referred to as discourse semantics because it focuses on text-size rather than clause-size meanings (Martin 1992: 1). This is one way of understanding Halliday's (1978: 135) view that 'a text is to the semantic system what a clause is to the lexicogrammatical system and a syllable to the phonological system'. Semantics encompasses three strands of meanings (i. e. ideational, interpersonal, and textual) at the same time (see Section 3. 3. 2 below). This diversification of metafunctions can be projected both upward to the variables of context of situation and downward to the lexicogrammatical realizations.

(ii) **LEXICOGRAMMAR** Lexicogrammar is the linguistic stratum realizing semantics. As was noted above, semantics and lexicogrammar stand in a natural rather than arbitrary relation to one another. They combine to form the content plane of the language system. Transitivity, mood structure, and the thematic structure and information structure are typically located on the lexicogrammar stratum, with clause taken as the basic unit of analysis (see Halliday 1985c, 1994/2000; Halliday & Matthiessen 1999, 2004). They primarily correspond to the experiential function, the interpersonal function, and the textual function respectively. Eggins (1994: 23) suggests that 'what is distinctive to systemic linguistics is that it seeks to develop both a theory about language as social process AND an analytical methodology which permits the detailed and systematic description of language patterns' (emphasis in the original).

(iii) **CONTEXT** While context is constructed as system of high-level in Figure 3 – 1, the relation of context to language is not simply one of expression, but a more complex natural dialectic one. This is the constructivist relation whereby language symbolizes the social categories and social realities, creating as well as being created by them.

The whole social context is divided into varying situations. Such varying situations are termed as context of situation, which is concerned with the most immediate contexts of communication events. In describing context of situation, SFL has found it most useful to use the three well-known contextual variables, namely, field, tenor, and mode. Since context of situation is the immediate context of communication, it is primarily responsible for semantic variations; this is the 'upward' point of view. Because of the constructivist relation between language and context, it is also possible to look at the same issue from 'downward' and see semantic variations as the linguistic system's response to pressures from the diversity of contexts of communication. The discussion here concerning context of situation and register has dipped into the heading of language as institution. I shall return to registerial variation later in this chapter.

Context of culture is concerned with the wider social and cultural context. According to Halliday (1978, 1999), context is interpreted in terms of potentiality[1]. More specifically, contexts of situation are considered as instances of the cultural potential. Hence, a context of situation is to context of culture what a specific text is to the language system (Figure 3 – 2).

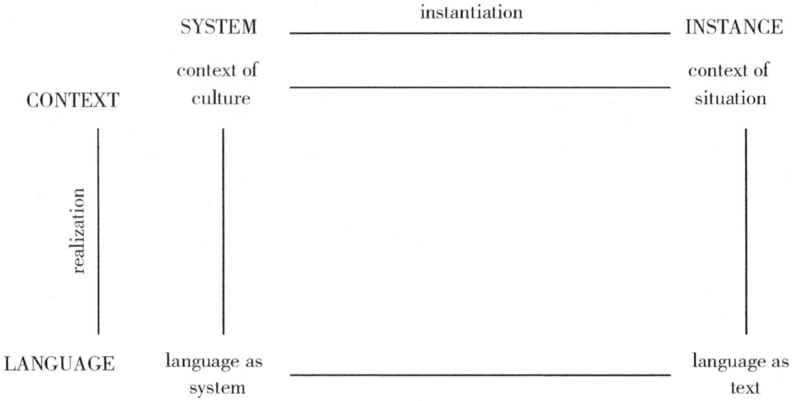

Figure 3 - 2 Language and context, system and instance (adapted from Halliday 1999: 8)

3.3.1.2 Metafunctional diversification

The best known aspect with SFL by other linguists outside the field might be its three metafunctions, one of the guidelines around which SFL is constructed. SFL hypothesizes that people use language to encode three types of meanings simultaneously, viz. ideational, including experiential and logical, interpersonal, and textual. They are called the three metafunctions and they locate on the semantic stratum. It is important to note that according to Halliday (1992/2003: 201), metafunction belongs to the theoretical categories rather than descriptive categories used in linguistic analysis. While descriptive categories such as clause, preposition, and theme are language-specific and have evolved in the description of particular languages, theoretical categories such as metafunction, system, and level are general to all languages and have evolved in the construction of a general linguistic theory.

The ideational metafunction 'represents the speaker's meaning potential as an observer', and 'it is the content function of language' (Halliday 1978: 112). It is language as a theory of reality and as a resource for reflecting on the world (Halliday & Matthiessen 1999). Responsible not only for representing the outside experiential world, but also for representing individual consciousness, the ideational metafunction expresses a variety of phenomena, everything that can be constructed as human resources and can be summed up as experience. The variety of phenomena can be divided into three categories of complexity, i. e. element, figure, and sequence, projected onto the lexicogrammar as group/phrase[2], clause, and clause complex respectively. Elementary and configurational phenomena are concerned with creatures, objects, actions, events, qualities, and states. Sequence as complex of figures deals with the kinds of relations figures can enter into. The more specific distinction of the ideational metafunction into the experiential function and the logical function corresponds to these two main parts.

The interpersonal metafunction is concerned with enacting interpersonal relation through language activities. More abstractly, it is the language function which involves speaking as doing. While the ideational metafunction involves the speaker as an observer, the interpersonal metafunction involves the speaker as an intruder. It focuses on the language in the practice of intersubjectivity. Martin (1997) breaks down the interpersonal metafunction into three semantic regions, i. e. speech functions (giving or providing information or goods-&-services), appraisal, and involvement.

While the ideational and interpersonal metafunctions are extrinsic if looked at 'from above', the textual metafunction is an intrinsic enabling function which organizes the ideational and interpersonal components into an integrated whole. This is another way of saying that we need the textual components in particular, apart from the ideational and the interpersonal, to produce texts. It is the textual metafunction that makes language relevant here and that is responsible for the texture.

When explaining how a clause can be seen as the configuration of the three modes of meaning, with English as the illustrative language, Halliday (1979/2002) associates the three modes of meaning with three structural types: 'experiential structures tend to be more elemental in character, interpersonal structures tend to be prosodic and textual structures tend to be culminative or periodic' (Halliday 1979/2002: 209). However, it is now believed that such structural types are not only found in English; rather, understood as a general tendency instead of a rule, these structural types are the regular structuring principles that the realizations of different metafunctions tend to follow (Halliday & Matthiessen 2004: 61). Outside SFL, such structural types of language are also recognized by K. L. Pike although he uses different terminologies (i. e. particulate, field, and wave) (see Halliday 1979/2002, Martin 1992: 548 – 549). Within SFL, Martin (1997) extends the three functional components and the structuring principles from the description of clause to the description of text. The modes of meanings and the structuring principles are summarized in Figure 3 – 3.

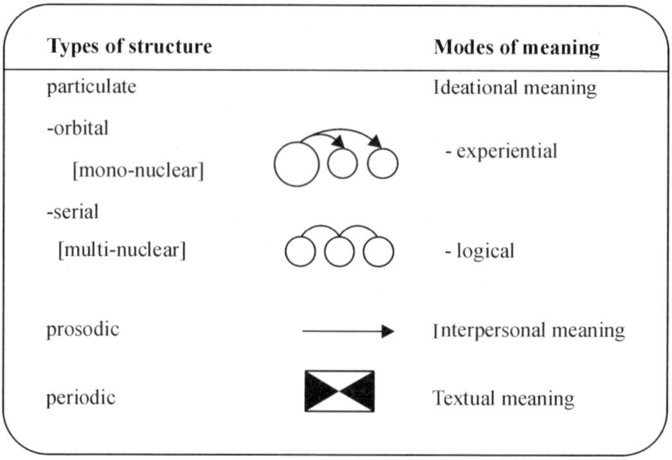

Figure 3 – 3 Types of structure and modes of meanings (from Martin 1997: 17)

Since semantics is the stratum locating between context and lexicogrammar, it would be useful to see how the metafunctional diversification is projected onto the two strata. I shall look at lexicogrammar first. There are basically three kinds of configuration making up a separate strand in the overall meaning of almost every clause: clause as a representation, clause as an exchange, and clause as a message. These three configurations are mapped onto each other, corresponding to the experiential, the interpersonal, and the textual metafunctions respectively. No single type of structure or mode of meaning is given priority in terms of significance; instead, all are considered equally important in the functions of the clause. Typical lexicogrammatical recourses for realizing these meanings are as such: clause as a representation basically involves transitivity; clause as an exchange involves the mood structure; clause as a message involves the thematic structure, information structure, and cohesion and coherence. The lexicogrammatical resources for the logical meaning are clause complex, whereby the logical independency relations and logico-semantic relations of the clauses involved are at stake. Regarding himself as a grammarian, Halliday has developed detailed methods of lexicogrammatical descriptions (Halliday 1985c, 1994/2000, also see Halliday & Matthiessen 1999, 2004; Matthiessen 1995). Due to the focus of this book, the introduction here is very brief and more details will be provided when specific lexicogrammatical resources are resorted to in the analysis.

In SFL, there are efforts to project the metafunctional diversification onto social context. More specifically, there is a match between the strands of metafunctions (i. e. ideational, interpersonal, and textual) on the one hand and contextual variables (i. e. field, tenor, and mode) on the other respectively. Such a match is between language and the immediate social context. This will be returned to in more detail later (see Section 3. 3. 2. 2 below). The metafunctional diversification also has its implication for the wider context of culture. For example, Lemke (2002a) attempts to project it onto the semantic relations of discourse formations and articulates a tripartite typology of semantic relation (i. e. thematic, axiological, and rhetorical-generic) (see Section 3. 4. 3 and Chapter 7 below).

3. 3. 1. 3 Metaphor and congruence

As a figure of speech, metaphor has been attracting the attention of rhetoricians for a long time. Although I shall focus on the conception of metaphor and congruence in SFL, there is no harm in starting the discussion from the traditional conception of metaphor, which is lexical in nature. Metaphor basically deals with verbal transference of various kinds. It is traditionally recognized as a figure of speech in which a word or phrase that ordinarily designates one thing is used to designate another, thus making an implicit comparison. Halliday (2003) provides simple examples of lexical metaphor so as to demonstrate how the view of lexical metaphor can lead to the conception of metaphor in grammar.

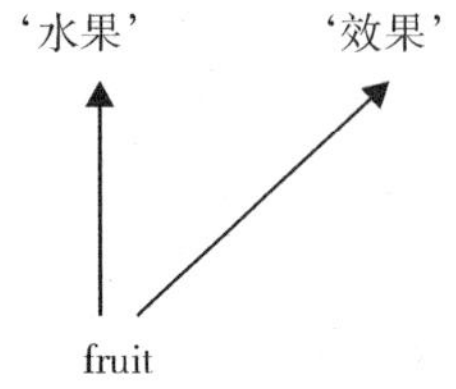

Figure 3 – 4 Metaphor seen 'from below'

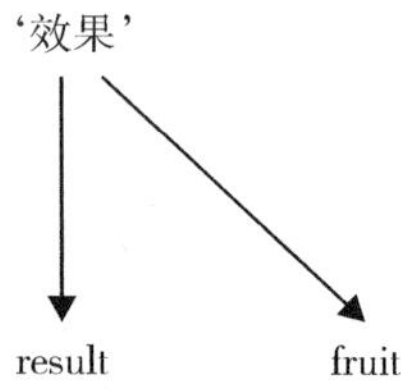

Figure 3 – 5 Metaphor seen 'from above'

As is indicated in Figure 3 – 4, the word *fruit* can be used to mean: (1) produce of the earth, edible covering on seeds of trees and shrubs; (2) outcome of an action, effect. The former is called literal meaning while the latter is called metaphorical meaning. The metaphor is seen 'from below' because we start from an expression (a word) and ask what it means. We can also look at metaphor from 'the above' and start with a meaning, asking how it is expressed (Figure 3 – 5). In Figure 3 – 5, the meaning 'the outcome of an action' can be expressed as *result* or *fruit*. *Result* is the congruent expression while *fruit* is the metaphorical expression. Of course *fruit* is the congruent expression for the meaning 'produce of the earth'.

These are all concerned with lexical metaphor whereby words are transposed. Considering transposing as the essential feature of metaphorical language, Halliday establishes his conception of grammatical metaphor, which involves transposing grammatical classes. It has been indicated that the relation between semantics (meaning) and lexicogrammar (form) is a realizational one. Specific semantic items have their typical lexicogrammatical realizations. Table 3-1 captures some of such typical realizations:

Table 3-1 Typical lexicogrammatical realizations of semantic components

Semantics	process	participant	circumstance	figure	sequence
Lexicogrammar	verbal group	nominal group	adverbial group/ prepositional phrase	clause	clause complex

If a semantic item is not typically realized and transposing occurs, grammatical metaphor is expected. For instance, the clause *The work needs modification.* involves grammatical metaphor, whereby a process (*modify*) has been coded as a noun (*modification*) and function as a participant in the clause.

Metaphorical and congruent realizations involve typical and atypical ways of encoding meanings. Since such typicality is implied in processes in which meanings are created, it is, therefore, useful to discuss metaphor in relation to the model of meaning creating processes, that is, semogenesis. Halliday (1989/2003) postulates that there are four dimensions of history that are forerunners of every sentence. These lines of thought are then developed into the semogenesis model for describing and explaining meaning creating processes.

The semogenesis model identifies three kinds of semohistory—logogenetic, ontogenetic, and phylogenetic, embodying different time scales respectively—that of the text, that of the individual, and that of the species (Figure 3-6). Phylogenetic history concerns with the evolution of the language system; ontogenetic history is concerned with the development of language in the individual from proto-language through a transition into adult language; logogenetic history involves the unfolding of text. Hence while phylogenesis provides the environment for ontogenesis, which in turn provides the environment for logogenesis, in the reverse order, logogenesis and ontogenesis provide the potential for change for what contextualizes it.

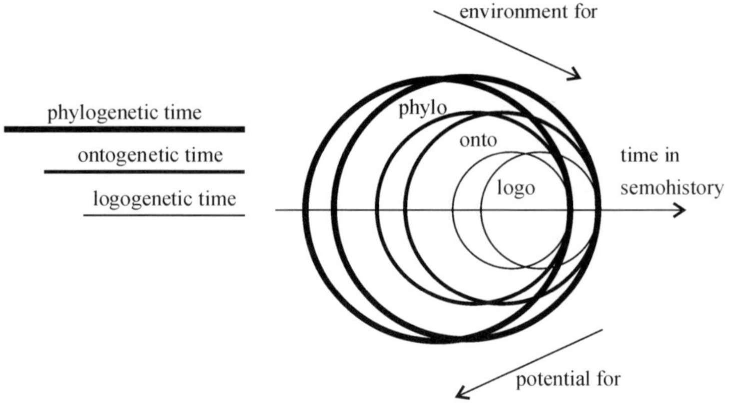

Figure 3 – 6 The model of semogenesis (from Matthiessen 1993: 265)

The semogenesis model with its three semogenetic histories provides a way to understand metaphorical versus congruent expressions. In terms of distinguishing between metaphorical and congruent expressions or deciding which expression has higher metaphorical value, semogenetic priority is an important principle. In simple terms, congruent expressions or expressions of lower metaphorical values will appear before the corresponding metaphorical expressions or expressions of higher metaphorical values, in each semogenetic history.

Halliday (1985c, 1994/2000) extends the transposing from lexical field to grammatical field. The conception of grammatical metaphor reveals the constructed nature of the term 'metaphor'. Halliday's treatment of grammatical metaphor is essentially based on cognition and indeed it easily reminds us of the Markedness Model reviewed in Chapter 2. I shall return to this when I consider code-switching in relation to metaphor and to Myers-Scotton's Markedness Model in Chapter 5 below. The conception of grammatical metaphor also demonstrates how we use different types of expressions to encode the 'same' meanings. The quotation implies that, as a choice grammar, systemicists also believe that 'the metaphorical lexicogrammatical realizations also construe new types in the semantic system itself and therefore expand its potential' (Matthiessen 1993: 262). This is also why metaphor is introduced as one organizing principle of language as system here.

3.3.2 Language as institution

The most salient feature about language as institution is language variation. In other words, language as institution is concerned with patterns of co-selections of linguistic features. Systemicists usually distinguish among three types of variation, i.e. dialect, code (semantic coding orientation in Benstein's sense), and register (Halliday 1978; Hasan 1973, 1989; Matthiessen 1993). Due to the focus of the present study, I shall skip codal variation and briefly introduce dialectal variation; registerial variation will be discussed in more detail because of its pertinence to the present study. The well-known distinction between dialect and register can be traced back to Halliday *et al.*'s (1964) discussion:

> A dialect is a variety of a language distinguished according to the user: different groups of people within the language community speak different dialects. It is possible also to recognize varieties of a language along another dimension, distinguished according to use. Language varies as its function varies; it differs in different situations. The name given to a variety of a language distinguished according to use is 'register'. (Halliday *et al.* 1964: 87)

Using Systemic Functional terms, dialectal variation and registerial variation differ in the locations of themselves and their higher-level constants (Hasan 1973, Matthiessen 1993). This can be summarized in Table 3-2.

Table 3-2 Dialetal and registerial variations and their constants across strata

	Lexicogrammar	**Semantics**	**Context**
Dialect	√		
Constant of dialect		√	
Register			√
Constant of register			

3. 3. 2. 1 Dialect

When discussing ‘institutional linguistics’ which in very general terms deals with the relation between a language and the people who use it, Halliday *et al.* (1964) distinguish between two types of varieties. The variety according to user is a dialect; the variety according to use is a register (Halliday *et al.* 1964, also see Gregory & Carroll 1978). Classical dialectology developed in Europe implicitly assumes a speech community to be a social unit whose members communicate with each other in a consistent way and all speak alike (Halliday 1978: 183). Although this is an ideal model of language, it highlights those lexicogrammatical and phonological/graphological variations with their semantic constants (see Table 3－2). This type of variation is the dialectal one, which is essentially variation between speech communities.

The term ‘dialect’ first and foremost pertains to regional or geographical variation. A case in point is varieties of Englishes in the world, which has become a field of academic studies. Unfortunately, the use of the term ‘dialect’ usually involves unsettling problems such as dialect versus standard dialect and dialect versus language. I would not go into detail about these issues but it is useful to point out that the distinction between dialect and language may sometimes be more political, historical or cultural rather than linguistic (Gregory & Carroll 1978: 17). Hence, differences between languages are in nature not so different from dialectal variation; the semantic constant is the link that makes translation possible.

Apart from geographical dialect, we also have social dialect whereby the speech communities can be defined as social classes or social categories. For example, in many societies there are upper class, middle class, and lower class, and people are thus grouped partly by the social dialects they are speaking. Social dialects can also be used to refer to dialects of genders or different age groups (in this case we actually often use ‘language’ and again this suggests that there is no clear-cut boundary between ‘dialect’ and ‘language’).

The dialect that a person speaks, no matter geographical or social, tells where he or she is from and generally who he or she is. This aspect of dialectal variation is rather different from that of registerial variation, which tells what he or she is presently doing or referring to. Halliday (1978: 34) notices that there is dialect switching where dialect comes to be an aspect of register. Indeed as our analysis will show, shifting of registers can be indicated by the shifting of social dialects, which are expressed in the code-switching patterns in the present case.

3. 3. 2. 2 Register

As is most basically formulated by Halliday, SFL traces its genealogy to the British linguist J. R. Firth. Firth (1957: 121 – 123) challenges the famous and widely accepted Saussurian notion of language as monosystemic in studying sound and prosodies. He argues that for different phonological contexts there are different lists of alternative phonemes. These lines of thought can be extended to argue that language behaviour was polysystemic, constituted of a range of different systems which vary according to social contexts and purposes. In other words, for Firth, language is a system of systems. This polysystemic hypothesis which sees 'the plurality of systems within a given language' (Firth 1957: 123) is pertinent to the conception of register. As is suggested by Matthiessen (1993), when the notion of 'context of situation' which Firth took over from Malinowski (1923) and the principle of 'polysystemicness' are read in conjunction with each other, it is theoretically reasonable to assume some sense of different systems of languages for systemically different contexts and hence the notion of 'register'.

Halliday (1978: 111) defines register as 'the configuration of semantic resources that the members of the culture associate with a situation type. It is the meaning potential that is accessible in a given social context'. Recall Table 3 – 2, where semantics is the stratum primarily responsible for registerial variation. This can be explained by the assumption that on the one hand semantics is the linguistic stratum which is the interface to context, and on the other hand the function of registerial variation is contextual. Different from dialectal variation, registerial variation does not have the higher-level constant. Its higher-stratal significance pertains precisely to diversification in context of situation (Matthiessen 1993: 234).

Context of situation is the contextual construct responsible for an individual text; situation type is to a register what context of situation is to an individual text. In describing context of situation or situation type, SFL has found it most useful to break it down into three variables: field, tenor, and mode. Intersections of different values of field, tenor, and mode combine to form the context of situation of a specific text or the situation type of a register[3]. This is what Hasan (1985) terms as contextual configurations (CCs). Hence a register has a situation type, which can be specified by its CCs, to correspond with it (Figure 3 - 7). In the present study, I shall term the context of situation and situation types as the immediate context of text and register respectively, which can be specified into context variables.

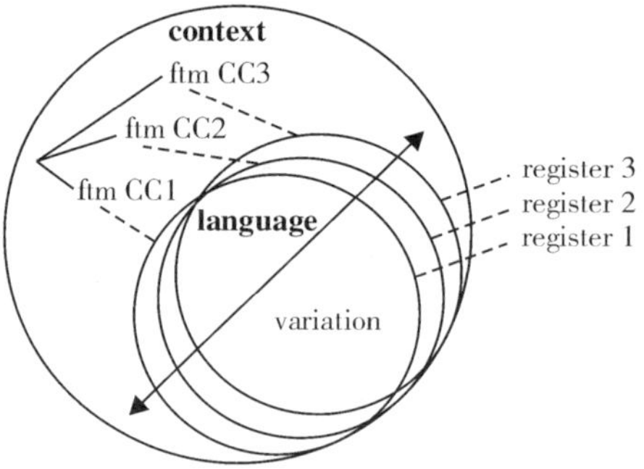

Figure 3 - 7 Contexts of situation characterized by CCs and corresponding registers (from Matthiessen 1993: 237)

As was mentioned in Section 3. 3. 1. 2, the principle of metafunctional diversification can be projected onto social context and a proportionality between contextual variables (field, tenor, mode) and metafunctions (ideational, interpersonal, and textual) is articulated (Figure 3 - 8). Such a hook-up hypothesis has important implications. That is, linguistic analysis can shed light on our understanding of context; on the other hand, the contextual factors can help us to predict some language patterns of texts. This has led Halliday (1978) to regard the register theory as a very simple and at the same time very powerful theory.

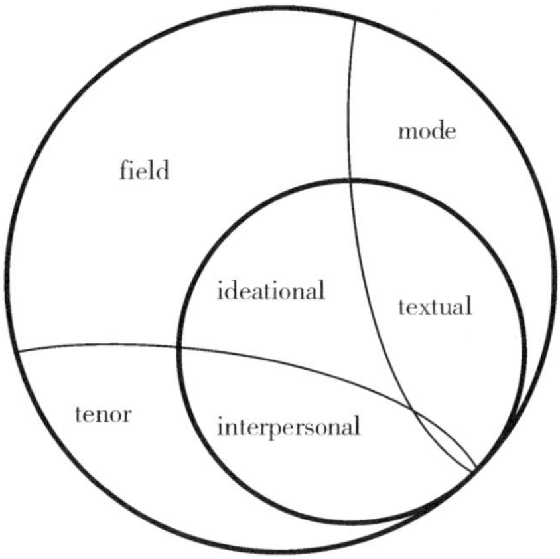

Figure 3 – 8 Functional diversification of language and social context (from Martin 1997: 5)

I have discussed that Halliday uses potentiality to model context, ranging from instantiated situations to cultural potential. It is possible now to provide a more complete picture by specifying an intermediate construct in the middle, namely, situation types as corresponding to register, which is also an intermediate construct between text as instance and language system as potential (Figure 3 – 9).

An understanding of a very similar term, genre[4], is closely related to the model provided. Both genre and register first of all seek to capture aspects of variation in language use and are constructs for grasping the notion of context. Halliday's main concern and contribution is about register rather than genre. In his early work, it seems that genre has a less serious theoretical status than register in that it is merely treated as involved in the

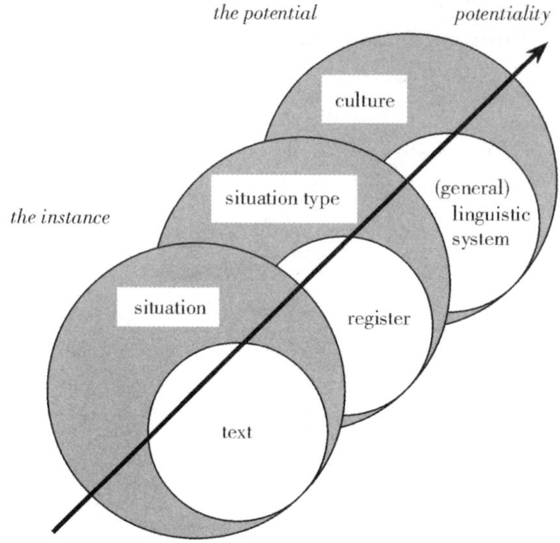

FFigure 3 – 9 Context of culture and context of situation along dimension of longterm potentiality (from Matthiessen 1993: 272)

realization of mode. Halliday argues that 'the concept of genre... is an aspect of what we here call the "mode"' (1978: 145). Elsewhere, he holds (Halliday 1978: 134) that 'the concept of generic structure can be brought within the general framework of the concept of register, the semantic patterning that is characteristically associated with the "context of situation" of a text'. Hasan's (1985) main contribution is the articulation of the Generic Structure Potential (GSP). The CC in the register analysis has a special status in explaining her GSP and its actual realizations. However, although using the very term of genre, Hasan seems to be inclined to use register and genre interchangeably to refer to a set of texts which are clustered by similar contextual factors (personal communication). Halliday and Hasan's point of view is adopted in the present study, while an overall tendency is witnessed and accepted that register analysis privileges the correlation between contextual factors and linguistic realizations while genre analysis takes text structure as its main concern with a special focus on the purpose of the interaction.

3.4 Rationale for a SFL approach to code-switching

In the previous sections, the underlying assumptions and basic principles of SFL were introduced. I am now in a better position to discuss why SFL is adopted to model the analyses of the collected data in this study and how SFL will help us to deal with the data.

Based on SFL, the present study is from an inter-organism perspective. The dichotomy between inter-organism and intra-organism perspectives unsettles the widely accepted tripartite typology of code-switching studies (i. e. functional dimensions, structural dimensions, and psycholinguistic dimensions; also see Section 2.1 above). It discloses that the established tripartite taxonomy is not well founded because it involves both phenomena aimed at by investigators (functions or structures) and theoretical perspectives (social or psychological). One result of this tripartite taxonomy is that the important implications of the variationist studies for the social and functional aspects of code-switching are neglected. Theoretically speaking, we only have two types of code-switching studies, one from an inter-organism perspective and the other from an intra-organism perspective. Hence while researchers such as Myers-Scotton and Jake are considering structures of code-switching, their research is in effect from a psychological and thus intra-organism perspective. On the other hand, the variationist studies (e. g. Bentahila & Davies 1995, Huang & Milroy 1995, Poplack 1980) which relate structures of code-switching to social categories provide important insights into our understanding of code-switching as a social phenomenon. The adoption of an inter-organism perspective in the present study means that language is seen as meaning making resources rather than as absolute rules, and if there is any investigation into the structural aspects of code-switching, it would be still from a functional approach. It is in this sense that code-switching is looked at as social practice.

In the remainder of this section, I shall consider theoretically a register analysis approach to code-switching and a multifunctional view on code-switching, and attempt to relate code-switching to a wider social context of culture.

3.4.1 Adopting a register analysis approach

The present study highlights intra-sentential code-switching and insertional code-switching (see Chapter 4 below) and I propose register analysis as a natural and necessary approach to the exploration of the code-switching highlighted in this study.

Intra-sentential code-switching is first and mostly explored by scholars who are interested in the structural and grammatical dimensions of code-switching (e. g. Poplack 1980, DiSciullo *et al*. 1986, Myers-Scotton 1993b) and its functional aspects are relatively neglected and have not yet been given systematic discussions. There are, however, some discussions on the type of code-switching with very frequent switches, usually with intra-sentential switching as its typical realization although inter-sentential switching may also be involved. Myers-Scotton refers to it as unmarked code-switching (1993a, also see Section 2. 3. 2 above); it is argued that each individual switch is not intended to convey a special social message and that it is the overall pattern which is intended to index simultaneous identities (1993b: 13). Similarly, some researchers (Alvarez-Caccamo 1998, Auer 1999, Franceschini 1998, Gafaranga 2000, Gafaranga & Torras 2001, Maschler 1998, Meeuwis & Blommaert 1998) argue that the code-switching pattern itself is a type of mode, medium, or lect (see Section 2. 3. 1 above). While there is still controversy concerning whether individual switches have certain meanings, one important implication of these studies is that apart from individual switches, code-switching pattern *per se* deserves our attention, especially for intra-sentential and insertional code-switching, and also for types of code-switching with not so very frequent switches.

In Section 2. 4, I mentioned that the variationist studies such as Poplack (1980) have important implications for the exploration of the functional and social dimensions of code-switching. In fact, the focus of these studies is on code-switching patterns and the variation of such patterns although it is not explicitly articulated. Scholars such as Bentahila & Davies (1995), Huang & Milroy (1995), and Poplack (1980) attempt to relate patterns of code-switching to social categories, for example, different generations of the community, speaker groups with different bilingual competence, and so on (see Section 2.4 above). In other words, these scholars look at code-switching pattern as a variable and examine its variation across different social categories, with different code-switching patterns as the variants. Code-switching pattern is then understood as an indexical feature of social categories.

Interpreted in conjunction with the distinction between dialectal variation and registerial variation (see Section 3.3.2), the variationist studies can be regarded as examining the dialectal variation of code-switching pattern since they look at variation according to language user. Then a natural question follows: can code-switching patterns also be examined with reference to registerial variation? It is very possible that code-switching will take on different patterns in different registers. This means that we look at variation of code-switching pattern according to language use. Few studies, if any, have attempted to look into this aspect of code-switching.

Since my collected code-switching data are from public written discourse, it would be more natural for me to relate code-switching pattern to newspaper registers rather than to the social dialects of different social groups in positivist terms as in Poplack (1980). However, dialect variation and registerial variation are in effect interconnected rather than sharply separated, especially when social dialect variation is involved. What we do is affected by what we are, and the registers a person has access to are a function of his place in the social structure (Halliday 1978: 2–3). Code-switching patterns as a feature of social dialects will be considered as an aspect of registerial variation. Adopting a register analysis approach to code-switching also helps researchers to relate practice of code-switching to the contextual configurations of field, tenor, and mode. As we shall see later, Chapter 4 is an overview of the code-switching in newspapers, where I will examine the differences of the code-switching pattern in different types of newspaper sections, seen as functional variations across newspaper registers; Chapter 6 attempts to explain the variations by resorting to contextual factors.

3. 4. 2 Developing a multifunctional view on code-switching

In Chapter 2 above, I reviewed the main studies aiming to address the functional aspects of code-switching. I also discussed the strong points and drawbacks of some studies or approaches (see Section 2. 3. 4 above). I shall now start from a SFL perspective and propose a multifunctional view on code-switching.

As was shown in Chapter 2, the checklist studies conducted by scholars such as Gumperz (1982: 75 –83), Grosjean (1982: 152), and Appel & Muysken (1987: 29 –31) have the strength of permitting a multifunctional view, which is however lacking in many theoretical models.

Many previous theoretical claims have focused on one metafunction or another of code-switching. Myers-Scotton's (1993a, 1999) Markedness Model concentrates on the negotiation of RO sets and hence negotiation of identities. Both this model and the situational/metaphorical code-switching opposition highlight the social values of language and the focus is always on the negotiation between interpersonal relationship as consequences of code-switching. In our framework, studies from a macro approach mainly deal with the interpersonal metafunctions of code-switching. Myers-Scotton (1993a) labels her Markedness Model as accounting for social motivations of code-switching; it is however important to note that the 'social motivations' she considers equal to only one aspect of context in our theoretical framework. On the other hand, studies from the micro approach concentrate on language intrinsic functions of code-switching or the contribution of code-switches to the organization of conversation. Functions of code-switching discussed in these studies include signalling side sequence or repair, indicating topic/comment contrast, discourse markers to mark discourse boundaries, indicating topic and frame, and the like (Auer 1984, Li & Milroy 1995, Maschler 1994, Nishimura 1995a). Since the principle of metafunctional diversification was already introduced, it seems natural for us to recognize that these functions can serve as specific examples of our textual metafunction and that they are contributing to the establishment of texture. This is another way of saying that while the macro approach highlights the code-switching functions as negotiating interpersonal relationships, the micro approach highlights the code-switching functions as organizing texts and creating texture. For a systemicist, there is little wonder that the two approaches should stand as inter-complementary; they correspond to the different metafunctions. If an analytical framework of code-switching functions aims to be applied to different bilingual communities with wider relevance, it should be a coherent framework into which the focal points of both approaches can be assumed.

More recently, Li (2001) looks at individual Cantonese/English code-switches in Hong Kong and argues that the code-switches in his data should be better understood as speakers' reluctance to translate English items into Cantonese in order to reserve the referential meaning (which roughly equals ideational metafunction in our terms). This study throws new light on our understanding of the code-switching in Hong Kong, whereby it is usually understood as that the overall pattern of code-switching indexes a double identity at the same time (cf. Chan 2004). Li's study has several implications and here are two important ones: first, although for one and the same bilingual community, if we focus on different aspects of code-switching (e. g. specific switches or the overall pattern), it is very possible that we are in a better position to see the multifunctional diversification of code-switching; second, in an analytical framework of code-switching functions with wider relevance, there should be a theoretical status for such ideational meanings as highlighted in Li's study.

A coherent view of these studies leads a systemicist to believe that a multifunctional view on code-switching such as SFL's metafunctional diversification is a useful alternative approach to the analysis of the functions of code-switching. This means that the present study will regard code-switching as social practice for making ideational, interpersonal, and textual meanings.

There is now only one final problem with the present diversified multifunctional approach to code-switching. It seems that I have chosen to adopt what Myers-Scotton calls a 'better-taxonomy' approach (see Chapter 2, Note 5), and I need to make sure that the present approach can tackle the challenges put forwards by Auer and Myers-Scotton (see Section 2.3.4). The introduction of SFL in this chapter has shown that the principle of metafunctional diversification has a sound theoretical basis and that the functions have clear definitions and criteria of their establishment. The present study accepts code-switching as a multifunctional social practice on a higher level and then zooms in to see how it is made possible in specific code-switching situations with specific switches. Metafunctional diversification is SFL's view on the abstracts of language function. Metafunctions do not refer to specific syntactic or communicative functions; They are concerned with abstracted functions and thus functions about functions. Because of their abstractness, the metafunction hypothesis is supposed to be a basic principle that underlies varying linguistic constructions in different languages. In other words, metafunction is a theoretical category rather than a descriptive one. Hence it is suggested that code-switching as social meaning making practice also involves the three metafunctions. This metafunctional diversification principle meets our needs in that it assumes a multifunctional view and permits dynamic descriptions and explanations in different code-switching situations. The interpretative and explanative power of the metafunctional analysis is further enhanced by the understanding that the metafunctional diversification can be projected onto social context, which can be specified as variables of field, tenor, and mode. In SFL, there is a constructivist relation between text and context, which is essentially how we can explain our language use. As has been made clear all throughout this chapter, a metafunctional approach should be deemed as belonging to what Myers-Scotton (1993a: 62) terms as 'better-theory' approach. This multifunctional view on code-switching will be taken up in Chapter 5, and Chapter 6 will try to relate it to the tripartite configurations of the immediate context.

3.4.3 Relating code-switching to a wider context of culture

In the summary of Chapter 2, it was mentioned as a gap in previous code-switching studies that few studies actually attempt to consider code-switching as meaning making practice which determines as well as being determined by the ideologies and value systems of particular cultures. On the other hand, in contact linguistics, although there is research which primarily discusses the spread of English and ideologies behind the English spread (e.g. Kachru 1986, 1994), unfortunately, discussions are usually not anchored onto specific textual description and analysis. However, putting the practice of code-switching in the context of culture is a necessary component of a study on language use in its context and should be regarded as a segment of a unified theory concerning code-switching.

It is really tempting for a systemicist to suggest a FLS approach to fill the gap when it is remembered that SFL 'develop(s) both a theory about language as social process and an analytical methodology which permits the detailed and systematic description of language patterns' (Eggins 1994: 23). In Sections 3.2 and 3.3 above, I explained how SFL sees language patterns as related to social factors. In doing so, most of the concentration was on linguistic features and the variables of context of situation and situation type. I now turn to the consideration of how systemicists bring the wider context (i.e. context of culture) into the picture.

As noted by Threadgold (1986), Halliday's context theory has been focusing on the register and the immediate semiotic construct of situation while the level of social analysis, which corresponds to Halliday's (1978) higher order social semiotic of social system, is much less-developed. This is why the introduction to context of culture is postponed to this section.

To relate text to the social context, it would be more manageable if intermediate level constructs can be established. We have seen that register is such a useful intermediate constructs for relating texts to the context (see Figure 3 – 8). However, as Lemke (2002a: 38) points out, 'the focus of register theory is on the relations of texts, and the semantic options they realize, to the immediate contexts of situation of their production and use'. Register analysis as on the intermediate level between language as potential and language as actually produced texts is very flexible in that it can be made delicate enough to specify a single text as a unique micro register on the one hand and be made to characterize a cluster of texts that have shared and recognized social and language features on the other. However, it seems that for the purposes of accounting for the co-patterning of more complicatedly connected meanings, the flexibility of the notion of register which essentially enables its shifting on the potential-instance scale is not 'flexible' enough here. Lemke (1983, 1985, 2002a) hence postulates discourse formation (also termed as discourse) analysis, the focus of which is on the relations of texts and webs of intertexts to their wider contexts of culture. In simple terms, discourse formation is used to describe the regular and repeatable, recognizably meaningful, and culturally and historically specific patterns of co-deployment of linguistic resources in a community. As a way to approach the context of culture, the principle of intertextuality or heteroglossia is highlighted in such a discourse formation analysis. Discourse formation can also be seen as an intermediate level construct. Discourse formation analysis looks at language activities as social behaviours and tries to reveal the usually naturalized ideologies and power relations constructed in and through discourse practice.

Focusing on code-switching, I shall argue that the embedded code, in the present study, introduces into texts certain voices and discourses which are connected to ideologies of specific cultures. Through intertextuality analysis, we expect to see how code-switches are employed in specific texts as quoting certain voices or discourses to serve its meanings and how the practice of code-switching helps to construe as well as being determined by a context of culture. Chapter 7 will be responsible for the exploration in this area.

3.5 Summary

This chapter is intended to provide the theoretical foundations for the study. I have introduced the underlying assumptions of SFL, which include: language is resources for creating meaning rather than grammatical rules; language is functional and is structured functionally; language is a social semiotic and should be analyzed in the social context; paradigmatic relation is given priority over syntagmatic one; the relation between text and context is a dialectical one. Starting from these theoretical assumptions, SFL has its distinctive ways to model the theory. Looking at language as system, I have primarily considered stratification, metafunctional diversification and metaphorical use of language. Looking at language as institution, I have focused on dialect and register.

In order to identify the conjunction of the SFL theory to the present study more explicitly, the rationale of a SFL approach to code-switching have also been provided. The study sets out from an inter-organism perspective and hence it is the functions of code-switching in its context that are highlighted. With SFL providing the theoretical basis and by reference to the previous studies, I have attempted to suggest that to study the code-switching in my data, a register analysis approach and a multifunctional view are needed. Also, I have indicated how code-switching can be discussed in relation to a wider context of culture.

Notes

1. According to Matthiessen (1993), there are at least three ways of modelling context of culture with relation to context of situation in SFL. These three ways have been using three different organizing principles respectively (i. e. rank, stratification, and potentiality). The principle Halliday is using is the last one, viz. potentiality, whereby context of situation is looked at as an instance of the context of culture.
2. Halliday (1994/2000: F47) distinguishes between group and phrase: 'A phrase is a reduced strain of clause, while a group is an enlarged strain of word.' Hence we have nominal group, adverbial group, etc. but prepositional phrase.
3. It is obvious that Halliday sees register and the contextual variables (i. e. field, tenor, mode) as belonging to different levels. He makes this rather explicit by saying that 'I would see the notion of register as being at the semantic level, not above it. Shifting in register means re-ordering the probabilities at the semantic level... whereas the categories of field, mode and tenor belong to one level up. These are the features of the context of situation; and this is an interface. But the register itself I would see as being linguistic; it is a setting of probabilities in the semantics' (Halliday in Thibault 1987: 610). Some other systemicists such as Martin (1992) and Eggins (1994) however treat register as belonging to the context stratum and hence a synonym of context of situation. There are two points worth noting here. One is that Martin (1999) views register and genre as very different abstractions of context in different levels. By contrast, in Halliday's or Hasan's conceptions, register and genre are modelled as constructs in the same level. The other point is that register is treated by Halliday and Hasan as phenomenon of language and the corresponding contextual term is *situation type* with *context of situation* reserved for the immediate context of a single text. On the other hand, Martin's *register* and *genre* are basically constructs in the context, and *context of situation* and *context of culture* are essentially their synonyms respectively. More theoretically, register is considered as state in functional variation by Halliday and Hasan while as connotative semiotic by Martin (also see Matthiessen 1993).
4. For more overall discussions on genre and register both inside and outside SFL, see Hyon (1996), Yunick (1997), and Zhang (2002).

4 Code-switching Patterns: A Registerial Variation Perspective

4.1 Introduction

I shall begin the analyses and discussions of the code-switching data by describing the code-switching in the several Chinese newspapers from a registerial perspective, which is what the present chapter aims to do. Primarily being descriptive, the present chapter will provide a basis for the following chapters, which endeavour to interpret and explain the practice of code-switching described in this chapter.

I shall first provide some information concerning the embedded English elements in the newspaper texts. Then I shall consider the code-switching examples in newspaper sections and discuss the code-switching data by reference to registerial variation.

4.2 The embedded English elements in the newspapers

As was indicated in Chapter 1, this study has chosen to focus on the code-switching instances in three newspapers published in Guangzhou (i. e. *Guangzhou Daily*, *Yangcheng Evening News*, and *Nanfang City News*). They are the most popular non-specialized newspapers in Guangzhou, and they, respectively, have a daily circulation of 1600 000, 1500 000, and 1030 000 (World Association of Newspapers 2003). Newspapers are a site for recording new ways of saying and the Chinese/English contact is reflected by the use of English elements in the newspapers.

Simply take the acceptance of the twenty-six English letters from *A* to *Z* for example. The English letters can be a system used to signify order or references. It is found that all the three newspapers use the format of English letters plus Arabic numerals (e.g. A2, B5) to number their sections. Also, expressions such as *A* 先生 (A xiānshēng, Mr A) and *B* 小姐 (B xiǎojiě, Miss B) often appear in the newspapers. When all of these come to us as no surprising, it needs to be noted that the English letter system is in effect replacing an indigenous system, i.e. the celestial stem and terrestrial branch systems[1] which can also been used to signify order or references. While it is true that the celestial stem and terrestrial branch systems might be much more complicated and hence inconvenient in signifying order, there are no obvious reasons why there is a tendency for 甲先生 (jiǎ xiānshēng, 'Mr jiǎ') and '乙小姐 (yǐ xiǎojiě, 'Miss yǐ') to be replaced by *A* 先生 and *B* 小姐.

Many researchers (e.g. Wu 2001, Yang 1999) notice a tendency whereby the Chinese language makes use of the English letters to form new lexical items such as 多 *D* (do1 di1, simply means 'more' with D as a particle), *Q* 版 (Q bǎn, 'cute version'), *N* 次 (N cì, 'N times' with N a mathematical symbol standing for 'indefinite number') etc. Sometimes a cluster of English letters is used as the acronym of a totally Chinese lexical item according to *hanyupinyin*, for instance, *MM* (měiměi, 美眉, literally as 'beautiful eyebrow' meaning 'beautiful girl'), *NB* (niú B, 牛 B, literally as 'cow B', adjective, meaning 'excellent'), *LG* (lǎogōng, 老公, literally as 'old man' meaning 'husband'), *LP* (lǎopó, 老婆, literally as 'old woman' meaning 'wife'), *GB* (guǎngběn, 广本, a shorted form for 广州本田, 'Guangzhou Honda'), etc. Most of such expressions are originated in and promoted by computer mediated communication (CMC); but they are also found in the newspaper texts.

Now I shall put aside these language contact phenomena, and focus my attention on the code-switching instances in the newspapers. Since the study is focusing on Chinese newspapers, it is natural to recognize all the code-switching examples as insertional code-switching, with Chinese as the matrix language and English as the embedded language, on the level of a whole newspaper.

Although many researchers follow Poplack (1980) in identifying inter-sentential code-switching, intra-sentential code-switching and sometimes tag code-switching, Huang & Milroy (1994b, 1995) challenge such a typology that tag switching is one type of intra-sentential code-switching; they follow Halliday to use clause as the analyzing unit (also see Bentahila & Davies 1995, Myers-Scotton & Jake 1997, Myers-Scotton 2002 using Projection of Complimentizer to refer to similar grammatical unit). Also, a Chinese sentence can be very long with many clauses separated simply by commas. Hence it would be more tenable to focus on clause rather than sentence for the data in the present study. In the collected code-switching data, the embedded English elements include words, groups and phrases, clauses, and even whole texts. Three types of code-switching are thus identified (i. e. inter-clausal switching, intra-clausal switching, and textual switching), examples of which are presented below:

Intra-clausal switching:

(1) "元点" BAND 队音乐 SHOW [YEN 30/9/2003 C8]
(The 'Yuandian' band's music show)

Inter-clausal switching:

(2) 这是最后一次扮孙悟空, Never Again, 因为真是太辛苦。[NCN 1/11/2002 B41]
(This is the last time I act Sun Wukong. Never Again, because it's so painstaking.)

(3) **Guangzhou Yunpu Baiyun Industrial Zone.**
Guangzhou Yunpu Baiyun Industrial Zone is a comprehensive development district approved by Guangzhou Municipal Government. Guangzhou Yunpun [*sic.*] Industrial Zone Baiyun Development Corporation is responsible for managing

the industrial zone. To meet the requirement of business expansion, we are looking for several high caliber candidates to join us.

Officer (Development Department) 发展部业务骨干

Requirements:

1. University graduate majored in international trade or English (TEM-8 is preferable)
2. Age below 35, good image
3. Familiar with the conditions of Guangzhou & Guangdong province
4. Able to work under pressure. Excellent communication & business negotiation skills
5. Knowledge of MS office, email & Internet is desirable

注：应聘者请将个人简历，学历证书，身份证复印件及近照在一周内寄至：广州市云埔工业区一路8号：广州市云埔工业区白云实业发展总公司发展部。邮编：510530。合则约见，勿电勿访。

[GZD 21/10/2002 10]

(***Guangzhou Yunpu Baiyun Industrial Zone***.

Guangzhou Yunpu Baiyun Industrial Zone is a comprehensive development district approved by Guangzhou Municipal Government. Guangzhou Yunpun Industrial Zone Baiyun Development Corporation is responsible for managing the industrial zone. To meet the requirement of business expansion, we are looking for several high caliber candidates to join us.

Officer (Development Department) Development Department Officer

Requirements:

6. *University graduate majored in international trade or English (TEM-8 is preferable)*
7. *Age below 35, good image*
8. *Familiar with the conditions of Guangzhou & Guangdong province*
9. *Able to work under pressure. Excellent communication & business negotiation skills.*
10. *Knowledge of MS office, email & Internet is desirable*

PS: Potential employees please send resume, education

certificates, a photocopy of ID card and a recent photo in one week to: Developing Department, Guangzhou Yunpu Industrial Zone Baiyun Development Corporation, 8th, the First Rd, Guangzhou Yunpu Industrial Zone. Zip code: 510530. Please do not call or visit us; we will contact you when we feel you are the person we need.)

Textual switching:

(4) **GROW WITH US**

HK Co. in GZ office wants:

1. Sales and Office Administrator
2. Accountant and Cashier (Guangzhou citizen)
3. Merchandiser and Shop assistant

· 3yrs + working experience;

· Good team player;

· Well with MS Office.

Please email Resume (do NOT use attachment) to:

HR@ncfindings. com ATTN: Ms Li

[GZD 21/10/2002 14]

On a lower level, some code-switches involve more balanced use of English and Chinese. Such code-switching is referred to as alternational code-switching, which usually takes place in the bilingual section titles such as 汽车周刊 *automobile weekly* 聚焦 *focus*, 时尚 *fashion*, 新生活 *lifestyle*, 娱乐大手笔 *celebrity entertainment column* etc. Some of such bilingual section titles are represented in Appendix I. In other code-switching examples, the two languages are usually not so balanced. Example (4) is totally coded in English. In texts such as Example (3), the matrix language is English rather than Chinese. Such examples are only found in recruiting advertisements.

In the data, all intra-clausal code-switching instances are concerned with English insertion into Chinese as the matrix language. The insertional elements include nominal group, adjectival group, verbal group, and preposition. For example,

Nominal group:

（5）这种配称法遵循“Mix & Match”的原则……［YEN 26/10/2002 C4］

(This way of matching observes the principle of ‘*Mix & Match*’.)

Adjectival group:

（6）金先生自小随父母移居国外，能说一口流利的英语，但中文就很“poor”，归国后在中信广场的一家公司从事高层管理工作。［YEN 7/10/2003 A5］

(Migrating to abroad with parents in childhood, Mr Jin speaks fluent English, but his Chinese is very ‘*poor*’. He works in a company as a higher level administrative officer in the Citic Plaza after coming back to China.)

Verbal group:

（7）……发誓要向身上的赘肉脂肪 say byebye［sic］，……［YEN 9/10/2003 C3］

(... promise to *say bye-bye* to the love handles, ...)

（8）现时广州，……到健身房 keep fit（瘦身），是都市女性的主流选择，……［YEN 1/11/2002 A5］

(Nowadays in Guangzhou, ... to *keep fit* (keep fit) in gyms is the main choice of city women, ...)

Preposition:

（9）出身背景：“草根阶层”VS 富家子弟［YEN 4/10/2003 B2］

(Family background: ‘grass roots’ vs. rich family children)

The data confirm previous studies (D. S. C. Li 1996, Yu 2001) in that most switches are nouns, and then come adjectives and verbs; there are only few instances of prepositional and adverbial switches.

Another feature of my code-switching data is that switched proper names have a high frequency. While some researchers (e. g. Myers-Scotton 1992: 29) treat cultural terms including proper names as unrelated to code-switching, I opt for an opposite stand, and I have strong reasons for this point of view.

First, to the extent that code-switching is understood as a sociolinguistic behaviour that is embedded in certain social-cultural context, there is no reason why cultural terms should be ruled out. The second reason is that Chinese and English are very different in terms of graphology. Although monolinguals may not have difficulties in recognizing switched proper names as such, they may have difficulties in memorizing and re-articulating the proper names. This means that switched proper names are similar to other code-switching items in that they are only accessible for bilinguals rather than monolinguals and hence belong to a phenomenon brought about by bilingualism. The third, and the more important, reason is that switched proper names can always have their translated Chinese names, at least by transliteration into Chinese characters, which are more acceptable by monolinguals; there must be motivations behind the use of English names, for in the data, many foreign proper names in certain sections are coded as what they are, with or without the Chinese translations.

4.3 Variation of Code-switching patterns across newspaper registers

In the previous section, I provided very general information about the code-switching in the data. In this section the code-switching in the data will be described from a register analysis approach, for which I provided theoretical account in Chapter 3. This means that the focus will be on the different patterns of code-switching in different registers.

4.3.1 Identifying newspaper registers

Before I embark on a register analysis of the data, there is one prior question: what registers do we have in the newspapers that I am examining? As we understand it, register is a notion which permits different degrees of delicacy. For example, while media texts can be counted as a register, sharing many common language features, it is still possible to find more registers along the delicacy if we decide to look into the media texts in detail. In the same way, it is possible to establish several registers for newspaper texts. For example, Bell (1991: 12) holds that genres[2] are the particular kind of media content in which readers are interested such as news, classified advertising, game shows, weather forecasts, and so forth. Similarly, Scollon (2000) classifies newspaper genres as officials meet, official statements, press conferences, sports, and China develops with sections such as editorials, financial reports, travel features, extended essays, arts and entertainments features also called genres.

With respect to code-switching in different newspaper registers, D. C. S. Li (1996) find that the prominence of domain as a crucial factor triggering code-switching is borne out in his data from Hong Kong Chinese newspapers, and among the favourite domains or topics in the newspaper, he identifies six where code-switching commonly occurs: computer, business (including administration, finance and investment, management, and marketing), fashion, food (including beverage), showbiz (covering film-making and music) and lifestyle.

Focusing on several Chinese newspapers in Guangzhou, Yu (2001) summarizes several newspaper discourse types whereby code-switching occurs frequently: computer discourse, academic discourse, advertising discourse, fashion discourse, and entertainment discourse.

While using different terminologies (domain and discourse), both D. C. S. Li's (1996) and Yu's (2001) are actually referring to what I call newspaper register here. Also, both of them then continue to describe the different patterns of code-switching in different domains and discourses.

As one of the pilot studies for the present one, we have undertaken a quantitative analysis of the occurrence of code-switching in different newspaper sections whereby usually code-switching can be found[3] (Lü, Huang, & Wang 2003, see Table 4 – 1). It is obvious that there are much more code-switching in entertainment and IT sections than others.

Table 4 - 1 Frequencies of code-switches in different newspaper sections (adapted from Lü *et al.* 2003)

sections	international news	national news	sports	entertainment	IT	others
percentage	7.9%	3.2%	6.6%	30.5%	37.9%	13.9%

With guidance from the media language studies and based on previous observations on code-switching in different newspaper registers, roughly several registers with special reference to the occurrence of code-switching can be set up: (i) hard news (including sports, health, travelling, and real estate for convenience of reference), (ii) IT & automobile, (iii) business, (iv) entertainment, (v) fashion (including shopping and lifestyle), and (vi) advertisement.

4.3.2 Code-switching patterns in different newspaper registers

In this section, the code-switching in several newspaper registers will be described. Hard news, where there are relatively few code-switches, will be discussed first and then I shall focus on several registers whereby code-switching is widespread.

(i) **HARD NEWS** In sections of hard news, sports, health, travelling, real estate, and so forth, code-switching instances are rarely found. When they do occur, the code-switches are usually accompanied by Chinese translations or explanations. For example,

(10) "Woman Power"（女人强权）已成为我们时代的特征之一。[NCN 2/11/2002 A2]
("*Woman Power*" (woman power) has become one of the features of our times.)

(11) SA 即 Sialic Acid（唾液酸）……［YEN 6/10/2003 C1］
(SA means *Sialic Acid* (Sialic Acid)...)

This is what Poplack & Sankoff (1988) term as flagged switching, whereby code-switching takes place together with translation, pause or other discourse markers. The following examples show that the treatment can be the other way round

(i. e. translations followed by switched items), resulting in what Newmark (1981: 75 –77) calls procedure of translation couplets.

(12) 这个神奇的小型机械臂被称作"幻影"(Phantom), 可以模拟出人类手臂的各种动作。[YEN 31/10/2002 A12]
(This amazing small-size mechanical arm is called 'Phantom' (*Phantom*); it can imitate the movements of human arms.)

(13) 近日, 美国航空航天局 (NASA) 的一份调查报告显示, 从国际空间站上的冒牌零件到月球岩石被盗, 去年以来 NASA 已经多次被承包商和自己的雇员欺骗。[GZD 1/11/2002 A15]
(Recently, a report of the National Aeronautics and Space Administration of U. S. (NASA) indicates that NASA has been cheated by contractors and its own employees for many times, including the fake spare parts in the space station and having the rocks from the moon stolen.)

Example (12) also makes use of 'translation label' (i. e. to use quotation marks to signal the translation so as to remind readers that this is actually a translation) (Newmark 1981: 75 –77). The code-switching in Example (13) is associated with the least effort principle. Similar to Example (12), when an acronym is first introduced into a text, its Chinese translation is usually provided; it is then the switched item that is used in the rest of the text. This bears out that switching to English acronym is for the sake of convenience. Acronyms such as that in (13), which usually involve names of institutions and organizations, are often found in these sections.

In the data, the only frequent used switch in the sports section is the preposition *vs* while in the real estate section, *shopping mall* is the one that can usually be seen.

(ii) **IT & AUTOMOBILE** Information technology, IT for short, and automobile are the register in which code-switching takes place frequently. Switches such as those in Examples (14) and (15) are found with a high frequency.

(14) ……都受到 RV 车，特别是 MPV 和 SUV 的强力挑战。[NCN 28/10/2002 C52]
(... meet great challenges from *RV*, specially from *MPV* and *SUV*.)

(15) 开始—运行—输入 dxdiag—显示，把 DirectDraw、Direct3D、AGP 纹理加速都启用。[YEN 9/10/2003 C4]
(Start — Run — input *dxdiag* — Display, and then invoke *DirectDraw*, *Direct3D*, and *AGP* texture acceleration.)

By contrast to the code-switches in the hard news register which are usually accompanied by Chinese translations, switched items in the IT & automobile register usually stand by themselves. Also, most of the switches are technical terms or jargon, many of which are acronyms. As a text in the automobile register indicates, 'there are more and more spare parts for modern automobiles and these state-of-the-art spare parts often have long names. For convenience's sake, English acronyms are usually used to replace these spare parts' long Chinese names, for example, ABS, BAS, EBD, PDC, etc.' [NCN 28/10/2002 C54].

Since the areas of IT and automobile are also closely related to business and marketing, embedded English items in this register include some proper names such as company names and brand names. This pattern is very much like that of the code-switching instances in the business section.

(iii) **BUSINESS** With the reform and opening up policy, China has been integrated into the international market. That is why many English or simply foreign names of enterprises, companies, brands, etc. have found their ways into the newspaper texts, especially in the business register. Usually the non-Chinese brand names will be quoted as they are, resulting in code-switching. For example,

(16) 超级市场和便利店经营商香港牛奶国际（Dairy Farm）公司日前与怡和太平洋控股（Jardine Pacific）达成协议…… [NCN 1/11/2002 C52]
(The supermarket and drugstore runner, the Hong Kong based

Dairy Farm (*Dairy Farm*) and the Jardine Pacific (*Jardine Pacific*) recently have come to an agreement . . .)

(17) 据 Venture One 研究公司和专业服务巨头 Ernst & Young 10 月 25 日发布的对风险投资基金的联合调查 …… [NCN 29/10/2002 C52]
(According to the combined investigation released on 25th, October, by *Venture One*, the research company and the service giant *Ernst & Young* on venture investment funds. . .)

(18) 这项诉讼还涉及百事可乐位于伊利诺伊州 Romeoville 的两家包装公司 RapakLLC 和 DSSRapakInc。[YEN 31/10/2002 A11]
(This lawsuit also involved Pepsi's two packing companies *RapakLLC* and *DSSRapakInc* in *Romeoville*, Illinois.)

As indicated by the above examples, while some proper names are provided with Chinese translations, others are not. Proper names can have inner structures of their own, such as *Dairy Farm*, *Venture One*. In this case, to the monolingual readers, the recognition of these foreign items as brand names outperforms the understanding of the lexical meanings of them.

(iv) **ENTERTAINMENT** The entertainment register is another site where code-switching is frequently found. The code-switching involves proper names including personal names and song titles, items related to music, items related to the Hong Kong show business, and some other switches that seem to create casual style.

Many foreign stars' names appear in the entertainment register in their original forms without translations. There is an interesting phenomenon, whereby super stars and VIPs are usually referred to by the Chinese transliterations of their names while small potatoes are on the contrary coded directly in English, without winning for themselves established Chinese translations of names, as in Example (19) below:

(19) 皮尔斯布鲁斯南的 30 岁女儿 Charlotte, ……Charlotte 并

非皮尔斯亲生女，是前妻 Cassandra 与前夫 Dermot 所生……［GZD 30/10/2002 B4］
(Pierce Brosnan's thirty-year-old daughter *Charlotte*, ... *Charlotte* is Pierce's stepdaughter; she is the daughter of his ex-wife *Cassandra* and her ex-husband *Dermot*...)

Note that in this example, Pierce Brosnan is coded in Chinese as 皮尔斯布鲁斯南（Píěrsībùlǔsīnán）which is a household name in China, while *Charlotte*, *Cassandra* and *Dermot*, with whom the Chinese audience are much less familiar, are simply quoted as they are.

There are many English song and movie titles inserted in the texts in this register. Some of them appear with their Chinese translations and most of them do not, which can be shown by the following examples,

(20) ……因为我非常仰慕她，我三四岁就在唱她的《Like a Virgin》了……［YEN 3/10/2003 B1］
(...because I adore her so much, and I sang her '*Like a Virgin*' when I was three or four years old...)

(21) 使用欧美老歌也似乎是韩片配乐的惯伎，《我的野蛮女友》有老掉牙的《My Girl》，这次也有《Do Wah Diddy Diddy》和《Happy Happy Shake》。［YEN 4/10/2003 B3］
(Using European or American old songs as the background music seems to be the old trick of Korean films. 'My Sassy Girl' has the hackneyed '*My Girl*'; this time we have '*Do Wah Diddy Diddy*' and '*Happy Happy Shake*'.)

(22) 这部毫不起眼的小成本电影打破了《12 怒汉》（12 Angry Men）创下的场景最小纪录。［NCN 21/10/2002 B35］
(This negligible low-cost film broke the record held by 12 *Angry Men* in using the smallest scene.)

It seems that the quick tempo of show business simply does not permit much time for many works in this field to have established translated names. This is confirmed by the fact that there are more song titles than movie titles coded directly in English. Also, reporters and editors seem to assume that those who are interested in this field should have some knowledge of English so as to recognize such foreign songs.

Some switches such as *base*, *hip-hop*, *rap*, *pop*, *drum' n' bass*, *house*, *big beat*, *encore* appear quite a few times in the data, without any translations. They are jargon of music and show business and in a sense similar to the technical terms in the IT & automobile register. These switches are invited by the topic of the register.

Some switched items are associated with the Hong Kong show business. Hong Kong is prosperous with its show business and also known as the Hollywood in the East. Some switches can be discussed by reference to the Cantonese-English bilingual Hong Kong (Chan 2003; D. C. S. Li 1996; Luke 1984, 1988). For instance, the Hong Kong based actors and actresses are sometimes referred to by their English names such as *Andy*, *Gi Gi*, *Jay*, *Karen*, *Kelly*, *Leon*, just to mention a few, which is one feature of the Hong Kong naming system (Li 1997). From time to timc, these actors' discourse is embedded with English items as in the following examples:

(23) 听到导演喊"Action",你就会很自然地躺下去,…… [YEN 3/10/2003 B1]
(When you hear the director say '*Action*', you will naturally lie down, ...)

(24) 他其实就是个很 down-to-earth(实际)的男人。[NCN 29/10/2002 B40]
(He is actually a man who is really *down-to-earth* (down-to-earth).)

Some other code-switches are manipulated to create a casual and humorous flavour (see Examples (25) and (26) below). This is in accordance with the entertaining function of the section.

(25) 至 hot 影视碟指引 [GZD 2/11/2002 B5]
(An introduction to the *hottest* movies, TV programs, and disks.)

(26) 2002 年，两位名嘴齐齐出道 10 年，又齐齐 30 岁，于是十年之养酿出了这个“10th · 30th Party!”。[NCN 29/10/2002 B44]
(In 2002, it has been 10 years since the two great talkers' commencer of their career and they are both 30 years old; hence it takes ten years to bring out this '10*th* · 30*th* *Party*!'.)

(v) **FASHION** This register including sections such as fashion, shopping, and lifestyle also witness many code-switching. Apart from the names of foreign designers and brand names, many code-switching instances are similar to those in the entertainment section in that they are used to encode a casual and fashionable flavour:

(27) 旧一点才是好的，破一点才是 IN 的。[YEN 26/10/2002 C4]
(Being old is good, and being worn-out is *in*.)

(28) 9 样发生在农林下路最 HIT 最 CURRENT 的事情，以流行榜的形式披露于各位面前，…… [NCN 1/11/2002 D70]
(9 most *hit* and most *current* things in Nonglinxia Rd, presented before you as Top 9...)

All these sections are associated with the motif of fashion. In this dimension, the motif of fashion is doubly coded both by the topic and by the style of language use.

(vi) **ADVERTISING** Advertising is another area of frequent code-switching. However, code-switching displays very different patterns in non-recruiting and recruiting advertising. The former chiefly involves intra-clausal and inter-clausal switching while the latter can even involves textual code-switching.

Usually both intra-clausal switching and inter-clausal

switching are employed to convey a 'foreign' and hence 'modern', 'fashionable' and 'technically-advanced' flavour. Below are an advertisement which contains code-switching:

(29) "因为有爱，所以永恒" / *William Blake*
就如 / "**Platinum with Love**" 以纯净、稀有、永恒的铂金及 **The Love Diamond**™完美结合，为您延续这段不变真挚 / 让爱变得璀璨，变得完美…… **My Platinum Wedding** *
[YEN 9/10/2003 B2]
("Eternity is in love with the production of time.' / *William Blake*
It's like / '*Platinum with Love*', a perfect combination of the pure, rare, and ever-lasting platinum and *The Love Diamond*™, and continue the forever feelings for you / let your love become resplendent and perfect …*My Platinum Wedding* *.)

Example (29) is Chow Sang Sang's advertisement of their wedding diamond platinum rings (see Appendix II for the whole advertisement). The first switch is the name of the famous poet, indicating that they are quoting foreign poems. The second and third switches are intra-clausal switching which are the names of collections of Chow Sang Sang. They are quoted as they are; the Hong Kong based Chow Sang Sang does not give Chinese names to these two collections. The last switch is an inter-clausal one. Together with other levels of strategies such as using foreign models, the code-switches invite a scene of a modern, elegant, and romantic wedding.

It is particularly frequent for advertisements to contain word play and it is found in the data that some wordplays are plays with code-switching.

(30) 黑白时尚条纹，我的年轻 *in* 记。[NCN 28/1/2005 A10]
(Black and white fashionable strips, my young *in* marker.)

Example (30) is a cell phone advertisement. The concept of 'in' is coded by both the lexical word and the embedded language. Intertextually, *in* here is replacing the homophonic Chinese character 印 since we have 印记 (yìnjì, 'imprint', 'marker') in Chinese. Then *in* fits well with 记 to mean 'a marker of being in'.

In some advertisements, the slogans are switched into English. Also, in many real estate advertisements, the advertisers are providing foreign names for their residences being promoted. Usually these switched elements are printed into artistic designs. Hence, it is supposed that the aesthetic function of these switched items and the created Western style are outperforming their referential functions. There will be more discussions on this in Chapters 5 and 7 below.

As for recruiting advertising (also see Section 4.2 above), some advertisements are totally coded in English such as Example (4); in some other cases such as Example (3), only the contact information is switched back to Chinese, which makes English the matrix language. Focusing on code-switching in recruiting advertising, Huang (2001: 291 – 292) argues that English is used to exclude Chinese monolinguals from becoming potential employees, serving the discrimination function.

4.3.3 Code-switching patterns and register analysis

The description in the previous section indicates that code-switching does not occur in a random fashion in newspaper texts; rather, the ways code-switching is employed vary across different newspaper registers. Code-switches rarely occur in the hard news register while the IT & automobile register witnesses a high frequency of English embedded items, which are usually technical terms. The entertainment register on the one hand parallels business register in that many proper names are directly coded in English and on the other, parallels the fashion register in that some nouns and adjectives are switched into English to achieve a fashionable flavour. Non-recruiting advertisements and recruiting advertisements display different patterns and functions of code-switching. The practice of code-switching in the former resembles that in the entertainment and fashion registers, while as concerns the latter, the whole or the main part of some advertisements might be coded in English, serving a discriminating function.

This means that code-switching pattern can be seen as a linguistic item which varies in different registers. In this light, the code-switching patterns described in the previous section are serving as candidates of indexical features (Halliday 1985a: 39) or realization patterns (Eggins 1994: 41 – 42) of specific registers. These indexical features of the registers contribute to a better understanding of the newspaper texts. Below is an extract of a text from the IT reports section (see Appendix III):

(31) …… 镶嵌闪片和烤印着 ET 图案的 T-Shirt 都是他的最爱。……我轻松地翻动滑板 kick-flip，接着冲上 U 型 [sic] 板的顶端，…… 我们爱闪，因为我们热衷最 FUN 的运动，崇尚最 IN 的理念，…… [NCN 29/10/2002 C55]
T-Shirt (s) with flashing pieces and *ET* pictures are his favourites... I kicked my skateboard with ease to make a *kick-flip*, and jump to the top of the *U* board,... We love flash, because we love the most interesting (*FUN*)④ sports, and we love the most *in* ideas.

Although the frequent occurrence of English items in Example (31) is one feature of the code-switching pattern in IT reports, also clear enough is that the inserted English items in the example are far from technical terms that usually take place in the IT & automobile register. Here comes the question of whether this text belongs to the IT register. If a reader goes through the whole text, he will find that this is a mobile phone advertisement rather than an IT report.

While scholars such as Bentahila & Davies (1995), Huang & Milroy (1995), and Poplack (1980) set up a link between code-switching patterns and subgroups of the communities, the link established by the present study is between code-switching patterns and registers. The attention of these scholars is on the variation of code-switching patterns according to user while the variation of code-switching patterns according to use is my focus.

Similar to the present analysis, some previous studies also describe different code-switching patterns in different newspaper registers (e. g. D. S. C. Li 1996, Yu 2001) although they use terminologies such as domain and discourse type (see Section 4. 3. 1). However, I would argue that recognizing the theoretical status of the variation of code-switching patterns as registerial variation can lead us further in exploring the social and functional aspects of code-switching.

As is implied by register analysis, a certain code-switching pattern is in effect one way of encoding the semantics within the meaning potentials defined by the register. As Ure & Ellis (1977: 197) point out, 'register is a certain kind of language patterning regularly used in a certain kind of situation. By making use of different kinds of register patterns, people show that they are aware of the social situation in which they find themselves'. Remember that it is discussed in Chapter 3 that the concept register is conceived as to capture the variation of language patterns in response to the contextual factors. Hence, the register analysis approach also permits discussing the practice of code-switching more systematically in relation to the contextual factors. This will be explored in Chapter 6 after I present a description of the functions of code-switching in Chapter 5.

4.4 Conclusion

In this chapter, I have first attempted to provide a general description of my Chinese/English code-switching data. The present data involve intra-clausal, inter-clausal, and textual code-switching and the insertional elements in intra-clausal code-switching examples include nominal group, adjectival group, verbal group, and prepositional phrase. The most frequently found switching type is intra-clausal switching with embedded English nominal group. Since this study focuses on Chinese newspapers, all the code-switching instances can be seen as insertional code-switching with Chinese as the matrix language and English as the embedded language in a level; in terms of individual texts, English is the matrix language and Chinese is the embedded one in some recruiting advertisements. On the whole, the code-switching data highlight intra-clausal and insertional code-switching.

The practice of code-switching in the newspaper sections has also been investigated. It is found that code-switching displays a patterned occurrence in the newspaper sections. Several newspaper registers (i. e. hard news, IT & automobile, business, entertainment, fashion, and advertising) can be set up, which have different code-switching patterns. The analysis indicates that for a description of the code-switching instances as collected in the present study, attention must be paid to the fact that code-switching displays different patterns in different registers. This is the approach I mentioned in Chapter 3 whereby code-switching is examined in relation to variation according to use.

Notes

1. The celestial stem system has ten elements, namely, 甲 jiǎ, 乙 yǐ, 丙 bǐng, 丁 dīng, 戊 wù, 己 jǐ, 庚 gēng, 辛 xīn, 壬 rén, and 癸 guǐ, while the terrestrial branch system has twelve elements, namely, 子 zǐ, 丑 chǒu, 寅 yín, 卯 mǎo, 辰 chén, 巳 sì, 午 wǔ, 未 wèi, 申 shēn, 酉 yǒu, 戌 xū, 亥 hài, corresponding with the 12 animals in the zodiac cycle. They can be used singly or together to signify order.
2. The term 'genre' used by Bell (1991) and Scollon (2000) can be seen roughly as equivalent with 'register' we are discussing. Also see Section 3. 3. 2. 2 above.
3. Lü *et al.*'s (2003) research is an early case study on newspaper code-switching in the sameproject with the present one. The data is collected from *Guangzhou Daily*, *Yangcheng Evening News*, *Nanfang City News*, *Nanfang Weekend*, and *Times* (Xìnxī Shíbào), during January, 2002 to May, 2003. The frequency count has been based on token rather than type.
4. The word 'FUN' is used as an adjective and a synonym of 'interesting' in some cases when it comes into the Chinese language.

5 The Metafunctions of Code-switching

5.1 Introduction

In the previous chapter, I provided an overview of the practice of code-switching in my data of several Chinese newspapers and suggested a registerial variation perspective to characterize it. In this chapter, based on SFL, code-switching is seen as a kind of multifunctional social practice and I shall set out to undertake a metafunctional analysis of the collected code-switching instances. I shall also attempt to extend the concept of metaphor in SFL to distinguish between metaphorical and non-metaphorical code-switching so that we have a better understanding of the forms and functions of the code-switching.

5.2 The metafunctions of code-switching

As was discussed in Chapter 2 and Chapter 3, many theoretical claims concerning the functions of code-switching mainly focus on one metafunction of code-switching. For example, studies from a macro approach highlight the interpersonal metafunction, while research from a micro approach mainly focuses the attention on the textual metafunction. On the other hand, some other studies which provide open-ended lists of functions of code-switching stop short of organizing any listings or insights into a coherent and comprehensive theoretical framework (e. g. Grosjean 1982: 152, Gumperz 1982: 75 –83). At least for my data, code-switching is a kind of multifunctional social practice which calls for a multifunctional perspective. In Chapter 3, I introduced the metafunctional diversification as one basic principle of the theoretical framework. Metafunction is a theoretical category (Halliday 1992/2003: 201) and it is supposed to be a basic principle that underlies varying linguistic constructions in different languages. Hence it is sensible to employ and test the principle of metafunctional diversification with code-switching data.

In this section, I shall consider the practice of code-switching in my data with regard to the experiential metafunction, the interpersonal metafunction, and the textual metafunction in turn. Then I shall sum up the three metafunctions and try to see what aspects of code-switching are being highlighted in discussing different metafunctions.

5.2.1 Switching code as tracing the experiential world

One important function of language is its capacity for us to articulate the experiential world around and inside us. This abstraction of language function is termed in SFL as the ideational metafunction, which can be divided into experiential metafunction and logical metafunction. Since the logical metafunction is mainly concerned with the logico-semantic relations between clauses and my data highlight intra-clausal and insertional code-switching (see Chapter 4), my discussion here will focus on the experiential metafunction. Below, I shall outline several factors or categories which alone or in some combination help to explain why code-switching can be seen as strategy of tracing the experiential world. These factors and categories are: (i) availability, (ii) specificity, (iii) translations already loaded with meaning, (iv) quotation, and (v) metalanguage.

(i) **AVAILABILITY** The most straightforward reason for code-switching in terms of experiential meaning may be whether what is encoded in the embedded items is available in the matrix language. In my data, I identify two categories where availability is usually in question. The first one and perhaps the most obvious one is proper names. The overview of the code-switching examples in the newspapers in Chapter 4 has illustrated that many proper names such as the names of persons, places, institutions, and organizations are directly coded in English, resulting in Chinese/English code-switching. Such switches are closely related to our experiential world in that proper names refer to persons and objects that are unique in the world and that these unique persons, objects, and organizations are simply called by those names. In many cases, there are no Chinese translations available for such proper nouns. Take the Korean brand *LG* for example; it seems that there is not yet any attempt to translate it into Chinese. Sometimes, the Chinese translations are not as popular as their original English names even in China. For example, the compact car *POLO* produced by Volkswagen was in recent years put into the China market by the Shanghai Volkswagen Com. Ltd. The producer provides no Chinese translation for the brand. While some people jokingly translated it into 菠萝（bōló, literally as ‘pineapple’）it does not outplay *POLO* in China.

Usually proper names are translated according to the pronunciations. However, this can also cause problems. As is indicated by one text in my data, the surname ‘Bergman’ is translated into Chinese sometimes as 伯格曼（Bógémàn）while as 褒曼（Bāomàn）some other times, and hence there might be some confusion about the referent [NCN 28/10/2002 E93].

Some of the switched proper names involve linguistic units such as group, phrase, and clause (e.g. the song titles and the movie titles), which are usually found in the entertainment register. Although they have their own structures, they parallel other proper names in that they also refer to something that has the feature of being unique. Chapter 4 indicated that the quick tempo of show business simply does not permit much time for many works in this field to have established translated names. Then it is natural to follow that quoting the song titles as they are is similar to the ‘Bergman’ example, helping to make the referents consistent.

The second category is culture-specific items. While proper names usually refer to specific objects in the experiential world, culture-specific items can be used to include more abstract concepts. Actually not many switched culture-specific items are found in the data. I wish the discussion of a simple word here can serve to illustrate my point. Let us take the simple word *party* for example. The meaning of the word *party* is ‘gathering of persons, by invitation, for pleasure’. It seems that the word has no real equivalent in Chinese. The usually used translations such as 集会（jíhuì），聚会（jùhuì），晚会（wǎnhuì）all have their obvious semantic gain or loss compared with *party*. In effect, it seems that we do not have such activities as party in its original sense in the Chinese tradition; we now have ‘party’ because it has been imported. It is also interesting to note that another term, 派对（pàiduì），the transliteration of *party*, is beginning to gain popularity. There are indeed many factors contributing to neology; one reason for 派对 to be accepted by the Chinese language is that 派对 is closer to *party* compared with other candidates such as 集会，聚会，and 晚会. The analysis here shows that code-switching is sometimes out of consideration of maintaining the semantic load as much as possible, although it is a matter of degree that how far we see the switched items as keeping the experiential meanings or as serving to represent styles（see Section 5. 3 below）.

（ii）**SPECIFICITY** For some embedded items, they do have Chinese translations; however, the embedded items and the translations are far from equivalent and usually different from specificity. Although many embedded English technical items in the IT & automobile register do have their rough Chinese translations, they are usually kept without being translating into Chinese for reasons of specificity. For example,

（1）Awave Audio 可将 MP3、WMA 和 WAV、CD Audio 等转成 RA。［YEN 29/10/2002 C2］
（*Awave Audio* can transform *MP3*, *WMA*, *WAV*, *CD Audio* and so on into *RA*.）

Switched technical items as those in Example（1）usually stand alone without any Chinese translations or explanations. For these items, if one does need to translate them into Chinese in other situations, one possible way is by using their hyponyms or superordinates as a method suggested by Baker (1992) when dealing items without equivalents. Then all the items in the example are probably translated into 音频格式 (yīnpín géshì, 'acoustic frequency format', music file format). However this translation method will not do here when it is remembered that what the text from which Example (1) is extracted, is dealing with the transformation between different music file formats. Hence, code-switching as a result of preserving the English items is pertinent to the expression of experiential meanings.

Similar enough to the above example, *outlook* appears in the data many times, always without any Chinese translation. Again, using a hyponym such as 电子邮件收发软件 (diànzi yóujiàn shōufā ruǎnjiàn, 'email receiving and sending software') is not relevant because usually the speakers are referring to that specific software *outlook* rather than other software with similar function such as Fox Mail, Dream Mail, etc.

(iii) **TRANSLATIONS ALREADY LOADED WITH MEANINGS** For some code-switching instances in the data, the potential Chinese translations are already loaded with other meanings. As a result, the English items are usually quoted as they are, sometimes with and sometimes without Chinese translations. Consider the following example that we have met in Chapter 4.

(2) 这个神奇的小型机械臂被称作"幻影"(Phantom),可以模拟出人类手臂的各种动作。[YEN 31/10/2002 A12]
(This amazing small-size mechanical arm is called 'Phantom' (*Phantom*); it can imitate the movements of human arms.)

In Example (2), a mechanism which can imitate the actions and movements of human beings is newly created and is named by using a common noun *Phantom*. A usual Chinese equivalent for *Phantom* has been 幻影 (huànyǐng), again a common noun. Obviously as a common noun, 幻影 in Chinese are already loaded with other meanings such as 'unreal image' and 'mirage' rather than one definite mechanism. In order to establish the link between the signifier and the referent, *Phantom* is also provided in brackets. This bears out that code-switching are sometimes used to indicate more exact experiential meanings.

In the real estate section, one frequent switch is *mall* or sometimes *shopping mall*. There are a few places whereby an attempt is made to translate *mall* into 摩尔（mó'ěr）. While shopping mall is a recently introduced item and consequently does not have its set Chinese translations, 摩尔 is obviously a translation according to the pronunciation. However, such a translation is questioned since 摩尔 in Chinese has been used to mean quite a different thing: the unit which measures the amount of substance, as a transliteration of 'mole'. Hence *mall* is usually directly quoted in English.

（iv）**QUOTATIONS** By now, what I have been discussing is all concerned with quoting the English original items as they are, which are usually words and groups. Let us now consider quotation, the more 'common sense' quoting, which usually involves a longer stretch of language. In SFL, this is called projection, meaning that something that has been articulated somewhere before is now projected into another text. Code-switching as a result of quoting can be deemed as an effort to keep as much as possible the features of another order of experience. The following example is found in the IT section where readers of the newspaper can write to editors and have their computer problems tackled.

（3）问：我在安装 Winxp 的时候，安装程序提示“... standard more：invalid DPMI return from 0387：o8ec ...”，到底是什么问题呢？我使用 HY/KingMax 64M SD 各一条，QDI 主板。[YEN 9/10/2003 C4]
（Q：when I was installing Winxp, the set-up program prompts that '*...standard more*：*invalid DPMI return from* 0387：*o8ec* ...'. What's wrong here? I use an *HY* 64*M SD*, a *KingMax* 64*M SD*, and a *QDI* mainboard.）

In Example（3）, the speaker is quoting what his computer

prompts, thus resulting in code-switching. In such cases, quoting the original is very much necessary because usually the speaker cannot figure out the problem and needs someone else's help to see what is actually happening there with his or her Win XP. The following are two similar examples whereby quoting the original seems more relevant.

(4) 把一些祝福或者表达的情感写在上面:"Happy day!"、"I LOVE YOU", …… [YEN 1/11/2003 C1]
(Print some wishing and caring words on them: '*Happy day*!', '*I LOVE YOU*', ...)

(5) 李小姐在 QQ 上打开一个朋友发过来的网址,蹦出的画面是大楼前路旁的一个指示牌,"Ms Li, Merry Christmas And Happy New Year",落款是自己同窗好友的签名。[YEN 27/12/2004 A13]
(Ms. Li clicked the website link sent from a friend. The picture that sprang out is that a guidepost saying '*Ms Li, Merry Christmas And Happy New Year*', and the inscription is the name of her classmate and good friend.)

Example (4) is taken from a text entitled 包装有话"说" (bāozhuāng yǒu huà 'shuō', 'Packages have their words to "say"') in the shopping section teaching people how to pack presents. One technique introduced in the text is to write some wishes or caring words on the presents. Hence what is exactly possible for presents to 'say' is much relevant here and the original wordings are quoted. The text also contains a photo to show how the packages look like with those caring words printed on them (see Appendix IV). Similarly, Example (5) is taken from a text entitled 电子祝福今年流行 DIY (diànzǐ zhùfú jīnnián liúxíng DIY, 'DIY electronic wishes are popular this year'). The text is reporting several instances whereby people created personalized web pages to send wishes to their friends. Example (5) describes such an instance and hence both the content and the language of the wishes are relevant in describing what kind of personalized features can be achieved by the way of

DIY.

In the data, there are some more 'common sense' switched passages as in quotations; for example,

(6) 几位外国朋友一边吃着手里的新疆风味烧烤，一边不停地说："Great! Great!"（好极了!）[YEN 6/10/2003 A1]
(Several foreign friends are saying '*Great*! *Great*! ' (Great!) while they are eating barbecues with the Xinjiang flavour.)

(7) "We will come tomorrow again（我们明天再来。）." David 让记者翻译给卖陶瓷的老板听。[YEN 4/10/2004 A3]
('*We will come tomorrow again* (We will come tomorrow again.).' David let the reporter to translate this for the boss selling ceramics.)

By using quotation, something that has happened and articulated is drawn into another order of discourse. This explains why quotations can often help to construe a vivid scene and to express objectiveness. Note that in discussing objectiveness we have slipped into the discussion of interpersonal components; however I would see objectiveness as a more general result of quotation and look at code-switching simply as a means to keep track of another order of experience.

(v) **METALANGUAGE** So far I have been concentrating on discussing code-switching as a strategy to trace the experiential world. However, code-switching can also be used to keep track of a special part of the experiential world, namely, the language system we are using. This is in the case of code-switching as a result of using metalanguage (Appel & Muysken 1987: 30). For example,

(8) 在现代，Mannequin 是指在橱窗示范衣饰产品的假人公仔，真人模特都叫 Model。不过，在 50 年前，活生生的模特儿不叫 Model，而叫 Mannequin。[NCN 1/11/2002 D66]
(In modern times, *Mannequin* refers to the dummy displaying dresses and accoutrements in shopwindows, with live models called *Model*. However, fifty years ago, live model was not

called *Model*, but *Mannequin*.)

(9) 全球知名语言网站“你的辞典”(yourdictionary. com) 24日公布了今年最热门的英文词排行榜，其中“无礼”(Incivility) 一词高居排行榜的榜首位。……因此热门词排行榜上排第二的就是“红州/蓝州” (Red States/Blue States)，指人群中出现危险的严重分裂。……在排行榜上列第三位的是“博客氛围”(Blogosphere)。[YEN 26/12/2004 A4]
(The world-famous language website ‘your dictionary’ (*yourdictionary. com*) released Words of Year lists on 24th, with ‘Incivility’ (*Incivility*) named as the Top Word... so the second Word of Year goes to ‘Red States/Blue States’ (*Red States/Blue States*), referring to the dangerously deep split of the people... The third goes to ‘Blogosphere’ (*Blogosphere*).)

It is in the sense that metalanguage is referring to a language system *per se* that we understand it as what Hjelmslev (1961: 114) terms as metasemiotic whereby the content plane itself (the words denoted) is a semiotic. When we focus on code-switching as a strategy to trace other areas of the experiential world rather than the language system, it is denotative semiotic that is involved.

5.2.2 Switching code as enacting interrelationship

We use language not only for reflecting and construing an experiential world, but also for establishing, negotiating, and maintaining interpersonal relationship. This component of language function is abstracted as the interpersonal metafunction. More specifically, systemicists look at three regions of interpersonal metafunction: negotiation of speech functions, appraisal or evaluation, and involvement (Eggins & Slade 1997, Halliday 1994/2000, Martin 1997, Martin & Rose 2003). Negotiation of speech functions is concerned with the exchange of information or goods-&-services between interactants (see Halliday 1994/2000) and hence the dynamics of speech functions are usually highlighted in conversations. Since the data I collected are of written mode, I shall skip the region of speech function negotiation and concentrate my discussions on code-switching as evaluation resources and involvement resources.

5.2.2.1 Code-switching as evaluation resources

As Thompson & Hunston (2000) point out, the expression of the writers' or speakers' opinions is an important feature of language and it needs to be accounted for in a full description of the meanings of texts. Appraisal and evaluation are concerned with the component of 'emotional charge' in a text, 'the kinds of attitudes that are negotiated in a text, the strength of the feelings involved and the ways in which values are sourced and readers aligned' (Martin & Rose 2003: 22). A variety of terminologies have been used by linguists to refer to this aspect of language functions in general and these include connotation, affect, attitude, evaluation, appraisal, stance, opinion, and so on. With regard to evaluation resources, Thompson (1996: 65) notes that with evaluation, we are on the edge of grammar since much of evaluation is expressed by lexical choices. Yang (2003) further argues that evaluation involves various systems of evaluative devices.

I am now trying to examine whether it is possible also for bilingual resources to encode evaluative meanings and how this is managed, which are much less explored in the literature to date. First of all, let us look at the following examples, some of which we have seen in Chapter 4.

(10) 9样发生在农林下路最HIT最CURRENT的事情，以流行榜的形式披露于各位面前，…… [NCN 1/11/2002 D70]
(9 most *hit* and most *current* things in Nonglinxia Rd, presented before you as Top 9...)

(11) 至hot影视碟指引 [GZD 2/11/2002 B5]
(An introduction to the *hottest* movies, TV programs, and disks.)

(12) 单色的西装已经完全 out [YEN 22/10/2003 C1]
(Homochromous business suit is completely *out*)

(13) 民族风由春夏一直吹到秋冬，设计师已将民族 Look 玩得不亦乐乎。[YEN 2/11/2002 C4]
(The fashion trend of China style has been in from Spring and Summer to Autumn and Winter, and the designers have been playing a great deal with the China *look*.)

(14) 真人模特儿里出现了 Super Model，假人模特儿也有明星。[NCN 1/11/2002 D66]
(While live models have their *Super Model*, there are also stars in dummies.)

In Examples (10) and (11), English has been used to indicate a flavour of fashion and modernization. In other words, the currentness, hitness and hotness are doubly coded by the attitudinal lexis on the one hand, and on the other by the switching into English. English as encoding modernization and foreign flavour is also found by Kamwangamalu (1992) and Huang (2001). It is in effect not necessary for the switching into English to be conflated with attitudinal lexis such as *current*, *hit*, and *hot*. Note that in Example (12), the switched item is *out*; it is sensible to suggest that although homochromous business suits are completely out, what the writer is talking about and the way he or she is talking are very in. Hence it does not matter so much which specific item is switched; what does matter is the switched-to language being English. 'Modern' and 'fashion' are the social values of the English language in this culture. In Examples (13) and (14), both of which are from the fashion section, it is noun and nominal group respectively that have been switched to English to express 'fashion'. Note that in Example (14), while 真人模特 (zhēnrén mótè, 'true-man models', live models) is contrasted with 假人模特 (jiǎrén mótè, 'artificial models', dummies), super model is parallel to 明星 (míngxīng, stars); both super model and 明星 trigger fashionable images, which are in line with the evaluative functions of code-switching.

We have looked at several instances whereby code-switching is serving as evaluation resources. Let me now see more theoretically the particular contributions of code-switching to the expression of evaluative meanings. In doing so, I shall need to refer to Martin and his colleagues' Appraisal system (Iedema, Geez, & White 1994; Martin 1997; Martin and Rose 2003; White 2001a, b) where they try to describe evaluation more theoretically and systematically.

In recent years, Martin and his colleagues establish the Appraisal system, within Halliday's interpersonal framework but develop it greatly, to account for the evaluative aspects of language. In this system, three dimensions are needed to account for appraisal, i. e. attitude, amplification, and source. Attitude can be divided into three categories: (i) Affect as resources for expressing feelings and emotions; (ii) Judgment as resources for judging character; and (iii) Appreciation as resources for valuing things. Amplifying attitudes involves graduation of attitudes. Resources such as intensifies, modality, metaphor, and swearing can be used to raise or lower, to sharpen or soften attitudes. Source refers to the immediate, intermediate, and ultimate sources of evaluative voices in discourses. Now I shall examine how code-switching as evaluation resources can be mapped onto the Appraisal system, when it makes its contribution to the expression of evaluative meanings.

It is felt that in the case of code-switching, the complexity of evaluation is intensified. In Example (12), the code-switch *per se* is capable of encoding evaluative meanings. The meanings of 'current' and 'fashionable' are implied by the embedded language used to code the item. Obviously code-switching can be considered here as Attitude: Appreciation. In Examples (10) and (11), however, it seems that the code-switching cannot be looked at merely as Attitude. In a sense, it is; but it can be also looked at as Amplifier serving to raise the volume of 'currentness' and 'hitness'.

The third region of the Appraisal system is the source of evaluation. Code-switching, the alternative use of two languages, in a natural way indicates 'otherness' and introduces other voices into texts (see Chapter 7 below for more systematic analysis). It is important that the source of an attitude is never a random choice. In the present case, the source of the voice as introduced by code-switching is also not accidental; rather, it plays an important role in expressing evaluation. Again take Examples (13) and (14) for instance. The introduction of the voice from English implies that what the authors of the texts are talking about is something that also happens in a Western discourse, which represents fashion and thus confirms the fashionable style of the texts and the sections. Hence the source of voices concerning evaluation serves to confirm, reinforce, and intensify the expressed evaluation and it is in this sense that the source of opinion is so important a dimension in analyzing evaluation. In this sense, code-switching as introducing other voices is also relevant to the amplification of evaluationl.

Code-switching as evaluation resources in the present data can also be perceived with reference to the tone of text or the key of a register. The overall tone or key for entertainment and fashion registers is considered as informal, entertaining, and fashionable; the practice of code-switching in these registers is in line with such a tone or key.

5. 2. 2. 2 Code-switching as involvement resources

Since we have looked at how code-switching is employed in the data to convey evaluative meanings, I now turn to code-switching as involvement resources. Martin (1997) finds in his Appraisal system that the grading resources also contribute to the negotiation of solidarity, but it is noted however that there are still some other resources serving the involving function and that we need to open up a separate region for this part of meanings. Indeed for any complete discussion of interpersonal components in a text, there should be a place for that component mediating involvement. Involvement is concerned with how much specialized the discourse is in terms of its readers and how interpersonal worlds are shared by interactants (Eggins & Slade 1997; Martin 1992, 1997; Poynton 1985). Eggins & Slade (1997: 143 –154) and Martin (992, 1997) detail a variety of resources for involvement, e. g. vocatives, slang, anti-language, taboo lexis, specialized and technical terms, standard and non-standard features. Although their treatments come down to very specific linguistic resources, it is useful to add that since involvement pertains to roles and identities, the employment of any linguistic feature of a social group would be an involving strategy for members of that group, and hence involvement resources are not restricted to vocatives, slang, anti-language, taboo lexis, swearing, and the like. This is concerned with social structure and is a conjunction between SFL and sociolinguistics (see Halliday 1978: 154ff.).

In very simple terms, we have different social categories and thus different language communities. This is made possible by the fact that there are always some links between social categories and language. Sometimes, the link between language and social categories is so strong, and variations of a single linguistic item, which can range from pronunciation, intonation to lexis and grammar, are enough to be an index of different social groups or categories (e. g. Labov 1972). The elicited logic is that the ways of using language can be social indices, indicating the location of the speaker in such social structures, and the speaker's identity is thus mediated and set up by, among other semiotic means, the language he or she is using. Since the link between language and social categories is first of all set up on the tension between homogeneity among group members and heterogeneity as to other social groups in linguistic terms, the issue of involvement not only indicates inclusions, solidarity and affiliation, but exclusion and alienation as well. They are the two sides of the same coin and sometimes referred to together as the 'boundary functions' (Tabouret-Keller 1997).

In bilingual situations, the link between language and social group can be more highlighted. One important factor in choosing one language over another is who the interlocutor in the interaction is. The most obvious case might be Gumperz' (1982) idea of 'we code' versus 'they code'. As was shown in Chapter 2, choosing to use code-switching as a mode of interaction can also be a way of indexing identity or negotiating involvement.

As was argued in Chapter 3 and demonstrated in Chapter 4, the present study has highlighted the variation of code-switching patterns across a variety of registers. This makes it possible to zoom in for examining the links between different patterns of code-switching and different social groups; usually different sections involve different reader populations (Kronrod & Engel 2001, also see Section 6. 4. 2 below). In other words, the code-switching patterns can be indexical of certain social categories and the way of using code-switching has the involving or excluding function.

In the registers of IT & automobile, business, entertainment, fashion and advertising, there are relatively more embedded English items, some of which are technical terms. In the IT & automobile register, the overloaded code-switches indicate a negotiation of the interpersonal relationship. By using overloaded code-switches, editors or authors of the newspaper texts are defining the boundary of the readership. For those IT or automobile technicians or at least amateurs, the code-switching pattern is what they are familiar with and in effect they are using. The code-switching pattern is hence inviting them to be readers of the register; laymen are not the target readers because of the overloaded use of English technical items. Likewise, the switching of song titles into English in the entertainment register is a strategy to involve western music lovers, and in the fashion register, keeping English brand names can be seen as a way of involving those people who are fond of western lifestyles.

Recruiting advertising is the site whereby the involving function of language can be most obviously witnessed. Some recruiting advertisements are completely coded in English except for the contact information such as address. As was noted, the collected newspapers are considered Chinese newspapers for the consumption by Chinese readers. Only those Chinese who have a command of English have access to the advertising coded in English. Hence, the textual code-switching in recruiting advertising demarcates its readership sharply, discriminating between bilinguals and monolinguals. Note that here the analysis has shifted back to the discussion of language choice.

The discussions here are closely related to interpersonal relationship as one variable of context. Hence the picture will be more complete until in Chapter 6 where the dialectics between the practice of code-switching and the immediate contextual factors is explored.

It is obvious that the highlighted aspects of code-switching for the experiential meanings and the interpersonal meanings of code-switching to be conveyed are quite different. While experiential meanings highlight the meaning differences between specific switched items and their potential counterparts in the matrix language, interpersonal meanings focus on code-switching patterns and their corresponding social values. As far as evaluation is concerned, the switching into the English language *per se* serves to encode and reinforce the flavour of fashion and modernization; as regards involvement, it is the overall pattern of code-switching that is highlighted albeit it is an empirical question how many code-switches would be enough to set off different readerships.

5.2.3 Switching code as organizing texts

As was introduced in Chapter 3 above, textual metafunction is an enabling function, making the ideational and interpersonal metafunctions into a semantic whole and generating the texture. It is concerned with the organization of texts and this is also why it is called the textual metafunction. In the code-switching literature to date, there some discussions on code-switching as discourse markers (Maschler 1994, Nishimura 1995a) or on its discourse-related status in conversation such as signalling side sequences (Auer 1984, Li & Milroy 1995). The functions of code-switching in such discussions are interpreted in the SFL framework generally as the textual metafunction, with reference to their contributions to the organization of texts. I shall in this section consider the contributions of the code-switches to the organization of texts. This, then, will be followed by a brief summary of the three metafunctions of code-switching.

Similar to other studies, some discourse markers such as *ok*, *by the way*, etc. are found in the data. By using these discourse markers, the speaker is actually articulating something like ‘so much for what we have been talking’ and ‘now I would like to talk about something else’. The contrast between the two codes involved highlights the organizing functions of the discourse markers. In other words, the functions of discourse markers as organizing the texts are doubly coded both by the items and by the fact of switching.

Some other switches are associated with the cohesion of texts. Let us first of all look at the following example which is taken from an interview with Carol Cheng Yu-Ling (郑裕玲, Do Do):

(15) 郑裕玲：……《男亲女爱》之所以这么受欢迎，就是男人普遍都有像余乐天那种 inferiority complex（自卑情结）。
……
记者：吕方会不会也有 inferiority complex?
[NCN 29/10/2002 B40]
(Cheng Yu Ling: ... The reason why War of the Genders gets so popular is because like Lok, men usually have *inferiority complex*...
Reporter: Does Lü Fang (Lui Fong) also have *inferiority complex*?)

There are altogether eleven code-switches (with nine types) in the whole text: two are concerning Cheng's program title ‘一笔 Out 销’ (The Weakest Link), eight occur in Cheng's turn and only one in the reporter's turn as in Example (15). As a Hong Kong based star, Cheng switches a lot while the Guangzhou based reporter switches only once and as Example (15) shows, the second *inferiority complex* can be seen as standing in an anaphoric relation to the first one in Cheng's turn and hence contributing to the cohesion of the text. It is what Auer (1984, 1988) terms as discourse-related insertion and it would be explained by Clyne (1991) as triggered by the first *inferiority complex*.

Similarly, in Chapter 4 we saw that in the register of hard news, after a code-switched acronym is introduced into the text, usually the English acronyms will be used in the rest of the text. While it is true that the principle of economy is playing an important role, the use of the English acronyms in the later part of a text can also be seen as establishing an anaphoric relation with the first occurrence of the English acronyms.

Let me now bring the three metafunctions together into a coherent story. At least in this Chinese/English language contact situation that I am focusing on, a description of the functional dimensions of the code-switching data calls for a multifunctional point of view. I have tried to show throughout Section 5. 2 that the code-switch instances in the data have their contributions to the expression of experiential meanings, interpersonal meanings, and textual meanings. To the extent that different metafunctions of code-switching are in focus, different aspects of it are being highlighted. When the experiential metafunction is in focus, we look at individual and particular switches; the switched items were compared to their potential Chinese translations, and the reason why they outperform their potential Chinese translations in terms of the expression of experiential meanings was discussed. In analyzing the interpersonal metafunction, I basically consider two regions of interpersonal meanings (i. e. evaluation and involvement). For evaluation to be conveyed, while the focus is on individual switches, it was also found that it does not matter which particular item is switched to English; what does matter is that there are switches into the language of English, whose social values are essential in the expression of evaluative meanings. As regards the region of involvement, the focus is however on the overall patterns of code-switching as discussed in Chapter 4. When the textual metafunction is concerned, the attention is on the contrast between the two codes and the locations of the switches. The contrast between the two codes highlights the discourse markers which are used to call for interactants' attention while the locations of the switches are important in discussing anaphoric elements and the like. It is then found that in the present study the realization of the three metafunctions of code-switching seems to coincide with the structuring principles of the metafunctions (see Section 3. 3. 1. 2 and Figure 3 – 3): 'particulate' for experiential function, 'prosodic' for interpersonal function, and 'periodic' for textual function. The correspondence is summarized in Table 5 – 1 below:

Table 5 – 1 Metafunctions of code-switching with different aspects of it highlighted

Metafunction	Types of structure	Aspects of code-switching highlighted
Experiential	particulate	specific individual and particular switched items
Interpersonal	prosodic	the Chinese/English code-switching pattern and its social values
Textual	periodic	the contrast between the two languages involved and the locations of the switches in the texts

While the overall tendency presented in Table 5 – 1 is found with the code-switching instances in this one specific language contact situation, it is suggested that such a tendency is by no means marginal and it can have wider relevance. For example, one important method employed by Li (2001) as a powerful illustration to show that it is more appropriate to see many English switches in the Hong Kong discourse as efforts to guard against semantic loss or gain in the referential meanings is to focus on particular individual switches and to compare them with possible Cantonese translations. In exploring the social motivations (equivalent to interpersonal metafunction here roughly) of code-switching, scholars such as Gumperz (1982) and Myers-Scotton (1993a) from a macro approach have accorded great importance to the social values of the codes and much attention has been paid to the switching to specific value-loaded languages when talking about metaphorical code-switching (Blom & Gumperz 1972) or marked code-switching (Myers-Scotton 1993a); or, they look at the overall patterns of code-switching to discuss identity establishment. Researchers taking a micro approach are mainly interested in the contribution of code-switching to the organization and development of the conversation, (i. e. the textual meanings in our terms). Such an interest and focus has led them to detach from conceptions such as social values of languages (Auer 1984) and resulted in their findings that sometimes the important points lie in the contrast between the two involved languages (e. g. Alfonzetti 1998).

5.3 Metaphorical and non-metaphorical code-switching

In the previous section, I attempted to analyze the code-switching instances in the data in terms of the three metafunctions (i. e. experiential, interpersonal, and textual) and their corresponding highlighted aspects. As for individual code-switches, it seems that some switches are taking on more experiential meanings than others which however take on more interpersonal meanings instead. For an explanation of this, a further distinction between different types of code-switching is needed. This section aims to provide explanations for this phenomenon and in so doing, the distinction between metaphorical code-switching and non-metaphorical code-switching is established. I shall first introduce these two types of code-switching and then I shall consider the implications of the distinction in relation to the expression of experiential and interpersonal meanings.

5.3.1 Distinction between metaphorical and non-metaphorical code-switching

In Chapter 3 above, I introduced the idea of grammatical metaphor in SFL. There are two points with Halliday's approach to grammatical metaphor that deserve our attention. One is that it helps to highlight the fact that metaphors are more prevalent in language than is often assumed and that metaphor is able to be working as a mechanism to extend the semiotics space. The other is that, as is pointed out by Halliday (1994/2000: 341), starting from his approach, we are asking not 'how is this word used?' but 'how is this meaning expressed?'. These two points make the distinction of congruent and metaphorical expressions relevant to the discussions on the meanings of code-switching here.

For the collected code-switching examples, metaphorical and non-metaphorical code-switching are distinguished. The code-switching with the technical terms in the IT & automobile register such as *MPEG*, *awave audio*, *outlook*, etc. are considered as non-metaphorical code-switching. They are called non-metaphorical because they are contrasted to the metaphorical ones that will be discussed below; and they are not called congruent code-switching since they do not have their corresponding metaphorical realizations. As was seen in Section 5. 2. 1 above, there might be no such things as equivalents to replace the non-metaphorical code-switching in the Chinese language. The switching is employed to guard for its experiential meanings. In other words, there are lexical gaps for the embedded items to fill and thus they are the most typical ways to encode the concerning conceptions.

Switched items which have their Chinese equivalents but are replacing their Chinese equivalents are considered to be metaphorical code-switching. Most of metaphorical code-switches such as *hit, hot, current, cute*, etc. are found in the registers of entertainment and fashion. Metaphorical code-switches are metaphorical realizations of the coded concepts, contrasted to their Chinese translations or equivalents as the congruent realizations. This means that we see the Chinese translations or equivalents as the more typical ways of expression.

Let me resort to the semogenesis model briefly (see Section 3. 3. 1. 3 above) for a further explanation of how the distinction between non-metaphorical code-switching and metaphorical code-switching is made. Halliday (1989/2003, also see Matthiessen 1993) uses the semogenetic system as a complementary solution to the distinction of the congruent and metaphorical realizations with regard to grammatical metaphor. Although the metaphorical use of language discussed here is not of the grammatical kind, the basic principle is believed to be relevant here. More associated to the analysis here are the phylogenetic and ontogenetic systems. Due to the fact that the type of Chinese/English contact is a learned one, metaphorical realizations such as *hot* and *cute*, which are elements from a learned foreign language will appear later than their Chinese counterparts 热（rè）and 可爱（kěài）. For non-metaphorical switches such as *MPEG* and *ADSL*, it is because they do not have Chinese translations that they are then used. Even if there were some Chinese translations, the Chinese translations can be metaphorical in the sense that *MPEG* and *ADSL* have appeared in the phylogenetic and ontogenetic systems earlier.

The discussion of metaphorical and non-metaphorical code-switching here is similar to Luke's（1984）distinction between expedient and orientational code-switching, although Luke's study seems to focus on informal situations. The discussion here also easily recalls Myers-Scotton's（1993a）marked and unmarked choices. However, while I am focusing on individual code-switches in considering metaphorical and non-metaphorical code-switching, Myers-Scotton's unmarked code-switching is concerned with code-switching patterns. If I have to do this, I would rather borrow Myers-Scotton's terminologies of marked switching and unmarked switching and reserve them for the descriptions of the overall switching patterns in different registers. I see the code-switching patterns across different newspaper registers found in Chapter 4 as unmarked code-switching in the sense that such patterns have been ingrained into our culture and are serving as indexical features of the newspaper registers.

Metaphor always involves discrepancy. While the discrepancy in lexical metaphor is the mismatch between the metaphorical meaning and the word which has its literal meaning, the discrepancy in grammatical metaphor is the mismatch between the metaphorical realization and the meaning encoded which has a more typical realization form, i. e. the congruent form（see Chapter 3）. It is natural for us to ask a similar question here: what discrepancy is to be found in the present kind of metaphor discussed concerning code-switching? I would be inclined to suggest that this is a kind of contextual metaphor since the mismatch happens between the context and the code used. In a very general sense of context, we can say that the Chinese language is used in the Chinese context of interaction and English in the context where interaction is undertaken between English speaking people. In the present case, the communication via the Guangzhou newspapers is typically in a Chinese context (in contrast with other situation such as Hong Kong and Singapore which officially involve both Chinese and English). It is in this sense that the discrepancy is found and the metaphorical use of language is discovered.

The way of looking at code-switching with reference to the mismatch of context reminds us naturally of Blom & Gumperz' (1972) pioneer work on code-switching whereby situational code-switching and metaphorical code-switching are distinguished (see Chapter 2 above). The distinction is essentially made on the basis of the correspondence between context/situation and the code used. While these lines of thought are also relevant here, it is noted that their study mainly deals with alternational code-switching or switching whereby speakers usually do not switch back, and that the concern of the present study is, however, on intra-clausal and insertional code-switching.

By using metaphorical code-switching, such as *hit, hot, current, cute*, etc. the 'English context' is activated and incorporated into the decoding of such metaphorical use of code-switching, namely 'modern' and 'fashionable' (see Section 5. 2. 2 above and Chapter 7 below). In Hjelmslev's (1961: 114) terms, the meaning expressed by the use of metaphorical code-switching is essentially of a connotative one in that for the meaning to be conveyed, the expression plane itself is a semiotic (Figure 5 – 1). In other words, the 'English context' first of all signifies modernization and fashion.

This is in effect what I analyzed as interpersonal meanings in Section 5. 2. The analysis here makes it more explicit that the discussions of interpersonal meanings expressed by code-switching should always take the social and ideological associations of the switched-to languages into consideration; this is also why I would like to discuss code-switching with relation to the context of culture in Chapter 7 below.

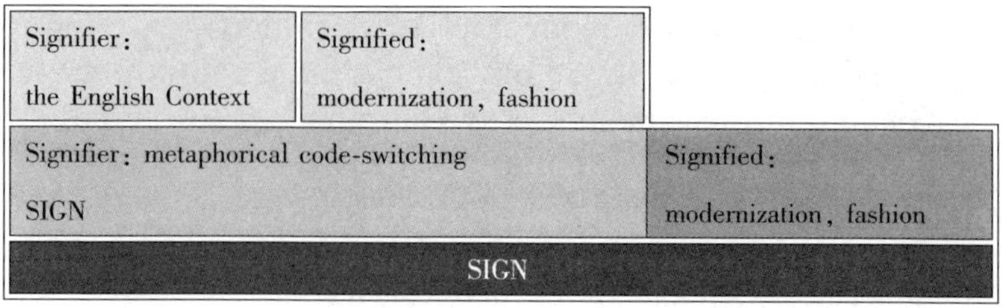

Figure 5 – 1 Metaphorical code-switching and connotative meaning

5.3.2 Implications on functions and forms of the code-switching

It is then suggested that since non-metaphorical switches are used to fill lexical gaps, they are mainly responsible for experiential meanings; on the other hand, since metaphorical code-switches take the place of their Chinese equivalents, the experiential meanings are not at stake and interpersonal meanings are generated from the fact of switching. All of this, of course, should be understood as a cline and a very general tendency (Figure 5 – 2).

Figure 5 – 2 Metaphorical and non-metaphorical code-switches with different metafunctions highlighted

With a focus on individual switches, it is the experiential metafunction that is at stake with the non-metaphorical code-switches such as *MPEG, awave audio, outlook* in the IT & automobile register. On the other hand, metaphorical code-switches such as *hit, hot, current, cute*, which are usually found in the entertainment and fashion registers, are responsible for more interpersonal meanings than experiential meanings. The affinities of non-metaphorical switches with experiential metafunction and metaphorical switches with interpersonal metafunction have implications for the forms of the code-switches.

On one level, we have seen that the most frequent switched items in the data are nouns and adjectives (see Chapter 4 above) and it is found that there is an overall tendency that switched nouns tend to be non-metaphorical switches while adjectives tend to be metaphorical ones. This can be explained by SFL's accounts of nominal groups. Technically, according to Halliday (1994/2000: 180 –191), the experiential structure of nominal group can be exemplified by ' Deictic + Numerative + Epithet + Classifier + Thing + Qualifier' . The Thing, which can be filled by common nouns, proper nouns, or pronouns, is usually used to name classes of persons, objects, institutes, and collectives[2], is the semantic core of a nominal group, being modified in one way or another by Deictic, Numerative, Epithet, Classifier, and Qualifier. As was shown in Section 5. 2. 1 above, some items are switched into English for the sake of referent consistency. This is closely associated with the functions of nouns as signifying referents and providing more elaborated taxonomies. Adjectives can fill the roles of Epithet, which is less objective, compared to Classifier, and can be used to express the speaker's subjective attitude towards the Thing. Hence it is little wonder that most of the metaphorical code-switches are conflated with adjectives.

Note that all of this should be understood as an overall tendency that permits exceptions. For instance, the code-switches such as *super model* and *look* are considered as metaphorical code-switches although they are nouns; similar to the switched adjectives such as *hot* and *cute*, they usually occur in the entertainment and fashion registers, where they are echoing the fashionable flavour of the registers. On the other hand, take the switches in the interview with Carol Cheng for example. In her speech, there are several switched adjectives including *youth-oriented*, *down-to-earth*, *up-dated*, *super aggressive*. Far from being interpreted as encoding an interpersonal meaning of being fashionable, these code-switches together with other switches *inferiority complex* and *He is a big man*! are associated with the speaker's Hong Kong background. Hence all the code-switches are followed by Chinese translations in brackets to ensure the experiential meanings can be understood. Note that while such a code-switching pattern is considered as unmarked choice for Hong Kongers (Myers-Scotton 1993a), the Guangzhou based readers will read it as marked choice and hence recognize the identity of the speaker as a Hong Konger. This has led us to the interpersonal region of involvement as discussed in Section 5.2.2.1.

On another level, code-switches that are responsible for experiential meanings should be managed in forms that enable readers to have access to the experiential meanings. In the data, this is made possible by two ways. One is to restrict the use of non-metaphorical code-switches, usually technical terms, to certain registers (e.g. the IT & automobile register) that have a specialized readership familiar with the English technical items. The other way is to provide Chinese translations for the switched items to reduce its metaphoricalness such as many code-switching instances in the hard news register. The fact of providing Chinese translations together with the embedded English items equals to saying that the experiential meanings are essential here and so both Chinese and English are offered. Metaphorical code-switches, on the other hand, are more concerned with the 'style', outperforming the experiential meanings of the switched items. It does not matter which items are switched into English; what matters is the switching to the English language *per se*. As a result, metaphorical code-switches are usually not translated into Chinese although they have their Chinese equivalents, with an implication that the recognition of the English language is more important than decoding the experiential meanings of the switched items. Sometimes the meanings of such items can be figured out from the context as in Example (13), whereby 民族 *look* is actually 民族风, and in

Example (14) whereby the meanings of *super model* can be inferred from 模特 and 明星. At other times, the clue might not be so explicit (e. g. Example (12)).

The forms of the metaphorical and non-metaphorical code-switching instances can be considered in relation to the Chinese/English language contact situation in China. As was mentioned earlier (see Chapter 1 above), the Chinese/English language contact in China is a learned one. One result of such contact is that there is a great difference with regards different people's English competence. Also, in the learned contact situation, with a same ethnical background, bilinguals, semi-bilinguals, monolinguals are not so separated distinctive social categories. These two factors are reflected in that the meanings served by the code-switches can be to some extent predicted by the forms of the switches. This also indicates that code-switching is not used far from randomly in newspaper texts. On the whole, switches that are motivated by the experiential metafunctions are accompanied with Chinese translations or explanations or meant for specialized readership, while interpersonal meanings of the metaphorical switches, as more or less indexed by the grammatical categories of the switched items and the register they occur, can be figured out by relating to the social value of the English language. These features of the code-switching have made it more acceptable by Chinese readers with different linguistic background concerning English and are a product of the present Chinese/English contact situation in China.

5.4 Conclusion

The present chapter has analyzed the functions of the collected code-switching instances. In doing so, I have adopted a multifunctional view and based on SFL's principle of metafunctional diversification.

The analysis in this chapter has demonstrated that the code-switches are employed to serve the three metafunctions, with different aspects of it being focused on: in the experiential metafunction, on individual and specific switched items; in the interpersonal metafunction, on the Chinese/English code-switching pattern and its social values; in the textual metafunction, on the contrast between the two languages involved and the locations of the switches in the texts. The different highlighted aspects of code-switching correspond to the structuring principles of the three modes of meanings in general. This means that at least in the language contact situation on which this book is focusing, a multifunctional view on code-switching is needed. In contrast to Myers-Scotton's (1993a) Markedness Model which mainly focuses on the interpersonal meanings of code-switching, the present study suggests that experiential meanings as motivations of many code-switches can never be neglected, especially when we are dealing with two languages with big differences, e.g. Chinese and English. The correspondence between the different highlighted aspects of code-switching and the structuring principles of the three modes of meanings is suggested to have a wider relevance rather than to be merely valid in the present case.

For a more in-depth understanding of the forms and functions of the code-switching, I have extended the conception of metaphor to consider my code-switching data. By distinguishing between metaphorical and non-metaphorical code-switches and analyzing their forms, we are in a better position to see how experiential meanings and interpersonal meanings are expressed. The descriptions of the forms and functions of the code-switches are related to the Chinese/English contact situation in China, which implies that different language contact types can involve different code-switching patterns.

Notes

1. Although Martin's Appraisal system (Martin & Rose 2003) articulates the importance of source of voice in analyzing appraisal and details how different voices can be introduced by certain lexical and grammatical means, it is a little bit disappointing to see that the system however does not spell out the interrelation between sources of voices and other aspects of evaluation. The analysis of code-

switching as evaluation resources reveals that the three dimensions of the Appraisal system might not be so cut and dried and need more exploration into the deceptively neat patterns.

2. 'Thing' can also name, by grammatical metaphor, phenomena that would typically appear as adjectives (qualities) or as verbs (processes and relations). These metaphorical 'things' often occur without further specification, since their referents cannot be said to have members in the usual sense.

6 The Immediate Context: Contextual Variables and Code-switching

6.1 Introduction

In the previous chapter, I discussed the functions of the practice of code-switching in the several Chinese newspapers. From time to time, I touched upon the context of the use of code-switches. This should not appear as surprising since semantics is the interface between language system and context as the higher semiotic system. The notion of context is central to a sociosemantic approach to language. In the last half century, there have been many researchers sharing a sense of its importance albeit concentrating on different aspects of context. Chapter 6 and Chapter 7 are devoted to the discussions of the context of code-switching with different focal points, the former on the immediate context (i. e. the situation types), while the latter on the wider social context (i. e. the context of culture).

The present chapter attempts to relate the practice of code-switching in the Chinese newspapers to the immediate context. Situation type is the contextual abstraction responsible for the immediate context of a register and the conception of immediate context would be more accessible if it is understood as a configuration of certain contextual variables. SFL has found it most useful to discuss the configuration of such immediate context in terms of three variables (i. e. field, tenor, and mode). In order to be more relevant to the discussions in Chapter 4 and Chapter 5, contextual configurations of situation types corresponding to the newspaper registers rather than the configurations of the contexts of situation corresponding to specific texts will be considered. In the rest of this chapter, a brief introduction of the contextual variables will first be provided. This will be followed by discussions of the three variables respectively, whereby I shall consider in detail how contextual factors, which are summarized as the three variables and their finer subheadings, contribute to the practice of code-switching.

6.2 Registers and the contextual variables

In Chapter 3 above, it was stated that the notion register can be related to Firth's polysystemicness and context of situation. Ideas in the writings of both Malinowski (1923) and Firth (1957) have been most important for the development of the notions 'register' and 'context of situation' in SFL. Malinowski (1923) studied the spoken texts of the peoples in the Trobriand Islands and found that it was impossible to convey the meanings and functions of those texts to a European audience without an extended description both of the social environment in which they operated and of their social purposes. He consequently coined the term 'context of situation'. Noting that 'the context of situation for Malinowski is an ordered series of events considered as in rebus', Firth believed that it is best used 'as a suitable schematic construct to apply to language event and that it is a group of related categories at a different level from grammatical categories but rather of the same abstract nature' (Firth 1957: 182). For Firth (1957: 182), such categories include:

A. The relevant features of participants: person, personalities
  (i) The verbal action of the participants
  (ii) The non-verbal action of the participants
B. The relevant objects
C. The effect of the verbal action

Firth's contribution to the establishment of 'context of

situation' is that he explicitly articulated the abstract nature of the notion and tried to break context of situation as a multifaceted and multiplex conception into several more manageable categories.

Following Firth's tradition, many researchers, including those who do not necessarily subscribe to the notion 'context of situation' or 'register', endeavour to propose categories of contextual factors. Young (1985) has provided a succinct summary of these studies. On the whole, to some degree there are agreements among researchers beneath a welter of conflicting terminology. Some of these studies are very important to and influential on SFL's theory of register and context (e. g. Ellis 1966, Ure & Ellis 1977, Gregory & Carroll 1978).

Inside SFL, in developing the notion of 'context of situation', Halliday and his colleagues (Halliday 1978, Halliday & Hasan 1985, Hasan 1977, Martin 1992) have built it into the whole system of language description and looked at it as the immediate context of a text. Also organized by the potentiality principle, context of situation is treated as the most foregrounded instance from the potential of situation type, which in turn is the instance from the potential of context of culture (see Section 3. 3 and Figure 3 − 9). Correspondingly, a register is a subdivision of a given language, a contextual-constrained variety constituted by a selection of choices from the total potential of linguistic options of one specific language. The discussion of a register pertains to its specific situation type.

In SFL, the semiotic construct of register is established from the very beginning to grasp the situation in which language is used. In other words, 'the notion of registers is thus a form of prediction, i. e. given that we know the situation, the social context of language use, we can predict a great deal about the language that will occur, with reasonable probability of being right' (Halliday 1978: 32). This articulation would be weak if the important theoretical question is left out: what factors exactly about the situation and social context would be needed to make such predictions? Systemicists have found it most effective to break down the context into three important headings. Halliday *et al.* (1964) articulate a typology of the contextual dimensions:

> While we still lack the detailed description of the registers of a language on the basis of their formal properties, it is nevertheless useful to refer to this type of language variety from the point of view of institutional linguistics. There is enough evidence for us to be able to recognize the major situation types to which formally distinct registers correspond; others can be predicted and defined from outside language. A number of different lines of demarcation have been suggested for this purpose. It seems most useful to introduce a classification along three dimensions, each representing an aspect of the situations in which language operates and the part played by language in them. Registers, in this view, may be distinguished according to **field of discourse**, **mode of discourse** and **style of discourse**. (Halliday *et al.* 1964: 9, emphasis added)

Halliday's 1964 typology has then been slightly modified in his later books (Halliday 1978, 1985a) where he replaces the term *style of discourse* with *tenor of discourse*. With respect to the covering range of the three headings, let me quote Halliday again:

1. THE FIELD OF DISCOURSE refers to what is happening, to the nature of the social action that is taking place: what is it that the participants are engaged in, in which the language figures as some essential component?
2. THE TENOR OF DISCOURSE refers to who is taking part, to the nature of the participants, their status and roles: what kinds of role relationship obtain among the participants, including permanent and temporary relationships of one kind or another, both the types of speech role that they are taking on in the dialogue and the whole cluster of social significant relationships in which they are involved?
3. THE MODE OF DISCOURSE refers to what part the language is playing, what it is that the participants are expecting the language to do for them in that situation: the symbolic organization of the

> text, the status that it has, and its function in the context, including the channel (is it spoken or written or the combination of the two?) and also the rhetoric mode, what is being achieved by the text in terms of such categories as persuasive, expository, didactic, and the like. (Halliday 1985a: 12)

This typology of contextual factors with their covering range has then been the most widely drawn-on version both inside and outside SFL. Taking this as the most basic schemata, systemicists such as Eggins (1994), Hasan (1977, 1985), Martin (1992), Poynton (1985) have worked towards more delicate descriptions of the three primary semiotic constructs by way of setting up subheadings. Their works are very important in that, by setting up more delicate links between context factors and linguistic realizations, we will be in a better position both to predict and explain language patterns of texts by referring to the context and to construe a context through analyzing the linguistic features of texts.

The following three sections will be devoted to the analysis of code-switching with special reference to the contextual variables. It would be more convenient and more explicit for me to do so if I relate the practice of code-switching to the three variables (i. e. field, tenor, and mode), of the context configurations respectively. I would hope this will not be understood as that the three variables influence the practice of code-switching independently; rather, as will be indicated by the following analysis, the three combine to bring out the whole picture interactively and interweavingly.

6.3 Code-switching and the variable of field

The first variable of situation type to be considered here is field, which may be the most obvious dimension of situation since it is associated with content, subject matter, and topic. After an introduction of the variable of field, I shall try to see whether the values of field have influenced the employment of code-switching and how this is made possible.

6.3.1 The variable of field

The reason for us to say that field may be the most obvious dimension of situation to be captured is that it refers to 'what is going on, the area of operation of the language activity' (Halliday *et al.* 1964: 90). It is 'that part of the structure of the social semiotic concerned with social actions with an institutional focus' (Benson & Greaves 1981). Under the heading of field, topic and technicality are usually discussed (Eggins 1994). Let me now look at these two important aspects of field (i. e. topic and technicality) below.

Topic is treated as one dimension of field in the current framework. Topic in the sense of subject matter refers to some domain of human experience, and so bears a close relationship to field of discourse (Hasan 1994: 139). One important implication of this treatment is that topic is not treated as a superordinate beyond the setting of the language activities. This stand is opposed to a generally accepted articulation that we use different ways to express the same thing in different situations. This articulation is deemed as an illusion in the SFL framework where form is the realization of meaning and there is no clear line between 'what' and 'how'.

Once topic is accepted to be one dimension of the situation, there is, however, a tendency to equate topic with the whole of field. Topic, meaning 'the manifest content or referent of speech' (Ervin-Tripp 1973), is treated as a subheading of field on several grounds. First, not glossing field as topic of situation would be more useful to capture the field in situations whereby language is simply accompanying actions. Halliday *et al.* (1964: 90 – 91) point out that 'in the type of situation in which the language activity accounts for practically the whole of the relevant activity, such as an essay, a discussion or an academic seminar, the field of discourse is the subject-matter' and also 'there are on the other hand situations in which the language activity rarely plays more than a minor part; here the field of discourse refers to the whole event'. Second, the fields of some registers are not limited to one single topic. Gregory & Carroll

(1978: 30) note that the fields of discourse such as gossip and casual conversation tend to involve shifts of topics which could be the realization of a dominant field of discourse. The most immediate and significant linguistic implication by topic may be the core vocabulary. Sometimes, a glance at the content words in a text would be sufficient to predict the topic involved. Such a core vocabulary can constitute lexical sets as an index of specific topics.

A further reason why topic is not considered as a synonym of field is that there is at least another dimension we need to consider with field of discourse. This is the dimension of technicality. Taking varieties of English as example, Gregory & Carroll treat technicality as the primary distinction of field:

> An important initial distinction in classifying a language such as English according to field of discourse might be between what are called Technical Englishes and non-Technical Englishes, between, that is, those Englishes in which the field-purposive role correlation so determines the language used that it becomes rather restricted to that role and to those acquainted with it (e. g. the English of Mathematics, Legal English, the English of Linguistics), and those Englishes which are not so restricted. (Gregory & Carroll 1978: 7–8)

These lines of thought are echoed by Eggins (1994: 71), who articulates that 'field varies along a dimension of technicality' and continues to ask for the linguistic implications of the technicality dimension. Eggins (1994: 71–74) thus identifies a technicality continuum of field with technical situation and everyday/commonsense situation as the two poles. This continuum enables her to locate a series of resulted contextual and linguistic continuums (see Table 6–1).

Table 6－1 Technical vs. everyday fields (based on Eggins 1994: 71－74)

Technical situations	**Everyday situations**
assumed knowledge of an activity / institution / area	'common knowledge' (no or little assumed knowledge)
deep taxonomies — detailed sub-classification	shallow taxonomies — limited sub-classification
technical terms — words only 'insiders' understande	everyday terms — words we all understand
acronyms	full names
abbreviated syntax	standard syntax
technical action processes attributive (descriptive) process	identifying processes (defining terms)

There are however some relations between topic and technicality. As observed by Gregory & Carroll (1978: 7), everyday situations have a number of possible related topics such as 'weather', 'health', 'projected holidays', 'current news'; also, the shifts of a sequence of topics as the realization of field are best thought of as an indication of the non-restricted, non-specialist nature of the field.

6.3.2 The values of field and code-switching

Let me now turn to the discussion of the influence of field on the practice of code-switching in the newspapers texts. I shall consider topic and technicality in turn.

The high code-switching frequency in the IT & automobile register is obviously associated with the topics of the registers. Recall an example we have used in the previous chapter, which is repeated here for the sake of convenience.

(1) Awave Audio 可将 MP3、WMA 和 WAV、CD Audio 等转成 RA。[YEN 29/10/2002 C2]
(*Awave Audio* can transform *MP3*, *WMA*, *WAV*, *CD Audio* formats and so on into the *RA* format.)

Example (1) is extracted from a text discussing the transformation between different music formats. If the switched items are singled out (i. e. *Awave Audio, MP3, WMA, WAV, CD Audio, RA*), they will give us a general impression of what the text is about.

Previous studies have shown that topic has an important role to play in language choice or code-switching (Ferguson 1959, Fishman 1965, Blom & Gumperz 1972). According to Blom & Gumperz (1972), switching to another language might have something to do with the change of the topic, or otherwise, changing the language without changing the topic metaphorically reminds the listener of that situation where the topic is involved. The common thread here is that certain topics are more associated with certain languages. While sometimes such association is social convention and can be much value-loaded, in other cases, this is because the knowledge of certain areas, as suggested by the notion 'topic', is mainly developed in a certain language, which makes it more convenient to discuss the knowledge of those areas in that language. Cases in point are IT and Internet with English and food with French. Many languages in the world have accepted quite a few loanwords from these languages in such fields. It follows that more English items, most of which are technical terms, are found in the IT & automobile register. Since we cannot talk about something without referring to it, the technical terms coded in English combine to form lexical sets of the register. The use of English items reflects that this embedded language has some advantages in the concerning areas, IT development and automobile production in the present case, and this embedded language has contributed more notions and concepts to our understanding of these areas of the experiential world. The following example vividly reveals the status of the English language in the IT area.

(2) 问：我的计算机启动时出现了这么的一句话：SMART failure predicted on primary master quantum fireball 1ct10 Immediately back-up your data and replace your hard disk drive A failure maybe imminet [sic.]。我得按 F1 才可进入 windows，不然就进不去。究竟怎么解决呢？ [YEN 29/10/2002 C1]

> (Question: This sentence appears when my computer starts up: *SMART failure predicted on primary master quantum fireball 1ct10. Immediately back-up your data and replace your hard disk drive. A failure maybe imminent.* I have to press F1 to enter Windows. Otherwise, I cannot get in. How can I solve this problem?)

Example (2) is found in the IT section. We have seen a very similar example in the previous chapter (Example (3) in Chapter 5) and there the code-switch was analyzed as a way to trace the experience. Both examples illustrate that the topic of IT is so closely related with English. Although we can use the Chinese operating system, it seems that English is the only choice, if not any computer language, when we need to communicate with the computer outside the Windows system.

Besides the IT & automobile register, other registers also have such English embedded items belonging to specific topics. For example, in the entertainment register, we find *Drum' n' Bass, House, Big Beat*, etc.

Obviously, more topic-related switches take place in the IT and automobile registers than in the entertainment register. Although this is partly because the English language is not so privileged in the field of music as in IT, there is more to field as influencing these code-switching patterns than the discussed topic that I am discussing. In my data, IT texts are usually more technical than texts in the entertainment register; thus, technicality is also a contributing factor.

In my data, there is a text entitled '新法治疗偏头痛' (Xīnfǎ Zhìliáo Piāntóutòng, 'New Solutions to Migraine'), in a section called 'Science'[1] [NCN 21/10/2002 B34 – B35]. The 'migraine' text is of high technicality and such texts are in effect rarely found in the several newspapers that we are focusing on. The technicality of this text has been expressed in its use of deep taxonomies, technical terms, technical processes, and also visual representation used to indicate the mechanism of migraine. The 'migraine' text contains a large number of code-switches, all of which are displayed in Table 6 – 2 except switched proper names.

Table 6 - 2 The switched technical items in the 'migraine' text

偏头痛 migraine
阿尔兹海默症 Alzheimer's disease
神经肽 neuropeptide
降钙素基因相关肽 cgrp [used several times without the Chinese translation after the first appearance]
托吡酯 topiramate
初级头痛 primary headaches
二级头痛 secondary headaches
丛集性头痛 cluster headache
休斯顿头痛诊所 Houston Headache Clinic
脑膜 dura
三叉神经 trigeminal nerve
"阈值" threshold
"导水管周围灰质" periaqueductal gray matter
"舒马曲坦" sumatriptan
"血清素" serotonin
神经递质 neurotransmitter
阿米替林 triptans
瑜伽 yoga
botox (without any Chinese translation)

It is noted that all the code-switches are concerning the core vocabulary of the topic and also deep taxonomies which we as laymen readers do not easily understand even though Chinese translations are provided. The switching of many technical items into English (Table 6 - 2) is also one way of construing, as well as being conditioned by, its high value of technicality. In other words, the technicality is doubly coded both by the use of deep taxonomies and by switching these deep taxonomies into English. The 'migraine' text is a Chinese translation from

English and this can also be one reason for so many code-switches. The code-switches in the text can be seen as the result of the translator's translation procedures such as translation couplets, translation labels, and transcription (Newmark 1981: 75 - 77). However, this is, again, the conditioning of the context: the employment of these translation procedures in dealing with the deep taxonomies still indicates its technicality, and why most of them have been translated into Chinese rather than transcribed is related to other contextual factors such as tenor.

High technicality usually indicates a restricted domain of knowledge and a restricted readership, and hence usually a set of unified taxonomies to facilitate communication between people with different language background. As observed by Gregory & Carroll (1978: 35), such specialized fields often show on one language the influence of another whose culture has been in the vanguard of the activity being verbalized. English as a global language has been serving as such a communication language in many specialized fields. Note that most of the international conferences are held in English and English technical terms are often found even in Chinese journal articles; both these two areas are supposed to involve high technicality. Although the registers of IT & automobile, entertainment, fashion are not technically enough to be regarded as belonging to the technical field and displaying restricted language, they are for those who are supposed to know or to be able to learn that field of activities being verbalized. As far as hard news is concerned, we see a shift of topics as the realization of the dominant fields and an indication of its low technicality. The technicality values of the registers with relation to the code-switching patterns can be summarized by a continuum in Figure 6 - 1.

Figure 6 - 1 shows that we are justified in stating that field, including topic and technicality, is a dimension of the immediate context that has its implications for the practice of code-switching. Note that the cline displayed in Figure 6 - 1 can be very similar to one used to indicate the degrees of association of different topics with the English language. In the present study, the relation between topic and technicality is indicated by their

Figure 6 – 1 Locations of the newspaper registers on the technicality continuum

similar implications for code-switching patterns. This in nature highlights the status of English as an international language and its intrusion into a wide range of knowledge domains.

It seems now quite clear that our discussions here are closely associated with the discussions in Section 5. 2 above, where code-switching is analyzed as employed to trace the experiential world and guard against referential loss or gain. Note that the field-related code-switches discussed here tend to be non-metaphorical code-switches with experiential meanings highlighted (see Section 5. 3 above). This is in line with the argument of Appel & Muysken (1987: 118) that all code-switches related to the topic tend to express referential meaning[2]. In other words, the hypothesis in SFL is confirmed that that part of situation as semiotically summarized by field is responsible for the experiential mode of meanings in semantics. Since we have considered how the switching to English helps to signify the referents in the experiential world more linguistically in Section 5. 2, I shall not plan to repeat the details here.

6. 4 Code-switching and the variable of tenor

Linguistic patterns are influenced by, as well as serving to construe not only the variable of field, but also the variable of tenor as well. This section aims to explore the dialectics between the practice of code-switching and the contextual variable of tenor.

6.4.1 The variable of tenor

Tenor is the variable which deals with the negotiation of the social relationships between the participants involved in interactions. The important role played by interactants in language events is emphasized by Gregory & Carroll (1978: 7-8) when they point out that 'in a general sense they [field, tenor, and mode] are all related to the role being played by the user in the language event'. More specifically, 'field of discourse is the consequence of the user's purposive role...the mode of discourse is the linguistic reflection of the relationship the language user has to the medium of transmission... the relationship the user has with his audience, his addressee(s), is the situational factor that is involved in tenor of discourse' (Gregory & Carroll 1978: 7-8).

One possible way to handle the multifaceted interpersonal relationships is to identify finer dimensions of tenor. Among the studies attempting to spell out the correlation between dimensions of tenor and the linguistic realizations is first of all Brown & Gilman's (1960) well-known study. Brown & Gilman examine the choice of the second person pronouns of address in several European languages such as French and German where there are different choices and they find that the choices are made primarily dependent on power and solidarity, which are elicited to be the two essential dimensions in their model.

There are many discussions on tenor within SFL (see Eggins 1994, Zhang 1998). Hasan (1977) discusses social distance between interactants as one dimension of tenor. She also articulates that of the role of the interactants can be described from three perspectives, i.e. textual role, social role, and participatory role. The first one refers to the role of the interactants as speaker or hearer, changeable during the unfolding the texts; the second one is concerned with roles as a social semiotic, for example teacher/student, vendor/customer and the like; the third one involves the question of who take the part of initiator or respondent[3]. Elsewhere more systematically Hasan (1985: 57) proposes three components of tenor: agent role, control or power, and social distance. Agent role seems to be a reprint of social role in the 1977 version and the dimension of social distance is also kept down. The added dimension of power concerns whether one party of the interaction is able to exercise power upon the other.

Starting from Brown & Gilman's study, Poynton (1985: 76 – 78) however critically argues that three dimensions of tenor rather than Brown & Gilman's two are needed. Specifically, in Poynton's model, Brown & Gilman's power is maintained while solidarity is broken into two separate notions, namely contact and affect. Contact is a social distance or intimacy dimension while affect is created to manage attitude or emotion towards addressee or field of discourse. Poynton's work is incorporated into and developed by Martin's (1992) and Eggins' (1994) studies on tenor.

This very brief review of the relevant studies shows that there is much overlapping between different researchers' classifications. Table 6 – 3 attempts to grasp the rough correspondences between the different systems of tenor although exactness of the correspondences is not claimed.

Table 6 – 3 Systems of tenor compared

Browm & Gilman (1960)	Hasan (1985)	Poynton (1985)
power	power/control	power
solidarity	social distance	contact
		affect
	agent role	

My analysis of code-switching with reference to the variable of tenor will be essentially based on the above reviewed studies. Before embarking on detailed analysis, I believe there are two points that we need to consider.

First, I would be inclined to push affect into the semantic stratum rather than to treat it as a dimension of tenor. There are two reasons for this. One is that both Poynton and Martin recognize that affect might not so independent upon power and contact; there are some systematic relations instead[4]. This means that affect is not so independent a dimension of tenor. The other is that according to Martin (1992: 525), affect is concerned with what Halliday (1978: 33) calls 'degree of emotional charge'; it seems that this aspect of language has been elaborated in the Appraisal system developed by Martin and his colleagues (Martin & Rose 2003; White 2001a, b; also see Section 5. 2. 2. 1 above).

Second, formality has long been recognized as one aspect of context which implies different language features. Eggins (1994: 65) discusses formal and informal situations as a way to bring typical tenor dimensions together. In the present case, I find it convenient and necessary to treat it also as a dimension of tenor to discuss its implications for the uses of code-switching (also see Wang & Huang 2004b).

6. 4. 2 The values of tenor and code-switching

Based on the previous discussions of tenor, I shall discuss code-switching in relation to the subheadings of tenor respectively: (i) social roles, (ii) power, (iii) distance, and (iv) formality.

(i) **SOCIAL ROLES** Participants always take on certain agent roles in communication with other participants. According to Kronrod & Engel's (2001) study on newspapers and my interview with newspaper reporters, different sections are meant for different populations. Hence it is believed that a more specific distinction of the target readers for different registers is highly relevant here. For example, hard news needs to use explicit language and as few as possible English items since the register is targeted at the whole reader population, part of which are Chinese monolinguals; the IT & automobile register on the other hand, uses embedded English jargon to target at IT technicians or amateurs, for otherwise laymen do not share the language habits of using a large number of English jargon. Since as a social being, an individual can take on different social roles, it is sensible to suggest that a reader's social roles keep changing as he or she consumes newspaper texts in different registers. Hence on the other hand, using different code-switching patterns is a way of negotiating involved social roles and construing situation types in terms of interpersonal relations. Recall our analysis of code-switching patterns as indexical features or realization patterns of registers in Chapter 4 above; different social roles would expect different code-switching patterns. These patterns are unmarked as regards the specific registers exactly because they are norms and conventions for these social roles as their target readers (also see Section 5.3 above). It is in this sense that code-switching patterns can be a way of indicating involvement (see Section 5.2.2 above).

(ii) **POWER** I have just considered social roles with special reference to different newspaper registers; it is also possible to look at social roles involved in print media in very general terms: reporters, editors and publishers on the one hand and readers on the other hand. With continuing economic reform, many newspapers now in China have to become self-sufficient and profit-oriented. As other consumables in the market, newspapers need to fight for the readers' attention and win more newspaper buyers. Such pressure is more obvious with the three newspapers that I am looking at since none of them is 'Party newspaper'[5]. In this analysis, readers obtain more power. Accordingly, editors and publishers have to take their target readers' language preference into consideration. If people in their daily life use English to refer to some automobile spare parts, editors or authors of the newspaper texts will follow such language habits (also see Section 5.2.2 above).

Recruiting advertisements, however, are an exception. In this case, the roles more relevant are advertisers as employer, and the readers as potential employee. Usually, the former obtains more power. Sometimes the power has been utilized to reserve the vacancies to those who have a good command of English and to block the access of Chinese monolingual readers to the advertisements by using embedded English texts. Gregory & Carroll's (1978: 61) remark is highly relevant here that tenors have the inclusive and exclusive social functions and they 'mark the boundaries of relationships, of group formations'. The present analysis illustrates that the inclusive and exclusive social functions can be more coherently viewed as the two sides of the same coin. To include the bilinguals at the same time indicates the exclusion of the monolinguals (see Section 5. 2. 2).

(iii) **SOCIAL DISTANCE** Hasan (1977) and Martin (1992) have shown that contact frequency and range of interaction are important factors in deciding the value of social distance. I would like to take a departure from what Hasan and Martin have postulated and try to suggest that the value of social distance is also associated with the degree of similarities in various aspects between the participants on a more abstract level, which can be called 'evaluative or ideological contact' (White 2001a: 4). More specifically, the same origin, common hobbies, or even similar opinions on specific issues are possible candidates of connector serving to reduce the social distance between two participants.

It is then possible to argue that in such registers as IT & automobile and business, the social distances between the editors/authors and the readers are shorter than those in registers such as hard news. The reason is that the former involves a more restricted domain of experience and hence has a more specifically targeted readership; the same interest in IT, finance, or automobile serves as a connector, linking the two parties. These are the registers where more embedded English items can be found, which is one way of understanding Martin's (1992: 531) idea of proliferation and contraction concerning social distance. Martin (1992: 531) holds that from the perspective of system, more contact, more choices available and vice versa; from the perspective of process, less contact means that the expressions need to be more explicit and more contact means that implicity can be more the case. Hence in the registers of shorter distance type, the interactants have one more code at their proposal and at the same time code-switched items are considered to be more implicit than their Chinese counterparts. The present analysis also indicates that the more technical the register is, the more evident will be this tendency. I displayed the locations of different registers on the technicality continuum (see Section 6. 3. 2 and Figure 6 - 1 above) and now let us see how it plays a role in the analysis here. Moving along the continuum to the left end, there will be lower technicality, more social distance, and consequently less code-switching; moving along the continuum to the right end, on the contrary, higher technicality, less social distance, and consequently more code-switching. The discussion of technicality has led us to stray into the variable of field; the nature of the role played by technicality here is a connector to reduce the social distance in the present analysis.

(iv) **FORMALITY** Formality is also a dimension of situation which has important implications for linguistic realizations. Joos (1967) defines five categories of style types according to formality (i. e. intimate, casual, consultative, formal, and frozen). The style types are actually delicate cuts on a cline. Here, I would merely treat formality as a continuum with formal and informal as the two end-points.

Studying the print media in China, Li & Bai (2001: 39 -41) generalize the functions of newspaper discourse in the Chinese context as providing information, propagandizing and educating, organizing people, and offering entertainment. Arguably the functions of propagandizing, educating, and organizing people are highlighted in the register of hard news. As texts of this register are usually meant to propagandize the guidelines and policies of the Party and the governments, the language of these texts should be formal so as to meet the formal and solemn feature of the register. By contrast, registers such as entertainment and fashion are intended to provide entertainments and therefore the informal style can be utilized to highlight the entertaining function. Code-switches seldom occur in formal registers such as hard news but take place frequently in those relatively informal registers such as entertainment and fashion. Formal registers usually witness non-metaphorical code-switches while informal registers witness metaphorical ones. The analysis here is also confirmed by Li's (1996) observation of the code-switching in the Chinese newspapers in Hong Kong.

Generally speaking, there are correspondences between formality and the distribution of power or the social distance, as is noted by Eggins (1994: 65); but it is not necessary that there would always be such correspondences. For instance, the IT & automobile register involves shorter social distance due to their relatively high technicality than registers of entertainment and fashion; but the latter is closer to the informal end on the scale than the former. These values of tenor are expressed in the choices of code-switching patterns: in the former, embedded are usually technical items as non-metaphorical code-switches while in the latter, the code-switches are usually common nouns and adjectives as metaphorical ones (see Section 5. 3 above). This is also the reason why formality is set up as an independent dimension of tenor in the present study.

With regard to the code-switching in advertising, Bell (1991) uses the notion of referee design to explain it. In his study of media language, Bell (1984, 1991) postulates a distinction between audience design and referee design, which correspond with two communicative dimensions respectively, i. e. responsive and initiative. According to Bell, in news reports, with the responsive dimension dominating the discourse, the addresser needs to refer to language conventions and the addressees' language habits, observing the audience design. By contrast, in genres with advertising as the most typical, it is the initiative dimension which takes the dominate role; the advertisers can resort to the language norms of a third party rather than the customers as a strategy to attract customers' attention and interest. Code-switching is such a referee design strategy. The dimension of formality I have been discussing is relevant here. In registers closer to the formal end, text producers are more constrained by social norms of language and thus have less room for creativity; in registers closer to the informal end, text producers are left much more room to 'play with' language to create interesting or even mysterious style, and this includes the use of code-switching.

In this section, I have considered aspects of tenor and discussed their implications on linguistic choices concerning code-switching. It is obvious that the analysis here is closely related to the discussions on the interpersonal metafunction of code-switching in Chapter 5. For example, the headings of social roles and power are pertinent to the involving function of code-switching, with code-switching patterns across different registers highlighted. Also, the formality of the registers is associated with whether metaphorical code-switching tend to occur and thus whether experiential meanings or interpersonal meanings are at stake. In other words, the overall tendency articulated by systemicists is confirmed whereby tenor is the corresponding contextual variable for interpersonal choices.

6.5 Code-switching and the variable of mode

I demonstrated in the previous two sections that contextual factors summarized as field and tenor are relevant to accounting for the code-switching instances in the newspapers. I shall now consider the last variable, that is, the variable of mode.

6.5.1 The variable of mode

The variable of mode refers to the role that language plays in realizing interaction. The most basic and well recognized distinction with regard to mode is that of spoken and written. It has long been generally accepted that spoken and written communications involve very different kinds of linguistic features and strategies. This aspect of language use has been attracting the attention of many scholars (e.g. Akinnaso 1982, Biber 1988, Halliday 1985b, Ong 1982, Stubbs 1980, Tannen 1982). More in SFL terms, the differences between written and spoken modes and their linguistic realizations are summarized in Table 6-4.

It is widely agreed that there is no absolute difference between spoken and written language. In SFL, there are efforts to construe semiotic space of mode to capture its more delicate dimensions and their linguistic implications (e.g. Gregory 1967, Gregory & Carroll 1978, Hasan 1985, Martin 1992).

Gregory & Carroll (1978) summarize some complex and important sub-varieties of medium as in Figure 6-2. This figure succinctly distinguishes between speaking and writing as two different modes while at the same time indicates the permutation of the two with delicate subvarieties.

Table 6 - 4 Spoken and written modes and their linguistic realizations (adapted from Eggins 1994)

	Spoken	**Written**
Situation	interactive, face-to-face	non-interactive, not face-to-face
	language as action	language as reflection
	spontaneous without rehearsal	planning, drafting and rewriting
	informal and everyday	formal and special occasions
Language	turn-taking organization	monologic organization
	context dependent	context independent
	dynamic structure	synoptic structure
	false starts, hesitations, etc.	indications of earlier drafts removed
	everyday lexis	'prestige' lexis
	grammatical complexity	grammatical simplicity metaphor
	lexically sparse	lexically dense

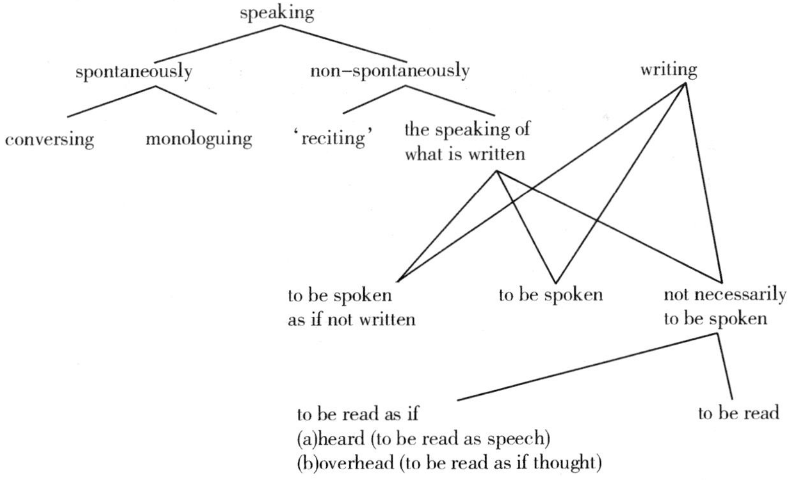

Figure 6 - 2 Permutations of writing and speaking (from Gregory & Carroll 1978)

More systematically, Hasan (1985: 58 - 59) postulates three subheadings of mode (Figure 6 - 3). The first one is the language role (i. e. constitutive or ancillary). This dimension examines whether language is used purely to constitute the activity or to accompany the activity. In other words, it is concerned with the degree to which the verbal activities tend to be self-sufficient. The second subheading is medium (i. e. spoken or written). 'Spoken' and 'written' are meant to be understood as the two poles of a continuum rather than a sharp dichotomy. This can be made more explicit with Hasan's third subheading of mode, i. e. the channel, which refers to the modality via which the text producer comes in contact with the message (i. e. graphic or phonic). Channel is devoted to the description of the physical feature of the message, either marks on paper or noises reaching the ear. Hasan's distinction between the notions of medium and channel is useful in accounting for situations such as 'written to be spoken' in personal letters to a friends and the like. The first two dimensions of mode are viewed as gradient rather than discrete and are indicated in Figure 6 - 3 by bi-directional arrows while the third is more of an either-or case.

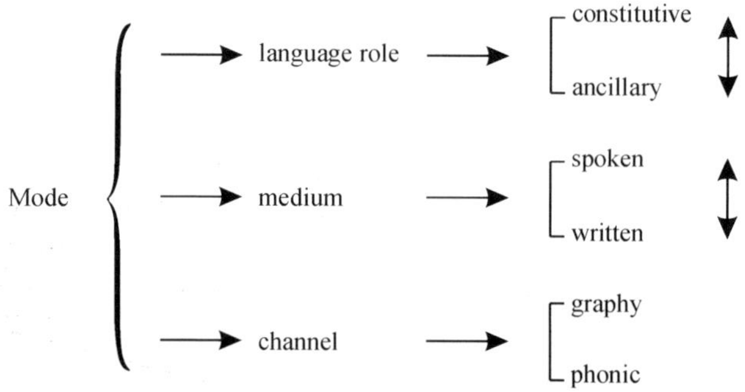

Figure 6 - 3 Three dimensions of mode (based on Hasan 1985)

In discussing mode, Martin argues that as with textual meaning, mode is concerned with symbolic reality and 'since symbolic reality has the function of constructing social reality, mode is oriented to both interpersonal and experiential meaning' (1992: 509). This viewpoint leads Martin (1992: 508–523, also see Eggins 1994: 53–63) to suggest two dimensions of mode which respectively describe two different types of 'distance' in the relation between language and situation, viz. the monologue/dialogue dimension and the action/reflection dimension. The former is concerned with interpersonal distance while the latter with experiential distance. These two dimensions can be viewed as continuums with many sub-categories.

6.5.2 The values of mode and code-switching

Since all the code-switches in my data are collected from print media, the channel of the texts under investigation is homogeneously graphic instead of phonic, and the language role here is constitutive rather than ancillary. However, registers of newspaper texts differ in their medium values and they show some combinations of spoken and written language features; it is this dimension of mode that is most relevant to the practice of code-switching here. As was introduced above, Gregory & Carroll (1978) identify several categories of the permutation of spoken and written. The relevant categories to newspaper texts would be 'written to be spoken' and 'written to be read'. Also, it would be sensible to add another category: writing as the record of spoken. In the case of 'written to be spoken' and 'written to be read', we are considering text of spoken or written mode directly. Indirectly, as Martin (1992: 521) points out, 'their verbalization may itself be experientialized'. This is basically accomplished by projection. For the present analysis, this can be further distinguished into two types. The first one is concerned with 'quote', where a stretch of spoken language is embedded into the written text. The second one is the 'transcription' of whole spoken texts into written ones. In newspapers, 'transcription' is usually the transcriptions of interviews, involving turn-taking. Hence generally the relevant mode values here include:

(I) Written to be read

(II) Written to be spoken
(III) Written as the record of spoken
(i) Quote
(ii) Transcription

These categories are located on different points on the medium continuum (Figure 6 – 4).

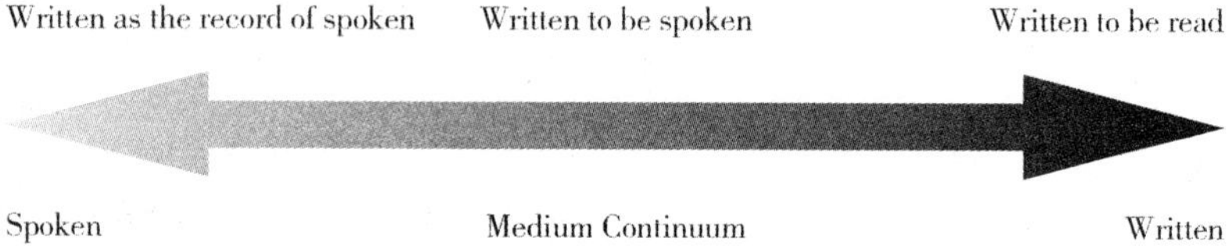

Figure 6 – 4 The medium continuum

The continuum as captured by Figure 6 – 4 is indeed not a delicate one. The category of 'written to be spoken' in effect should be understood as a continuum itself and it may be in some cases very similar to 'written as record of spoken'. My task now is to see whether the code-switching in newspapers are sensitive to these mode values.

Obviously, the newspaper registers locate on different points of the medium continuum. Studying on the orality in Hong Kong Chinese print media, Wu (2000) suggests that there are mainly three forms of orality identified in the written media discourse: (1) question-answer pairs; (2) general emphatics, first person pronouns and second person pronouns; (3) colloquial Cantonese. All these orality forms can be found in collected newspapers in the present study and it is generally observed that these forms have a higher frequency in registers of entertainment, fashion, and some advertisements than in the hard news texts.

It is reasonable to suggest that hard news, especially political news, is considered to have the mode value of 'written to be read' and is closer to the written end of the continuum. Usually registers such as hard news require using formal languages and it is the monolingual norms that tend to prevail

(Li 1996: 42). On the other hand, registers of fashion and entertainment are concerned with 'written to be spoken' mode value and are closer to the spoken end which permits informal use of language, including the alternative use of two codes.

'Written to be spoken' is the type of mismatch between medium and channel that has been discussed with special attention in the literature to date. However, it is useful to suggest that there are other cases where there is also interaction between written and spoken, which is made possible by projection. Many code-switches are found in quotations and transcriptions of interviews, such as in the following examples:

(3) "自《孤男寡女》、《龙在江湖》开始，观众所见到的都是木口木面的刘德华，当时我立下决心，我要观众 Read my mind（看我的头脑）并非我的表情……" [YEN 30/12/2004 B2]
("Since Needing You and A True Mob Story, the audience has been looking at a dead-pan Andy. I made up my mind, I want the audience to *read my mind* (read my mind), but not my countenance.")

(4) "……Fashion 呀，Baby!" [NCN 2/11/2002 B33]
("It's *fashion*, *baby*!")

Although the use of code-switching in some of the above examples is also associated with the identities of the speakers as Hong Kongers, there is no denying that the mode value of 'quote' has a role to play here since the texts that these examples are embedded in are actually of graphic channel. Note that the reporters and the editors opt to quote rather than to report[6] as a treatment of the projected contents. Together with the projected speech, the spoken and informal medium is also projected in the somewhat more written and formal medium of the newspaper texts. In other words, there is projection of the medium of the embedded texts. As Thompson (1996: 206-207) holds, 'the projected paratactic quote does not need to fit in with the projecting clause in Mood, reference, register, dialect, etc'. The fact that more code-switches are found in quotes and transcriptions of spoken texts indicates that with quotes more capable than report in reserving the features of original texts, it is the casual and unprepared features of spoken texts that have been projected into the projecting environment and brought the code-switches from spoken texts into the written ones. Note that all the newspaper texts except advertising are 'reports' of something that has happened in the experiential world, and to a large extent they are manipulated and reconstructed as written texts as what we read in print media.

By far I have been discussing chiefly how the values of medium determine the occurrence of code-switching. It is also noted that our discussions of medium easily lead us into the interpersonal components of texts, especially when I discuss formal and informal languages. Gregory & Carroll (1978: 46) state more explicitly that there are relations between mode and language's interpersonal function by way of personal and functional tenors: formal and written tend to go together as do informal and spoken. Following these lines of thought, it would be natural to suggest that mode can also influence interpersonal semantic choices, including choices concerning code-switching.

More directly related to the spoken medium are some discourse markers such as *ok, by the way*, etc., which are typical features of spoken medium because they are organizing texts as action rather than as reflection (Martin 1992, Eggins 1994). As regards the case of 'transcription' such as the interview with Carol Cheng (see Section 5. 2. 3 above), it was demonstrated that the anaphoric relations between switched items can be established between turns by different speakers, which is concerned with the dialogue rather than monologue feature of texts (Martin 1992: 508–523). These values of mode influence the employment of code-switching as strategies of organizing texts.

6.6 Conclusion

In this chapter, I have been analyzing the practice of code-switching by relating it to the situation types. The analysis has illustrated that the practice of code-switching in different newspaper registers is conditioned by the situation types. The contextual variables (i. e. field, tenor, and mode) with their subcategories have been found to be useful semiotics in accounting for the code-switching instances and the code-switching patterns. The discussions of field, tenor, and mode also correspond to the experiential meanings, interpersonal meanings, and textual meanings of code-switching analyzed in Chapter 5. During the discussions, it is also found that the three variables of situation types are in effect not so separated headings. For instance, the technicality dimension of the situation can be a connector to reduce social distance between participants in verbal activities and hence condition the interpersonal choices. The values of medium are associated with formal and informal aspects of situation and they thus stray into the expression of interpersonal meanings.

Notes

1. Such a 'Science' section rarely appears in the newspapers and hence is not counted as a usual newspaper register in Chapter 4; this treatment however does not intervene in the dialectics between linguistic realizations and context with regard to code-switching.
2. Appel & Muysken's (1987) referential meaning equates roughly to the experiential meaning in SFL.
3. As we can see, the first and the third categories of roles are then almost effaced from Hasan's later discussions of tenor. One possible reason is that these two categories of roles can be more operationally useful with texts of spoken mode than with texts of written mode.
4. For example, Poynton (1985: 78) holds that affect can be marked or unmarked (absent) in discourse and 'whether or not affect is marked will depend on what kind of power and contact choices have been made: in particular, the subordinate in an unequal power relationship is less likely to choose affect than the superior, while in interactions characterised in terms of greatest contact, i. e. intimacy, affect is expected'. Martin (1992: 533) also expresses the same principle with his terminology in saying that 'it [affect] is much more likely to be realized in involved than uninvolved contact situations; and as far as status is concerned, it is more

probable with equal than with unequal status'.

5. With continuing economic reform, newspapers have been told by the governments to become financially self-sufficient. The pressure from marketing is more obvious for those that are not provincial and municipal government newspapers as known as 'Party newspapers'. On the one hand, Party newspapers are usually subscribed to by different levels of governments and administrative institutions and hence have a relatively stable distribution. On the other hand, Party newspapers are still considered the 'voice of the Party,' and they still cannot very well become too commercialized and have less freedom to appeal to general readers. Party newspapers may establish branch papers, weekend editions with separate names, and other offspring, which are allowed more freedom to appeal to readers and sell advertisements. As a matter of fact, NCN can be seen as such a branch newspaper.
6. In simple terms, according to Halliday (1994/2000), one dimension of the interrelationship between clauses is logico-semantic description, which includes expansion and projection. There can be two types of projection, i. e. quote and report, which respond to direct speech and indirect speech in terms of traditional grammar.

7 The Wider Context: Discourse and Code-switching

7.1 Introduction

In Chapter 6 I attempted to discuss code-switching with reference to the configurations of the situation types, where I was only touching upon the inner circle of the context (i. e. the immediate context). In decoding certain meanings of the code-switching, I made use of some 'facts' and 'common sense', whereby, for example, the English language signifies modern, fashionable, and technically-advanced flavours. This chapter goes beyond the situation types to get into the wider socio-cultural context in which the former is embedded, and examines how such signification is made into 'fact' or 'common sense' that then becomes meaning making resources. In the rest of the chapter, I shall first introduce several theoretical concepts which are important in exploring the context of culture such as discourse formation, ideology, and intertextuality. This will be followed by discussions relating the practice of code-switching to several discourses and to some viewpoints that have been naturalized as ideologies in this culture. Code-switching as a value-loaded and ideological practice in this culture will then be considered in relation to the power of English as an international language and to the Chinese/English learned contact situation.

7.2 Language in context of culture

To discuss language with relation to culture, it would be difficult for us to relate language directly to the social context. This calls for an intermediate level of analysis. The register concept has been proved to be a useful notion of such intermediate level; however, its strength lies in the correlation between linguistic forms and factors of the immediate context (i. e. configurations of the context of situation or situation type). In this section I shall introduce the concept 'discourse' or 'discourse formation' as a flexible intermediate construct which can best meet our needs here. This social construct of discourse is particularly useful for illuminating the dialogism in the instantiated texts, which is now more uniformly termed as the principle of intertextuality. With the help of the conceptions of discourse and intertextuality, language use can be discussed in relation to the wider context of culture. Thus, this section is devoted to some more theoretical discussions of discourse, intertextuality, and ideology.

7. 2. 1 Context of culture and discourse

As is implied in the previous section, by using code-switching, people are making use of certain 'facts' or 'common sense' as the meaning making recourses. Focusing on the immediate context of communication only enables us to see these meaning making recourses as neutral 'facts' or 'common sense'; but in order to account for them, a focus on the wider context of culture is needed. As noted by Halliday,

> The context of situation, however, is only the immediate environment. There is also a broader background against which the text has to be interpreted: its CONTEXT OF CULTURE. Any cultural context of situation, the particular configuration of field, tenor, and mode that has brought the text into being, is not just a random jumble of features but a totality — a package, so to speak, of things that typically go together in the culture. People do these things on these occasions and attach these meanings and values to them; this is what a culture is. (Halliday 1985a: 46)

One aspect of language which is often emphasized by

systemicists and other discourse analysts is the dialectical rather than mechanistic relationship between it and social reality including social structures, role relations, situation, etc. This means that on the one hand, as a mode of social action, linguistic interactions presuppose a segment of social reality, and on the other hand, social reality is construed and produced by more specific social actions or linguistic interactions. One implication of the latter aspect is that specific and particular interactions, albeit 'micro' as they are, should never be reduced as merely locally significant; rather, every linguistic interaction contributes to the construction and production of 'macro' realities.

Such exploration is a necessary component of a study on language use in its context and should be regarded as a segment of a unified theory concerning code-switching, if being a sociological issue implies that the issue should be also studied in relation to culture and social values. Regrettably, this aspect of code-switching is much less explored in the code-switching literature to date. There are indeed discussions concerning code-switching in relation to social values and social norms of specific communities and societies. Such discussions, however, are quite loose and unsystematic. By this, I mean the discussions are similar to ours in previous chapters in that social values and ideologies are touched upon as background information. Other research on the spread of English with regard to power and ideology (e. g. Kachru 1985, 1986, 1994; Phillipson 1992) otherwise usually does not come down to detailed analysis of bilingual texts. In considering the practice of code-switching by reference to the context of culture, I share the concern with other researchers (e. g. Fairclough 1995a, b; Fowler 1991; Lemke 1983, 1995, 2002a; Thibault 1989, 1991), who on the one hand explore the socio-cultural context of language events, and on the other hand insist that the discussions of the socio-cultural context should be undertaken through detailed textual analyses.

In several places, I indicated that the notion of register alone may not be enough for our purposes here. Lemke (1985: 279–280) argues that the notion of register, even in its language-relevant typology of situational context, does not capture many of the socially most important kinds of relationship among the texts made in a community, though it does contain elements of a useful theoretical framework for doing so. In the present study, I shall follow Lemke (e. g. 1983, 1985, 1995, 2002) to use discourse formation or simply discourse as a flexible intermediate social construct to meet our needs with a special focus on the wider socio-cultural context (i. e. context of culture). Lemke (1995: 102) uses semiotic formations to describe 'the regular and repeatable, recognizably meaningful, culturally and historically specific patterns of co-deployment of semiotic resources in a community', and uses discourse formations to refer to 'social semiotic formations in which the deployment of linguistic resources is essential to the social meaning of the result'. In other words, networks of semantic relations are built up from the common or similar deployment of the same kinds of lexicogrammatical resources and patterns across different specific texts in the same discourse formations[1]. Discourse formation provides an intermediate level of conceptual analysis between the microsocial utterances and texts and the macrosocial institutions, classes, and ideologies.

The word 'flexible' is used to describe the notion, primarily implying two things. The first one is that there can be a diversity of discourse formations on the basis of different semantic relations. For instance, we have technology discourse, encounter discourse, discourse of teacher-student talk, etc. This means that it is possible to focus merely on one dimension of a set of texts, which are connected with each other precisely by a semantic relation of such a dimension. The second is that such discourse formations can be discussed with a stretch of language of any length. In other words, even particular lexicogrammatical items can activate the discourse formations or other texts with specific semantic relations as the background of the items. It is obvious that this second aspect highlights the principle of intertextuality and dialogism (see Section 7. 2. 2 below).

Discourse as the abstract conception of social practice involves social groups or categories. An important implication is that the values and points of views contained in a certain discourse are in effect value judgments of certain social groups and categories. These value judgments can be naturalized in instantiated texts both by linguistic strategies and by other discourses.

7.2.2 Discourse, intertextuality, and ideology

A specific text is related to certain discourses by intertextual connections. A central assumption of intertextuality is that the meaning of a text depends directly on the kinds of connections made in a particular community between it and other texts (Lemke 1995). The principle of intertextuality makes it possible for a diversity of social discourses to be built into specific texts. Although in Halliday's (1999: 8) model of 'language and context, system and instance' (see Chapter 3 above and Matthiessen 1993) there is no obvious status for such concept as intertextuality, he considers intertextuality as one way of understanding the constructive relation between text and context:

> ... But in fact the relationship between text and context is a dialectical one: the text creates the context as much as the context creates the text. 'Meaning' arises from the friction between the two. This means that part of the environment for any text is a set of previous texts, texts that are taken for granted as shared among those taking part. (Halliday 1985a: 47)

Halliday then continues to call this principle of relating text to its previous texts intertextuality, which he regards as the way of drawing on previous texts as meaning making resources. Although intertextuality is used in quite different ways from that language is used as system and potential, intertextuality is by no means less important than the latter. Intertextuality is an essential principle in demonstrating how the specifics of texts can be related to patterned social meaning making practice and in illustrating social positions of the community members and their ideologies.

The principle of intertextuality is usually traced back to

Bakhtin's (1981) theory of dialogism and heteroglossia. For Bakhtin, the meanings of the utterances do not arise from their pure linguistic forms, but should be from their connectedness with previous meaning making practice in the community. In this way, the utterance always originates in and functions as part of a social dialogue and instantiates the dialogized heteroglossia. Heteroglossia then serves as the basic condition governing the operation of meaning in any utterance. According to Bakhtin (1981: 262–263), the diversity of heteroglossia includes 'social dialects, characteristic group behaviour, professional jargons, generic languages, languages of generations and age group, tendentious languages, language of the authorities, of various circles and of passing fashions, languages that serve the specific sociopolitical purposes of the day, even of the hour', which he calls 'internal stratification' of every language. Bakhtin's varieties of heteroglossia or his social voices are in effect intermediate social construct and are similar to constructs such as registers, genres, and discourse formations. However, for Bakhtin, the notion of heteroglossia is actually a notion of dialogized heteroglossia and his attention is on the dialogism of this heteroglossia in specific utterances or texts. The dialogized heteroglossia of Bakhtin was later articulated more explicitly by J. Kristeva who coined the term 'intertextuality' as now generally accepted.

Intertextuality is first and foremost the connectedness between texts[2]. However, the intertextual relations can be seen not only from the focus on a text to other specific texts, but also from a text to the abstract discourse formations (Lemke 1985: 280–281). This view is in accord with Halliday's idea of viewing language as potential and text as instance (see Section 3.3 and Figure 3–2); it makes the principle of intertextuality more relevant here with the discussion of texts as specific and discourse formations as general.

Feeling that Bakhtin has left the principle of intertextuality or heteroglossia to be further specified and that we need to understand how members of a community read one text against the background of some, and not other, texts to construct its meanings, Lemke (1995: 25) tries to explore different types of semantic relations of discourses. Lemke's early work (1983) chiefly focuses on what he calls 'thematic system', which is used to describe more abstract thematic patterns in texts. Thibault (1989), while accepting Lemke's concept of thematic formation (a later version of 'thematic system'), later traces back to Bakhtin and identifies 'a discursive system of what we commonly refer to as "attitudes", "opinions", "beliefs", and evaluative orientations'. This is the dimension of heteroglossia Bakhtin (1981: 337) terms as 'axiological dimension'. Halliday's (1985a: 47) insight into intertextuality is essentially corresponsive to his principle of metafunctional diversification. These lines of thought are followed by Lemke to develop a rather neat typology of such semantic relations of discourse. His basic argument is that the Hallidayan tripartite semantics are not only made within a text but from text to text as well, and that all meaning is intertextual (Lemke 1995: 41). He then further identifies three types of semiotic formations, viz. thematic, axiological and rhetorical-generic, corresponding the ideational, interpersonal, and textual metafunctions respectively (Lemke 2002).

The notion of discourse and the principle of intertextuality are only useful tools; the aim is to discover the naturalized ideologies in a particular culture. Ideology is a protean notion which has different emphasis for different researchers. According to Lemke (1995), 'the central insight which the concept of ideology tries to sum up is simply this: there are some very common meanings we have learned to make, and take for granted as common sense, but which support the power of one social group to dominate another'. Similarly, Fairclough (1995a: 14) understands ideology as meaning in the service of power and he argues that 'ideologies are propositions that generally figure as implicit assumptions in texts, which contribute to producing or reproducing unequal relations of power, relations of domination'. Starting from K. Marx, Hodge & Kress (1988: 3) articulate that ideology viewed as false consciousness represents the world 'upside down' and in inverted form and that ideology 'also displays an image of the world as it ought to be as seen from the vantage point of the dominant, or from the dominated group'. Such Marxist conception of ideology as 'deliberately misleading system of ideas' (Bottomore & Rubel 1963, cited in Hasan 1996: 133) is deconstructed by Hasan (1996: 133) who sees ideology as a socially constructed system of ideas which appears as if inevitable. Similar to Hasan, I would prefer a less politically radical conception of ideology whereby it is a system of ideas, which community members have learned to produce and make use of, usually as naturalized common sense, which reflects the beliefs and interests of certain groups, societies, nations, political systems, etc., and which underlies social actions including language interactions. Ideology tends to be naturalized and is seen as 'fact' which is simply 'self-evident'. In most cases, such implicit assumptions are working politically for certain groups or classes, but for more cases, whether or not they work politically, these assumptions index the values a community lives by. Such values are ingrained as part of particular cultures.

Ideologies and discourses are meaning making resources in particular cultures and determine the way how meanings are articulated and decoded. They get realized as voices in a variety of instantiated texts. These instantiated texts, on the other hand, by way of integrating the voices, contribute to construing, reproducing, and reinforcing the concerning discourses and naturalize certain discourses into ideologies of particular cultures.

7.3 Code-switching, discourse, and ideology

Texts containing code-switching examples provide a site to explore social heteroglossia. It is not accidental that we recognize some common ground in 'diglossia', a key term in sociolinguistics, and 'heteroglossia', a key term in the studies of discourse. Introducing into a text a stretch of other language is introducing a voice into the text. Hill & Hill (1986, cited in

Myers-Scotton 1993a: 70) base on Bakhtin's theory and argue that 'different languages bring with them different world views or ideologies, which may engage in battle, an engagement in which rules can be broken in order for one voice or another to achieve domination of the dialogue and impose its own point of view'. In this section, by using discourse and intertextuality analysis, I shall try to illustrate what voices have been introduced into specific texts and what ideologies the practice of code-switching serves to maintain. I shall first revisit the expression of evaluative meanings considered in Chapter 5 and the main point is that for the evaluative meanings to be conveyed, there is, in this culture, a conspiracy of certain points of view which are in fact our ideologies that we resort to as meaning making resources. In doing so, I undertake detailed analysis of two advertisements. Then I shall consider the mode of code-switching as quoting the voice of certain discourses.

I deliberately chose advertising texts for analysis because it is a register where the persuasive aspect and the interpersonal component are highlighted (see Zhu & Yan 2001: 40). On the whole, it is felt that the interpersonal component of semantics and interpersonal relationship are more ideologically potent (Hasan, personal communication). The first text for analysis is a real estate advertisement selling villas. The whole text is presented in Appendix V and the most relevant part of the copy is represented below.

(1) The top villas in the world
just you want [sic.]
甲天下别墅园，您真正想要的别墅
美国别墅 本质再版
[YEN 1/10/2003 A11]
(*The top villas in the world*
just what you want
The top villas, the villas you just want
A reprint of American villas)

In Example (1), the embedded English element is followed

by a roughly equivalent Chinese translation (it is actually difficult to decide which is the original, the English or the Chinese). Let me now consider Example (1) with the analytical tools proposed in this chapter. Example (1) as a social practice, involves interplay of different voices. The embedded English has introduced to the text a voice which represents a certain discourse. The membership of a participant in a community is indexed by his or her ability to navigate the network of intertextual relations which are habitual in the community so as to produce and consume specific texts. As members of this society, we are able to read the English element as encoding an international, modern, and fashionable flavour. In more technical terms, the switching to English in Example (1) as the play of voices connect to the internationalization discourse and an axiological discourse formation whereby the American culture and life style or more generally, the western culture and life style are positively valued. For the sake of convenience, I would here call this axiological discourse the better-West discourse.

This analysis can be confirmed by the Chinese sentence that follows: 'a reprint of American villas', where the evaluative meanings are expressed more implicitly, since something that is reprinted is supposed to be simply 'good'. In the copy of this advertisement, the villas are described with expressions such as 世界至佳户型 (shìjiè zhì jiā hùxíng, 'the best layouts in the world') and from the information concerning the prices, it can be seen that roads in the advertised residence block are named 纽约大街 (Nĭuyuē dàjiē, 'New York Avenue'), 圣约翰路 (Shèngyuēhàn lù, 'St. John Road') and 林肯大道 (Línkĕn dàdào, 'Lincoln Road') (see Appendix V). These again activate the internationalization discourse and highlight the better-West discourse.

Compared with other evaluative expressions, code-switching is an implicit one, but no less a forceful one. As a referee design (Bell 1991, also see Section 6.4 above), the embedded English elements quote the voice of a discourse concerning the lifestyle of the west. Quoting this voice in the advertisement as a way to persuade the reader shows that people believe that the American architecture, and usually more generally the Western culture, is good, and implicitly better than the indigenous one. In the data, there are quite a few similar real estate advertisements which resort to code-switching as an evaluative strategy. This confirms that the better-West discourse which is axiological in nature has been accepted as 'common sense' or 'fact' which are then utilized in the meaning making in and through the actualized texts. The reason why it is able to be disguised as 'common sense' or 'fact' is that it has become ideological and has been ingrained into this culture.

Let me now turn to another advertisement for analysis. Example (2) is a trickier one in that it further guises something that is actually ideology into 'fact' to manipulate its readers. This example is a hospital advertisement. The relevant extract is presented below for convenience of analysis; for the whole text, please see Appendix VI.

(2) 诊疗方法：引进国际先进设备美国威视 VISX 准分子激光系统和德国新一代设备爱丽丝 ESIRIS 准分子激光系统，汇集国内知名眼科教授专家，采用 LASIK 术在短时间内治愈近视、远视、散光达国际先进水平…… [GZD 31/10/2002 A27]

(Treatment: introducing the internationally state-of-the-art equipments, the Wēishì[3] *VISX* excimer laser system from U. S. A. and the new-generation Ailìsī *ESIRIS* excimer laser system from German, gathering nationally well-known ophthalmologists, using *LASIK* technology to heal myopia, hyperopia, and astigmatism in short period of time, reaching the world advanced level...)

This is an advertisement where a hospital is selling their medical services. I shall first analyze the code-switches in Example (2) using the method I have suggested in Chapter 5 and 6 above. The advertiser (the hospital) would hope to use the advertisement to promote their products (technology) and persuade customers (patients) to consume their products (receive their treatments). The field can be seen as involving technology. It seems that there is nothing 'special' with this advertisement; the way of using code-switching is exactly what we encounter many times in newspaper reading: switching of nouns, switching of technical terms and very possibly acronyms, switching accompanied by Chinese translations, and non-metaphorical code-switching as I suggested to term in previous analysis. I deliberately chose this 'common' text with an aim to emphasize that some naturalized use of language is in effect an index of our value judgment and a context of culture.

On the other hand, note that the readers of the advertisement are patients or their families and friends rather than doctors or technicians. Neither can it be warranted nor is it necessary that they would understand the embedded items. However, by switching into English, the advertiser is implying that the equipments are really 'internationally state-of-the-art equipments' from Germany and the U. S. A., hence making readers believe that the hospital is providing good treatments. In other words, the ideological function outperforms the literal meanings of the embedded items. Similar to Example (1), as members of this society, we are able to resort to, again, the better-West discourse for interpreting the functions of the code-switching.

Example (2) is trickier in that the pattern of switching technical terms is a way of naturalizing the axiological discourse and hence a particularly effective way in manipulating readers. In Chapter 4 above, it is concluded that switching technical terms into English is one indexical feature of IT reports. With the establishment of intertextual relation to technical discourse, the code-switching is guised as being used merely because of technicality. The introduction of the voice of technical discourse here has naturalized the evaluative meaning of the code-switches I analyzed in the previous paragraph; it is packed as a fact that western technologies are better than those in China, and hence more English jargon is employed. Furthermore, note that the semantic motivation of introducing the voice of technical discourse here is again also an axiological one. As we remember, the readers of Example (2) are patients or their families and friends, rather than technicians or doctors. Chinese monolinguals are to be deflected from the lexical meaning of the English terms to the ideological values associated with the printed form of the language open to them. In other words, the embedded English items can be merely viewed in the same way as other graphical elements in advertising. The English items imply 'westernness' or 'advantageous technology' for some Chinese readers and thus help the advertisers to achieve their marketing purposes.

In the code-switches in Example (1) and Example (2), the English language is associated with fashionable architecture in the former and state-of-the-art technologies in the latter. In either case, the use of English leads to the internationalization discourse, whereby English is naturally connected to internationalization and fashion and the better-West discourse, whereby something from the West is thought as better than something from Beijing or Shanghai. Recall my discussions on the interpersonal meanings of the code-switches in Chapter 5; people in this culture have made use of such value judgment to form connotative semiotics for interpersonal meanings to be expressed. These naturalized ideologies determine the way we encode and decode the meanings concerning the Chinese/English code-switches; meanwhile, they are sustained and reproduced by the actual meaning making practice including the practice of code-switching as in the examples.

Let me now turn to the mode of code-switching *per se*. The practice of Chinese/English code-switching can be seen as the voice of those elites in this culture who are usually Chinese/English bilinguals. A command of English which is a global language is a must for the elites; it is both an important tool for getting well-informed and an essential gateway to better jobs and higher financial and social positions. The relation of the practice of code-switching in print media to the bilingual elite discourse is a natural one when we remember that the code-switching under discussion is one result of the learned contact between Chinese and English.

While quoting the voice of the bilingual elite discourse is far from meaning that the texts will only be consumed by bilingual elites, it does mean that elite is a symbol of better capability, high social positions, more income, etc. and hence positively valued. This ideology ensures the sustaining and reproduction of the bilingual elites discourse. One way for this to be achieved is by quoting the voice of this discourse into many actualized texts.

On the basis of P. Bourdieu's sociological vision whereby language is considered as a form of cultural or symbolic capital which is available to be exchanged in the 'marketplace' of social interaction, Mejía (2002) argues that elite bilingualism can be seen as symbolic resources which receive certain values on the market and the possession of such symbolic resources helps to gain access to valuable social, educational and material resources, which constitute symbolic resources in turn. Forming a circle, the quoting of the voice of this social group enables the group to have access to more resources and obtain more interest. Note that the insertion of English items in the newspaper texts favours the bilingual elites' language capacity rather than the monolinguals'. As a more obvious case, some recruiting advertisements are mainly coded in English, undisguisedly giving the privilege to the bilingual elites. Chinese monolinguals are totally denied such resources. In other words, language is used in a pattern that involves conflict and inequality. The conflict and inequality, as van Dijk (1998: 63) suggests, are characteristically organized in a polarized way, i. e. represented as Us versus Them. The Us versus Them is expressed here by whether an additional language is in hand.

Hence the practice of code-switching as quoting the voice of the elite discourse is ideology-loaded; it sustains and reproduces conflict and inequality, and also the dominance of the elite discourse. In other words, while the dominance of the elite discourse determines the language use in the actual texts, the actual texts by quoting its voice serve to construe and reinforce the elite discourse and the ideology. The two are dialectically linked. We thus see that 'the power of discourse in facilitating and maintaining discrimination against "members" of "groups" is tremendous' (Fowler 1991: 94).

7.4 Code-switching and the power of English

In the last section, I considered the practice of code-switching in the newspapers as quoting the voices of certain discourses. This helped us to see more clearly some ideologies in this culture. Obviously, the discourses and ideologies discussed are associated with the embedded language (i. e. English), which as an international language has an essential role to play. In this section, the practice of code-switching will be located in the context of English spread and be considered by reference to the power of English.

The analysis in the previous section has shown that the English language in China is being looked at as a prestigious one ideologically and sociopsychologically although not statistically or politically. A series of symbolic functions (e. g. internationalization, modernization, fashion, eliteness) are attached to the English language. Such symbolic functions are not only found in the present-day China, but also in other communities as is indicated by Kamwangamalu's (1992) cross-culture study on code-mixing involving English. English gains such symbolic functions from its spread around the world and from being an international language. The increased mobility of products, goods, services, labour, technology, and capital or 'globalization' has a concomitant need for globalized communication. This has resulted in the spread of English. As is noted by Phillipson & Skutnabb-Kangas (1996), 'English is the dominant language of the U. S., the UN, the World Bank, the International Monetary Fund, the Organization for Economic Cooperation and Development, many other world policy organizations, and most of the world's big businesses and elites in many countries worldwide; it is the language in which the fate of most of the world's citizens is decided'. The command of English enables communication with the outside world and participation in a range of fields internationally.

The power of English to connect a nation to the international community is more obvious with the Third World countries which are usually facing pressure of economic development. Kachru (1994) observes that many Expanding Circle[4] countries see the English language as a vehicle for entering the twenty-first century, and that 'even the most anti-Western nations are not reluctant to use English for national development — internal and external reasons conspire in favour of assigning English an important role'. Similar situation is witnessed here in China. It was mentioned in Chapter 1 that China is going to great lengths to promote the learning of English (see Section 1.2 above), which seems to be a natural trend in the pedagogic discourse. On the level of individuals, English learners are looked at as active agent of pragmatism to gain more social resources while on the level of the whole country, the command of English is seen as a way leading to modernization and internationalization (see D. C. S. Li 2002). These stances are highlighted by political discourse on the level of government with regard to issues such as meeting the challenges of entering the World Trade Organization and welcoming the 2008 Olympic Games. Note that this is also the environment whereby the Chinese/English learned contact came about and got intensified. There are hence also pedagogy discourse and business discourse concerning English learning that contribute to naturalizing such stances. In such a context, the discussed discourses and ideologies in the last section are taken for granted and seen as common sense. As Kachru (1986: 124) points out, 'the attitudes towards "mixing" with English provide a good indication for the cross-cultural and cross-language power of English'. In effect, the Chinese/English learned contact situation and the English rush in the present-day China (see Section 1.2 above) are results and evidence of the power of English.

However, it is important to note that modernization and internationalization are only part of English's power. Focusing on the spread of English as an international language in the Outer Circle and Expanding Circle countries, Kachru (1986: 136) recognizes a list of labels representing the power of English.

Table 7 − 1 Labels representing the power of English (from Kachru 1986)

Positive	**Negative**
national identity	anti-nationalism
literary renaissance	anti-native culture
cultural mirror (for native cultures)	materialism
modernization	westernization
liberalism	rootlessness
universalism	ethnocentricism
technology	permissiveness
science	divisiveness
mobility	alienation
access code	

It seems that the Outer Circle countries are more aware of such different labels for the power of English. While it is connected to modernization, technology, mobility, etc., some people in Iran, Pakistan, Nigeria, and India argue that introducing Westernization causes both conscious and unconscious linguicide and dislocation of native cultural tradition, and they see English as a tool of economic exploitation and domination (Kachru 1986: 136). Although in China introducing Westernization will not necessarily and easily cause lingocide or dislocation of native cultural tradition, there is indeed anxiety about the impact of the English language on the Chinese culture and on the national identity (He 2004). Also, we have seen that the practice of code-switching in a general sense indicates a boundary between monolinguals and bilingual elites. This can cause unequal access to resources and thus lead to alienation between social groups.

Furthermore, it should be noted that ideologies are usually ideologies in particular cultures. Kachru (1986) indicates that the symbols of English are different from Circle to Circle. For example,

> In psychological terms, English now has support groups in the Outer Circle which have given it credit for cultural renaissance, spread of nationalism, pan-regional literary creativity, and neutrality. It is due to these psychological reasons that there is a strong emotional attachment to the English language: this type of attachment is unprecedented in the history of language spread. It is interesting that the native speakers of English in the Inner Circle have as yet not recognized the psychological factor. (Kachru 1986: 137)

This quote is important in that it helps us to see that although our attitudes concerning English in this culture are naturalized as common sense, they are only ideologies in this specific culture. The English speaking countries, mainly U. K. and U. S. A., are selling English as a commodity in the international market, which enables them to gain more interests. Promoting English as a global language that can be shared by people from different ethnic backgrounds in international communication in turn helps to keep hold the market. This is where Phillipson' (1992) proposes the concept of linguistic imperialism, which is defined as that 'the dominance of English is asserted and maintained by the establishment and continuous reconstitution of structural and cultural inequalities between English and other languages' (Phillipson 1992: 47).

To return to the issue of code-switching, the practice of code-switching in the newspaper is indexing our attitudes towards English, which are ideologies in this specific culture. They are naturalized in the internationalization discourse and the bilingual elite discourse concerning English as a global language, in the name of 'globalization' and with the power of English. Different practice of quoting the voices of English consciously or unconsciously reinforces the power of English and construes, sustains, and reproduces the different ideologies concerning English in this culture.

7.5 Conclusion

The concern of this chapter has been to relate the practice of code-switching in the Chinese newspaper texts to a wider social context (i. e. context of culture). For this concern, I mainly drew on Lemke's (1983, 1985, 1995, 2002) and Thibault's (1989, 1991) studies, followed the intertextual principle, and used discourse formation as an intermediate construct which mediates language and the wider social context. This has enabled me to relate the practice of code-switching to some discourses and to spell out some ideologies in this context of culture that are being taken for granted. It is found that the practice of code-switching is determined by, as well as construing a context of culture. The use of code-switching to encode evaluative meanings involves the internationalization discourse and the axiological better-West discourse; the mode of code-switching *per se* activates the bilingual elite discourse. The former quotes the voices of internationalization discourse and the better-West discourse whereby English symbols internationalization, modernization, fashion, and so on; the latter serves to give priority to the interests of the elite group over other social groups. These ideologies are naturalized by the power of English as an international language in the context of its spread and are confirmed in the discourses of pedagogy, business, and politics in the present-day China. Relating the practice of code-switching to the wider context of English spread, the study also points out that while the power of the English language leads to modernization and globalization, it is also possible that it can create anxiety of blurred identity and alienation between social groups in the nation.

Notes

1. It is obvious that 'discourse' is used here in a different sense from 'text'. The terms 'text' and 'discourse' are usually used interchangeably in many SFL works (Eggins 1994, Halliday 1994/2000, Martin 1992). This might be because the focus of these studies is primarily on lexicogrammatical realizations and the semantics (termed by Martin as discourse semantics). Thibault (1991: 119) argues that the distinction between 'text' and 'discourse' cannot be adequately

demonstrated if disjoined from social practice. Text is regarded as a product of the social semiotic processes. It is a social site whereby we on the one hand see the specific realizations in lexicogrammatical terms and on the other as an instance of a plurality of social discourses. Text and semantics ('textual meanings' in Thibault's term and 'discourse semantics' in Martin's term) are made possible in and through social discourse which are 'patterned, limited ways of meaning and ways of doing that function both to regulate and deregulate human social activity and the social formation itself' (Thibault 1991: 120). In simple terms, we use 'text' when we focus on the specifics of an interaction and we use 'discourse' when we focus on the patterns and commonality of different texts.

2. In the present study, the notion of intertextuality will be reserved to refer to meaning relations between different texts rather than relations occurring both between portions of a single text and between whole texts as in Lemke's (1985, 1994) sense. While I acknowledge that sometimes it is difficult for researchers to demarcate boundaries of distinct texts, my treatment of the notion is out of two considerations. First, I am using newspaper texts as the demonstrative data and therefore the graphic channel of the texts make it possible to reasonably recognize distinct texts. Second, relations inside a single text have been taken up for analysis in Chapter 5 when we were discussing the textual metafunction of code-switching.
3. I use the *pinyin* system to translate the Chinese characters which are actually transliterations of *VISX* and *ESIRIS*.
4. Kachru (1985) identifies three Concentric Circles of English to represent three types of countries whereby English is used: the Inner Circle (e. g. U. S. A., Britain, Canada, Australia, and New Zealand), the Outer Circle where institutionalized varieties of English are used (e. g. India, Singapore, and Nigeria), and the Expanding Circle, where English is used as a foreign language (e. g. Egypt, Japan, and China). The English teaching in the latter two types of countries are correspondingly called as ESL and EFL (Richards, Platt, & Weber 1985).

8 Conclusions and Implications

8.1 Introduction

In the previous chapters, I characterized the Chinese/English code-switching in the Chinese context and focused on the Chinese/English code-switching examples in several Chinese newspapers published in Guangzhou. For a description and explanation of the practice of code-switching from an inter-organism perspective, I chose to depend on SFL as a theoretical framework. This theoretical framework enabled me to ascertain how the code-switching can be characterized linguistically and how it is conditioned by as well as construing the immediate and the wider contexts. Through these analyses, I am now in a better position to answer the research questions raised at the beginning of this book. I shall first summarize the analyses in the previous chapters and their conclusions. Implications of the study with special reference to language standardization and language planning will then be provided. Finally I shall offer suggestions for future studies.

8.2 A retrospect of the study

This book has set out to investigate the Chinese/English code-switching as social practice in several Chinese newspapers published in Guangzhou, and the analyses have been based on SFL as a theoretical framework. I shall sum up the main points and findings of the present study so as to offer response to the research questions and aims of the study. In the introductory chapter I asked the following research questions:

(1) What are the features of the Chinese/English code-switching in the newspapers?
(2) What functions do the code-switches play in the newspapers?
(3) In what way is the practice of code-switching conditioned by, as well as construing, the immediate and wider contexts in which it is embedded?

To answer the above questions, this book has unfolded the analyses of code-switching across the strata of language, the immediate context, and the wider context in turn.

In Chapter 4 I examined the code-switching in the three Chinese newspapers from a registerial variation perspective in order to tackle the first research question. In my data, the code-switching examples involve intra-clausal, inter-clausal, and textual code-switching. The insertional elements in intra-clausal code-switching include nominal group, adjectival group, verbal group, and preposition. The most frequently found switching type is intra-clausal switching with insertion of nominal group. Since all these English elements occur in the Chinese newspapers, all the code-switching instances can be obviously seen as insertional with Chinese as the matrix language and English as the embedded language on one level; in terms of individual texts, English is the matrix language and Chinese is the embedded one in some recruiting advertisements. It is argued that for a description of the data that highlight intra-clausal and insertional code-switching, a register analysis approach is needed. From this approach, it is found that code-switching does not occur randomly or homogeneously in different newspaper sections. In the hard news register (also used to include sports, health, travelling, and real estate for convenience of reference), code-switching rarely occurs and if there are some English elements inserted, Chinese translations or explanations usually will be provided. The IT & automobile register witnesses a large quantity of code-switches, most of which are technical terms and acronyms. In the business register, many proper names concerning the names of companies, institutions, and brand names are quoted as they are in the English language. Similarly, the titles of many English songs and movies are coded in English in the entertainment register. In this register, there are also some English items concerning the topic of music and what I later termed as metaphorical code-switching indicating fashion and entertainment. In the fashion register (also including shopping and lifestyle), apart from the names of foreign designers and brand names, there are also some metaphorical code-switches encoding a casual and fashionable flavour. Such metaphorical code-switching also occurs in commercial advertising while as regards recruiting advertising, there are some instances whereby the whole texts or the main part of the texts are coded in English. This means that code-switching pattern *per se* can be treated as a linguistic item and its variations across different registers as functional variations can be examined. The code-switching patterns can be viewed as indexical features of different registers.

I suggested in Chapter 3 that the exploration of the functional aspects of code-switching calls for a multifunctional perspective. More specifically I adopted a diversified metafunctional approach for answering the second research question and Chapter 5 used such an approach to examine the functions of code-switching in the newspapers. The analysis illustrates that the code-switches are employed to serve the three metafunctions, with different aspects of code-switching being focused on: in the experiential metafunction, on individual and particular switched items; in the interpersonal metafunction, on the Chinese/English code-switching pattern and its social values; in the textual metafunction, on the contrast between the two languages involved and the locations of the switches in the texts. This means that at least in the language contact situation that this study is examining, a multifunctional perspective on code-switching is needed. Two types of code-switching (i. e. metaphorical and non-metaphorical) are distinguished. Metaphorical switches tend to be represented by adjectives, involve connotative semiotics, and encode interpersonal meanings; non-metaphorical switches, usually in the form of nouns, tend to be responsible for experiential meanings. This pattern is closely related to the Chinese/English contact situation as a learned contact type, which implies that different language contact types can involve different code-switching patterns.

One assumption of SFL is that language is functional in social context and the relation between the two is a dialectical one. The third research question asked how this is made possible with regard to the practice of code-switching and its social context. Chapter 6 and Chapter 7 are two kinds of attempt to answer this question with different focal points on the social context. Concentrating on situation types as the immediate contextual environment for registers, Chapter 6 examined the relation of the practice of code-switching to the variables of situation types (i. e. field, tenor, and mode). Specifically, I considered several subheadings under these three variables: topic and technicality of field, social role, power, social distance and formality of tenor, and medium of mode. The analysis demonstrates that the distribution of code-switching across different registers, including frequencies and the types of the code-switches, is sensitive to the values of the aforementioned contextual variables. The analysis also suggests that there are general correspondences between the field, tenor, and mode on the one hand and on the other hand the experiential metafunction, the interpersonal metafunction and the textual metafunction of the code-switching.

While Chapter 6 focused on the inner circle of the context, Chapter 7 concentrated on the wider context, that is, the context of culture. Chapter 7 complemented Chapter 6 in illustrating that some meaning making practice treated as social norms or common sense in Chapter 5 and Chapter 6 is far from neutral coding of the natural reality; rather, they are dialectically linked to certain ideologies of this particular culture. In Chapter 7, I relied on discourse as an intermediate construct and intertextuality as an important principle to explore the dialectics between the practice of code-switching and the context of culture. It is found that the practice of code-switching is determined by, as well as construing a context of culture. The use of code-switching to encode evaluative meanings involves the internationalization discourse and the axiological better-West discourse, and the practice of code-switching in general activates the bilingual elite discourse. The better-West discourse assumes that something from the West such as technologies and lifestyles are good and implicitly better than the indigenous ones; the bilingual elite discourse positively values Chinese/English bilingualism and serves to give priority to the interests of the bilingual elites over other social groups. The axiological components in these discourses are made used of as meaning making resources and are introduced as voices by the practice of Chinese/English code-switching into instantiated texts to get realized. The practice of code-switching in texts, on the other hand, relying on the power of English as a global language and in the name of globalization, helps to naturalize the axiological discourses into ideologies of this particular culture. The analysis reveals that something we think as facts or common sense is actually ideologies and points of view in this culture. By relating the discussion to the wider context of English spread, I have also pointed out that while the power of the English language, which it gains from its prestigious status as a global language, can lead to modernization and globalization, it is also possible that the power of English causes anxiety of blurred identity and alienation between social groups in this nation.

To sum up, the practice of code-switching in the Chinese newspapers published in Guangzhou cannot be simply reduced as non-standard use of language or examples of language pollution; on the contrary, throughout this book, I have been showing that code-switching is not practiced randomly and that the practice of code-switching is socially and functionally motivated. On the one hand, code-switching displays a patterned occurrence in newspapers, and the functions of the code-switching can be summed up as experiential meanings, interpersonal meanings, and textual meanings, with different aspects of it brought into focus. On the other hand, the forms and patterns of the code-switching data are the results of the present Chinese/English learned contact situation. More semiotically, both the forms and functions of the code-switching are conditioned by, as well as construing the situation types of newspaper registers and this particular context of culture. Since the present study focuses on code-switching as an outcome of bilingualism in its formative stage in a learned contact situation, to which few studies, if any, have paid attention, it can possibly shed new light on the understanding of code-switching.

More theoretically, as one of the initial attempts to introduce SFL into the studies of code-switching, this study has tested the applicability of the theory to bilingual issues. The theoretical categories in SFL (e.g. system, metafunctions, realization and construing, and instantiation and potentiality) are proven to be valid and relevant in analyzing bilingual data. At least for the code-switching instances in the language contact situation that the present study has been examining, SFL has successfully helped to tackle the research questions. Since SFL is a theory concerning language in use, it is natural to suggest that the analytical perspectives offered by SFL in this study are by no means marginal. These include looking at code-switching *per se* as a variable to examine its variation across registers, offering a multifunctional perspective, and discussing the practice of code-switching in relation to the context of culture. The practical applicability of SFL in this study serves as an addition to the growing literature on code-switching.

8.3 From descriptive to prescriptive: Implications for language standardization and language planning

In the introductory chapter, it was stated that the present study is mainly a descriptive and explanative one and that it was hoped that the present study will provide implications for language standardization and language planning. During the book writing, I was often asked by both academic researchers and laymen friends of my attitudes towards code-switching, positive or negative, for or against. Essentially I deem myself as a descriptivist; the task of this book is to characterize the code-switching that is found in the several Chinese newspapers in Guangzhou and to ascertain their conditioning factors, instead of arguing for the pros and cons of code-switching or setting down rules for language use. However, using language for communication always involves language standardization or more broadly language planning. These pertain to two important traditions in linguistic studies, viz. descriptivism versus prescriptivism. According to Crystal's explanation,

> In its most general sense, prescriptivism is the view that one variety of language has an inherently higher value than others, and that this ought to be imposed on the whole of the speech community. The view is propounded especially in relation to grammar and vocabulary, and frequently with reference to pronunciation. The variety which is favoured, in this account, is usually a version of the 'standard' written language, especially as encountered in literature, or in the formal spoken language which most closely reflects this style. Adherents to this variety are said to speak or write 'correctly'; deviations from it are said to be 'incorrect'. (Crystal 1997: 2)

It follows that language might be decaying, deteriorating, or, being polluted if the prescriptive rules fail to be observed. Opposed to prescriptivism is descriptivism. By contrast, a descriptive perspective would aim to record and explain the rules and regularities that languages obey rather than to evaluate language variety or halting language change. In other words, descriptivists notice the factual uses of language and try to explain them rather than set down rules as prescriptivists do. This is because they believe that there is no objective scientific reason for the preference or priority to the 'correct' forms over the 'incorrect' forms although there are social ones. Descriptivism has been one of the important tenets of modern linguistics.

Nevertheless, descriptive and prescriptive viewpoints are in effect not so conflicting as the terms themselves suggest. Between prescriptivism and descriptivism there is a mutual interest in such matters as acceptability, ambiguity, and intelligibility (Crystal 1997: 3). Gregory & Carroll (1978: 93–94) point out that 'there can be nothing but health in prescriptions for how to use language well and effectively if they are based upon sound and thorough descriptions of the appropriate linguistic and situational conditions of the type of text in question'. Since the code-switches discussed are from the print media, which are believed to have the capacity of setting up examples of language use for community members, I would like to consider the Chinese/English code-switching from a prescriptive perspective and briefly discuss the implications of the present study on language standardization.

Since the foundation of the People's Republic of China, the government has inaugurated a series of language policies and language reforms. Many specifications are released aiming at standardization of different aspects of language use, mainly focusing on the standardization of Chinese characters and the promotion of Putonghua. In 2000, the first law concerning language use in China, namely, *Law of the People's Republic of China on National General-purpose Language and Characters* (2000) was passed and became effective from January, 2001. In these specifications, some regulations are concerned with the use of foreign language elements in Chinese texts. For example, according to *Law of the People's Republic of China on National General-purpose Language and Characters*, if foreign languages should be used, there should be corresponding explanations in Chinese. According to the *Temporary Specification of Language Use in Advertising* (State Language Work Committee, 1998), if foreign language elements should be used in advertisements, the main part of the advertisements should be using Putonghua and standardized Chinese characters, with foreign language elements only as complement; two languages cannot be both used in one sentence. Also, as was mentioned in the introductory chapter, some researchers are looking at alternative use of Chinese and English in one text as non-standard language use and as a threat to the pureness of the Chinese language. Since prescriptive studies should first of all base on descriptive and explanative research, the present study has several implications for language standardization and language planning.

First, it is obvious that the aforementioned regulations are far from effective, with many code-switching examples discussed in the present study going against the regulations. In spite of this fact, code-switching cannot be regarded simply as non-standard language use. The analysis demonstrates that as the result of the Chinese/English learned contact situation in the present-day China, the Chinese/English code-switching in the newspapers is practised in a pattern which is more or less acceptable by monolinguals. For example, non-metaphorical code-switches are usually accompanied by Chinese translations and the meanings of metaphorical code-switches can be roughly figured out from the social values of the embedded language and the tones of the registers where the metaphorical code-switches are found (see Section 5. 3. 2). Meanwhile, as Chapters 4, 5, and 6 combine to show, the code-switching patterns in different registers can be seen as a strategy to follow the language preferences of target readers of these registers. Hence, generally speaking, my data indicates that the practice of code-switching might not cause serious communicative problems, which are an important consideration in language standardization. This can be confirmed by the fact that people also keep using code-switching in their daily life, regardless the regulations. What should be pointed out here as a problem is that there are some examples of non-standard use of English in the data (also see Huang 2001: 294 –296). Note that in several examples I used 'sic' to indicate that there are errors or mistakes there. As I repeatedly point out, the Chinese/English contact in this country is a learned one and some people may then follow suit.

Second, in this specific case, many switched item in the data are technical terms, usually in the IT field. These are often the category which makes up certain lexical gaps. Usually, people just use them for the sake of convenience, and providing explanations in Chinese is usually not relevant. This is usually due to the rapid development of modern science and technology, and is concerned with modernization as one aspect of language planning in modern society (Xu, Tao, & Xie 1997: 205). These items can be treated in the same way as other Chinese neologies. We can take a relatively permissive stance and allow the Chinese language to have its say about whether these items can be absorbed into the language system. Indeed the Chinese language has accepted quite a number of such items composed of English letters such as *CPU, CDMA, DNA, DOS* in recent years (see *Dictionary of Modern Chinese* 2002). It is the job of linguists to follow up such expressions and compile them into dictionaries in due course. Authoritative organizations can also provide unified translations of technical terms, which usually turns out to be a tough job (Saraireh 2002, Zhang 2002). The standardization of technical terms has been seen as one important component in language planning, but there are few satisfactory results (Xu, Tao, & Xie 1997: 205).

Third, this study has shown that code-switching is not merely a linguistic issue; rather, throughout the analyses, I have been showing that the practice of code-switching is motivated by social context and associated with social values. Broadly speaking, while the above two points pertain to corpus planning, this last, but not least aspect pertains to status planning, which involves language attitudes (see Daoust 1997, Hu 1993). It has been illustrated in previous chapters that the practice of code-switching has something to do with certain ideologies in this culture. In other words, our attitudes towards the English language play an essential role in the practice of code-switching in this culture and indeed more and more researchers agree that language attitudes are all-important in determining language change (Daoust 1997, Thomason 2001). It is equally important to point out that language policies and language planning are also not ideologically free. As Crystal (1997: 3) points out, 'the prescriptive approach provides a focus for the sense of linguistic values which everyone possesses, and which ultimately forms part of our view of social structure, and of our own place within it'. According to Daoust (1997: 441–445), ideologies involved in language policies and language reforms include linguistic pluralism, linguistic assimilation and nationalism, purism, internationalism, and vernacularization. The language policies concerned in the present-day China can be seen as involving purism, internationalism and the clash between them. On the one hand, learning English which is an international language helps to promote modernization and participation in the world trade and technology. Such a highlight has a constructive relation to the ideologies, as was discussed in Chapter 7. On the other hand, there are nationalist feelings where purism is insisted, that is, there should not be mixing of two languages. The clash between the two makes this aspect of language standardization and language planning a long-term activity. In terms of language standardization and language planning, raising people's language awareness is essential and this calls for the combined efforts of language users and language planners. As far as print media is concerned, it is proposed metaphorical code-switches are ruled out. Similarly, recruiting advertisers can always translate their advertisements into Chinese; why should we need English for intra-group communication (since most of the staff of foreign companies in China are still Chinese)? Linguists and sociologists can inform people that something they are looking at as common sense is simply ideologies, which are simply points of view in this culture, and that we can do better if we make some changes to our point of view. Since the Chinese/ English bilingualism in China is still in its infancy, as I repeatedly point out in this book, before language policies are made, much fact-finding research concerning English (e. g. language functions, the range of its use, language competence, language attitudes, etc.) is needed (see Wang 1999).

8.4 Suggestions for future studies

The present study is one of the first attempts to base on SFL in analyzing code-switching and hence it is basically exploratory. Based on the empirical descriptions and theoretical discussions in this study, there are several suggestions of possible areas that follow-up studies can continue to explore.

First, the present study has chosen to focus on the

variations of code-switching patterns across different newspaper registers. In doing so, I have suspended the differences between the three newspapers. Researchers can examine the variations of code-switching patterns in different newspapers and then ask for the social motivations. Cursory observation reveals that magazines may usually have specialized readership and some magazines in China contain quite a few code-switches. It would be useful to focus on one magazine or one type of magazines to investigate the occurrences of the code-switching. Also, researchers can discuss code-switching in literary works, which can be considered as the language style of the writers or by reference to the themes or motifs of the literary works. In the former case, personal style as idiolect can be seen as the site where the two types of language varieties, (i. e. variation according to use and variation according to user) meet if they are described in more and more delicate terms. In the latter, discussions of code-switching may involve looking at different orders of context.

Second, this study has confined its discussions to code-switching in written mode. Also, few studies have tried to examine Chinese/English code-switching in China in the spoken mode. Different from the present study on public discourse, many conversational code-switching instances (except those in radio discourse) are private. This implies that in talking about tenor, researchers will be able to obtain more specific information than the present author. Also, while spoken code-switching data can involve other approaches such as CA, it might also be a challenge for analysts to base on SFL again for exploration, since SFL has been proven to be also useful in analyzing conversation (e. g. Eggins & Slade 1997). Besides the traditional spoken and written modes, the development of technology today has created for us some other modes of communication. Studies on code-switching in television programs will probably involve multimodal discourse or multimedia semiotics (Lemke 1998, 2002b) and highlight the interaction between code-switching and other semiotic means such as pictures, icons, sounds, animations, etc. CMC is a new area for linguistic studies and it is also a site witnessing the spread of English in the Internet. It would be useful and interesting to investigate code-switching in CMC texts.

Third, In terms of the semogenesis system (see Chapter 3), the present study has focused on logogenesis; I have chosen to focus on one point of history. This is also the aspect most of the code-switching literature sets out to examine. Many other studies which aim to investigate bilingual acquisition might be seen as from an ontogenetic point of view. Few studies, however, have attempted to investigate code-switching from a phylogenetic perspective (e. g. Bentahila & Davies 1995, Ye & Qin 2004). Future studies can investigate the change of code-switching patterns over a period of time, in relation to social change. Halliday points out that linguistic changes 'are also a source of new insights into the nature of cultural change, changes in the reality that each one of us constructs for himself in the course of interaction with others' (Halliday 1978: 163). Since the founding of the People's Republic of China in 1949, there have been many different foreign language policies, closely related to the role China is playing in the international community. Researchers can look at the change of code-switching pattern with different language policies as one way of examining the social changes.

Last but not least, since the three theoretical perspectives (i. e. registerial variation, metafunctional diversification, and context of culture) provided by SFL on code-switching are developed from discussions on this specific Chinese/English language contact situation in the mainland of China, more empirical data from other language pairs in other bilingual situations are needed so as to examine the extent to which such perspectives are pertinent in characterizing code-switching instances. For example, I have ventured to suggest that registerial variation is most relevant to intra-clausal and insertional code-switching. With regard to metafunctional diversification, while the data in the present case call for such a perspective, it is possible that in other bilingual situations, one or two metafunctions of code-switching over the other are highlighted. Then questions arise such as: is there any systematic relation between forms of code-switching and its highlighted metafunction? or, is whether one metafunction is highlighted or not largely determined by the bilingual situation type? and then can SFL provide more detailed and dynamic analytical tools if one metafunction is highlighted? To answer these questions, much more data and theoretical exploration are needed. However this is worthwhile because these are more theoretically orientated questions, which contribute on a larger scale to a coherent view of code-switching and will also shed light on SFL.

8.5 Envoi

In this chapter, I have summarized and discussed the main findings, significance, and implications of this study. Suggestions for future studies are also provided. As has been indicated, code-switching is a multifaceted research topic, involving different language pairs, different language contact situations, and different approaches. With the ever developing mobility and intercultural communication in the modern world, the complicatedness of code-switching is increasing rather than decreasing. This means that this field of study will continue to be open both as a problem shooting area and as a theory testing ground. As for the present study, i. e. a Systemic Functional account of the Chinese/English code-switching as social practice in several Chinese newspapers, I decide that I shall stop here.

References

Adamson, B. 2004. *China's English: A History of English in Chinese Education*. Hong Kong: Hong Kong University Press.

Akinnaso, F. N. 1982. On the differences between spoken and written language. *Language and Speech*, 25: 97–125.

Alfonzetti, G. 1998. The conversational dimension in code-switching between Italian and dialect in Sicily. In Auer, P. (ed.) *Code-switching in Conversation: Language, Interaction and Identity*. London and New York: Routledge, 180–211.

Alvarez-Cáccamo, C. 1998. From 'switching code' to 'code-switching': Towards a reconceptualisation of communicative codes. In Auer, P. (ed.) *Code-switching in Conversation: Language, Interaction and Identity*. London and New York: Routledge, 29–48.

Appel, R. & Muysken, P. 1987. *Language Contact and Bilingualism*. London: Arnold.

Auer, P. 1984. *Bilingual Conversation*. Amsterdam: Benjamins.

Auer, P. 1988. A conversation analysis approach to code-switching and transfer. In Heller, M. (ed.) *Code-switching: Anthropological and Sociolinguistic Perspectives*. Berlin: Mouton de Gruyter, 187–213.

Auer, P. 1995. The pragmatics of code-switching: A sequential approach. In Milroy, L. & Muysken, P. (eds.) *One Speaker, Two Languages*. Cambridge: Cambridge University Press, 115–135.

Auer, P. (ed.) 1998a. *Code-switching in Conversation: Language, Interaction and Identity*. London and New York: Routledge.

Auer, P. 1998b. Introduction: Bilingual conversation revisited. In Auer, P. (ed.) *Code-switching in Conversation: Language, Interaction and Identity*. London and New York: Routledge, 1–24.

Auer, P. 1999. From code-switching via language mixing to fused lects: Toward a dynamic typology of bilingual speech. *The International Journal of Bilingualism*, 3: 309 –332.

Azuma, S. 1993. The frame-content hypothesis in speech production: Evidence from intrasentential code switching. *Linguistics*, 31: 1071 – 1094.

Backus, A. 2000. Review of 'Code-switching in Conversation: Language, Interaction and Identity'. *Journal of Pragmatics*, 32: 831 – 838.

Baker, M. 1992. *In Other Word: A Coursebook on Translation*. London: Routledge.

Bakhtin, M. M. 1981. *The Dialogic Imagination*. Austin: University of Texas Press.

Basic Rules for Hanyu Pinyin Orthography (汉语拼音正词法基本规则, Hanyu pinyin zhengcifa jiben guize). 1996. National standard of People's Republic of China, GB/T 16159 –1996. Beijing: State Education Commission, State Language Work Committee, and the Committee of Hanyu Pinyin Orthography.

Bataens Beardsmore, H. 1982. *Bilingualism: Basic Principles*. Clevedon: Multilingual Matters.

Bell, A. 1984. Language style and audience design. *Language in Society*, 13: 145 –204.

Bell, A. 1991. *The Language of News Media*. Oxford: Blackwell.

Benson, E. J. 2001. The neglected early history of codeswitching research in the United States. *Language and Communication*, 21: 23 – 36.

Benson, J. D. & Greaves, W. S. 1981. Field of discourse: Theory and application. *Applied Linguistics*, 2: 45 –55.

Bentahila, A. & Davies, E. D. 1995. Patterns of code-switching and patterns of language contact. *Lingua*, 96: 75 –93.

Bhatia, T. K. 1989. Bilinguals' creativity and syntactic theory: Evidence for emerging grammar. *World Englishes*, 8: 265 – 276.

Biber, D. 1988. *Variation across Speech and Writing*. Cambridge: Cambridge University Press.

Blom, J. P. & Gumperz, J. J. 1972. Social meaning in linguistic structure: Code-switching in Norway. In Gumperz, J. J. & Hymes, D. (eds.) *Directions in Sociolinguistics*. New York: Holt, Rinehart and Winston, 407–434.

Bloomfield, L. 1933. *Language*. New York: Holt.

Bokamba, E. G. 1989. Are there syntactic constants on code-switching? *World Englishes*, 8: 277–292.

Bolton, K. 2003. *Chinese Englishes: A Sociolinguistic History*. Cambridge: Cambridge University Press.

Bottomore, T. B. & Rubel, M. (eds.) 1963. *Karl Marx: Selected Writings in Sociology and Social Philosophy*. Harmondsworth: Penguin.

Bourhis, R. Y., Giles, H., Leyens, J. P., & Tajfel, H. 1979. Psycholinguistic distinctiveness: Language divergence in Belgium. In Giles, H. & Clair, R. St. (eds.) *Language and Social Psychology*. Oxford: Blackwell, 158–185.

Brown, R. & Gilman, A. 1960. The Pronouns of power and solidarity. In Sebeok, T. A. (ed.) *Style in Language*. New York: Massachusetts Institute of Technology Press, 253–276.

Chan, B. H. S. 2003. *Aspects of the Syntax, the Pragmatics, and the Production of Code-switching: Cantonese and English*. New York: Lang.

Chan, B. H. S. 2004. Hybrid language and hybrid identity: The case of Cantonese-English code-switching in Hong Kong. Paper presented at The International Conference on East-West Identities: Globalization, Localization and Hybridization. Hong Kong: Hong Kong Baptist University.

Chen, E. Q. (陈恩泉) 1994. Lun shuangyu jiaorong guocheng zhong ciyu de guifan (论双语交融过程中词语的规范, 'On the standards of lexicalisation in bilingual contacts'). In Chen, E. Q. (ed.) *Shuangyu shuangfangyan* (Vol. 3) (双语双方言(三) 'Bilingualism and Bidialectism'). Hong Kong: Sinology Press, 16–33.

Chen, X. F. (陈小枫) 2000. Difang baozhang biaoti zhong de yumazhuanhuan chuyi (地方报章标题中的语码转换刍议, 'A preliminary study on code-switching in artical titles in local newspapers'). *Zhongshan renwen xueshu luncong* (中山人

文学术论丛, 'Yat-sen Journal of Humanities'). Gaoxiong: Chinese Department, National Sun Yat-sen Univeristy. 289 – 333.

Cheng, C. C. 1982. Chinese varieties of English. In Kachru, B. B. (ed.) *The Other Tongue: English cross Cultures*. Urbana, I. L.: University of Illinois Press.

Clyne, M. 1987. Constraints on code switching: How universal are they? *Linguistics*, 25: 739 –764.

Clyne, M. 1991. *Community Languages: The Australian Experience*. Cambridge: Cambridge University Press.

Clyne, M. 1997. Multilingualism. In Coulmas, F. (ed.) *The Handbook of Sociolinguistics*. Oxford: Blackwell, 301 – 314.

Crama, R. & van Gelderen, H. 1984. Structural constraints on code-mixing. MA thesis in linguistics, Universiteit van Amsterdam.

Crystal, D. 1997. *The Cambridge Encyclopedia of Language*. (2nd Edition) Cambridge: Cambridge University Press.

Daoust, D. 1997. Language planning and language reform. In Coulmas, F. (ed.) *The Handbook of Sociolinguistics*. Oxford: Blackwell, 436 –452.

de Bot, K. 1992. A bilingual production model: Levelt's speaking model adapted. *Applied Linguistics*, 13: 1 – 24.

de Groot, A. M. B. & Kroll, J. F. (eds.) 1997a. *Tutorials in Bilingualism: Psycholinguistic Perspectives*. Mahwah, N. J.: Lawrence Erbaum Associate.

de Groot, A. M. B. & Kroll, J. F. 1997b. Introduction and overview. In de Groot, A. M. B. & Kroll, J. F. (eds.) *Tutorials in Bilingualism: Psycholinguistic Perspectives*. Mahwah, N. J.: Lawrence Erbaum Associate, 1 – 16.

Dictionary of Modern Chinese (现代汉语词典 (增补本), Xiandai hanyu cidian). 2002. Beijing: The Commercial Press.

DiSciullo, A. M., Muysken, P., & Singh, R. 1986. Government and code-mixing. *Linguistics*, 22: 1 – 24.

Eggins, S. 1994. *An Introduction to Systemic Functional Linguistics*. London: Pinter.

Eggins, S & Slade, D. 1997. *Analyzing Casual Conversation*.

London: Cassell.

Ellis, J. 1966. On contextual meaning. In Bazell, C. E., Catford, J. C., Halliday, M. A. K., & Robins, R. H. (eds.) *In Memory of J. R. Firth*. London: Longman, 79 – 95.

Ervin-Tripp, S. M. 1973. An analysis of the interaction of language, topic, and listener. In Ervin-Tripp, S. M. *Language Acquisition and Communicative Choice*. Stanford: Stanford University Press, 239 –261.

Fairclough, N. 1995a. *Critical Discourse Analysis: The Critical Study of Language*. London: Longman.

Fairclough, N. 1995b. *Media Discourse*. London: Arnold.

Fan, G., Lee, T., Lun, C., Luke, K. K., Tung, P., & Cheung, K. H. 1993. *The Cantonese Romanization Scheme*. Hong Kong: Linguistic Society of Hong Kong.

Ferguson, C. A. 1959. Diglossia. *Word*, 15: 325 –340.

Firth, J. R. 1957. *Papers in Linguistics* 1934 – 1951. London: Oxford University Press.

Fishman, J. A. 1965. Who speaks what language to whom and when? *La Linguistique*, 2: 67 –88.

Fowler, R. 1991. *Language in the News: Discourse and Ideology in the Press*. London & New York: Routledge.

Franceschini, R. 1998. Code-switching and the notion of code in linguistics: Proposals for a dual focus model. In Auer, P. (ed.) *Code-switching in Conversation: Language, Interaction and Identity*. London and New York: Routledge, 51 – 72.

Gafaranga, J. 2000. Medium repair vs. other-language repair: Telling the medium of a bilingual conversation. *The International Journal of Bilingualism*, 4: 1327 –1350.

Gafaranga, J. & Torras, M. C. 2001. Language versus medium in the study of bilingual conversation. *The International Journal of Bilingualism*, 5: 195 –219.

Ge, X. Q. & Ge, S. B. (葛西劝、葛素表) 1996. Dui xinwen yuyan zhong xinciyu yingyong de yidian kanfa (对新闻语言中新词语应用的一点看法, 'Some comments on the use of neologies in news discourse'). *Yuyan jiaoxue yu yanjiu* (语言教学与研究, 'Language Teaching and Research') (2):

143 – 146.

Gibbons, J. 1987. *Code-Mixing and Code Choice: A Hong Kong Case Study*. Clevedon: Multilingual Matters.

Giles, H. & Smith, P. M. 1979. Accommodation theory: Optimal levels of convergence. In Giles, H. & Clair, R. St. (eds.) *Language and Social Psychology*. Oxford: Blackwell, 293 – 308.

Green, D. W. 1986. Control, activation, and resource. *Brain and Language*, 27: 210 –223.

Gregory, M. 1967. Aspects of varieties differentiation. *Journal of Linguistics*, 3: 177 –198.

Gregory, M. & Carroll, S. 1978. *Language and Situation: Language Varieties and their Social Contexts*. London: Routledge & Kegan Paul.

Grosjean, F. 1982. *Life with Two Languages: An Introduction to Bilingualism*. Cambridge, M. A.: Harvard University Press.

Grosjean, F. 1997. Processing mixed language: Issues, findings and models. In de Groot, A. M. & Kroll, J. F. (eds.) *Tutorial in Bilingualism*. Mahwah, N. J.: Erlbaum, 225 –254.

Grosjean, F. 1998. Studying bilinguals: Methodological and conceptual issues. *Bilingualism: Language and Cognition*, 1: 131 – 149.

Gross, S. 2000. Intentionality and the markedness model in literary codeswitching. *Journal of Pragmatics*, 32: 1283 – 1303.

Gumperz, J. J. 1982. *Discourse Strategies*. Cambridge: Cambridge University Press.

Halliday, M. A. K. 1973. *Explorations in the Functions of Language*. London: Arnold.

Halliday, M. A. K. 1978. *Language as Social Semiotic*. London: Arnold.

Halliday, M. A. K. 1979/2002. Modes of meaning and modes of expression: Types of grammatical structure and their determination by different semantic functions. In Allerton, D. J., Carmey, E., & Hodcroft, D. (eds.) *Function and Context in Linguistic Analysis: A Festschrift for William Haas*. / In Webster, J. (ed.) *On Grammar*. London:

Continuum, 196–218.

Halliday, M. A. K. 1985a. Part A. In Halliday, M. A. K. & Hasan, R. *Language, Context and Text: Aspects of Language in a Social-semiotic Perspective*. Geelong, Vic.: Deakin University Press, 1–49.

Halliday, M. A. K. 1985b. *Spoken and Written Language*. Geelong, Vic.: Deakin University Press.

Hilliday, M. A. K. 1985c. *An Introduction to Functional Grammar*. (1st Edition) London: Arnold.

Halliday, M. A. K. 1989/2003. The history of a sentence: An essay in social semiotics. In Bosinelli, R. M. B. (ed.) *Language System and Cultural Systems: Proceedings of the International Symposium on Bologna, Italian Culture and Modern Literature*. University of Bologna. / In Webster, J. (ed.) *On Language and Linguistics*. London: Continuum, 355–374.

Halliday, M. A. K. 1992/2003. Systemic grammar and the concept of a 'science of language'. *Waiguoyu* (外国语, '*Journal of Foreign Languages*') 78. / In Webster, J. (ed.) *On Language and Linguistics*. London: Continuum, 199–212.

Halliday, M. A. K. 1994/2000. *An Introduction to Functional Grammar*. (2nd Edition) London: Arnold. / Beijing: Foreign Language Teaching and Research Press.

Halliday, M. A. K. 1999. The notion of 'context' in language education. In Ghadessy, M. (ed.) *Text and Context in Functional Linguistics*. Amsterdam and Philadelphia: Benjamin, 1–24.

Halliday, M. A. K. 2003. On metaphor in grammar. Lecture given in the 2nd Systemics Week. Guangzhou: Sun Yat-sen University.

Halliday, M. A. K. & Hasan, R. 1985. *Language, Context and Text: Aspects of Language in a Social-semiotic Perspective*. Geelong, Vic.: Deakin University Press.

Halliday, M. A. K. & Matthiessen, C. M. I. M. 1999. *Construing Experience through Meaning: A Language-based Approach to Cognition*. London: Continuum.

Halliday, M. A. K. & Matthiessen, C. M. I. M. 2004. *An*

Introduction to Functional Grammar. (3rd Edition) London: Arnold.
Halliday, M. A. K., McIntosh, A., & Strevens, P. 1964. *The Linguistic Sciences and Language Teaching*. London: Longman.
Halmari, H. 1993. Structural relations and Finish-English code switching. *Linguistics*, 31: 1043 – 1068.
Hasan, R. 1973. Code, register, and social dialect. In Bernstein, B. (ed.) *Class, Codes and Control Vol 2: Applied Studies towards a Sociology of Language*. London: Routledge and Kegn Paul, 253 – 292.
Hasan, R. 1977. Text in the Systemic-Functional model. In W. Dressler (ed.) *Current Trends in Textlinguistics*. New York: Walter de Gruyter, 228 –246.
Hasan, R. 1985. Part B. In Halliday, M. A. K. & Hasan, R. *Language, Text, and Context: Aspects of Language in a Social-semiotic Perspective*. Geelong, Vic.: Deakin University Press, 51 – 118.
Hasan, R. 1989. Semantic variation and sociolinguistics. *Australian Journal of Linguistics*, 9: 221 – 275.
Hasan, R. 1994. Situation and the definition of genres. In Grimshaw, A. D. (ed.) *What's Going On Here: Complementary Studies of Professional Talk*. Norwood, N. J.: Ablex, 127 –172.
Hasan, R. 1996. *Ways of Saying: Ways of Meaning*. Edited by Cloran, C., Butt, D., & Williams, G. London: Cassell.
He, S. J. (何世健) 2004. 'Yingyure' yu wenhua shengfen jiaolü ("英语热"与文化身份焦虑, '"The English rush" and the culture identity anxiety'). Retrieved Jun. 6th, 2004, from http: //lal. szu. edu. cn: 88/research/papers/20041120. htm.
Heller, M. (ed.) 1988a. *Code-switching: Anthropological and Sociolinguistic Perspectives*. Berlin: Mouton de Gruyter.
Heller, M. 1988b. Strategic ambiguity: Codeswitching in the management of conflict. In Heller, M. (ed.) *Code-switching: Anthropological and Sociolinguistic Perspectives*. Berlin: Mouton de Gruyter, 77 –96.
Hill, J. H. & Hill, K. C. 1986. *Speaking Mexicano*. Tucson,

Ariz.: University of Arizona Press.

Hjelmslev, L. 1961. *Prolegomena to a Theory of Language*. Madison, Wisconsin: University of Wisconsin Press.

Hodge, B. & Kress, G. R. 1988. *Social Semiotics*. Cambridge: Polity Press.

Hu, Z. L. (胡壮麟) 1993. Yuyan guihua (语言规划, 'Language planning'). *Yuyan wenzi yingyong* (语言文字应用, 'Applied Linguistics') (2): 11 – 20.

Hu, Z. L., Zhu, Y. S., & Zhang, D. L. (胡壮麟、朱永生、张德禄) 1989. Xitong gongneng yufa gailun (系统功能语法概论, 'A Survey of Systemic-Functional Grammar'). Changsha: Hunan Education Press.

Huang, G. W. (黄国文) 1999. *Yingyu yuyan wenti yanjiu* (英语语言问题研究, 'Explorations in English Language and Linguistics'). Guangzhou: Zhongshan University Press.

Huang, G. W. (黄国文) 2001. *Yupian fenxi de lilun yu shijian* (语篇分析的理论与实践, 'Theory and Practice of Discourse Analysis'). Shanghai: Shanghai Foreign Language Education Press.

Huang, G. W. & Milroy, L. 1994a. Evaluating ways of identifying the matrix language in code-switching utterances. *Newcastle University Studies in Language and Speech*, 5: 1 – 37.

Huang, G. W. & Milroy, L. 1994b. Language choice and code-switching behaviour. *Newcastle University Studies in Language and Speech*, 8: 1 – 41.

Huang, G. W. & Milroy, L. 1995. Language preference and structures of code-switching. In Graddol, D. & Thomas, S. (eds.) *Language in a Changing Europe*. Clevedon: Multilingual Matters, 35 – 46.

Hudson, R. A. 1980. *Sociolinguistics*. Cambridge: Cambridge University Press.

Hyon, S. 1996. Genre in three traditions: Implications of ESL. *TESOL Quarterly*, 30: 693 – 722.

Iedema, R., Geez, S., & White, P. R. R. 1994. *Media Literacy*. Sydney, Disadvantaged Schools Program, NSW department of Scholl Education.

Jake, J. L. 1994. Intrasentential code switching and pronouns:

On the categorical status of functional elements. *Linguistics*, 32: 271 – 298.

Jake, J. L. & Myers-Scotton, C. 1997. Codeswitching and compromise strategies: Implications for lexical structure. *The International Journal of Bilingualism*, 1: 25 – 39.

Jakobson, R. 1953. Results of the conference of anthropologists and linguists. *IJAL* Supplement. Memoir No. 8: 19 – 22.

Jiang, Y. J. 2003. English as a Chinese language. *English Today*, 19 (2): 3 – 8.

Joos, M. 1967. *The Five Clocks*. New York: Harcourt, Brace & World.

Joshi, A. K. 1985. Processing of sentences with intrasentential code switching. In Dowty, D. R., Kattunen, L., & Zwicky, A. M. (eds.) *Natural Language Parsing: Psychological, Computational and Theoretical Perspectives*. Cambridge: Cambridge University Press.

Kachru, B. B. 1978. Code-mixing as a communicative strategy in India. In Alatis, J. E. (ed.) *Georgetown University Round Table on Languages and Linguistics*. Washington, D. C.: Georgetown University Press, 107 – 124.

Kachru, B. B. 1983. On mixing. In Kachru, B. B. (ed.) *The Indianization of English: The English Language in India*. New Delhi: Oxford University Press, 193 – 207.

Kachru, B. B. 1985. Standards, codification, and sociolinguistic realism: The English language in the outer circle. In Quirk, R. & Widdowson, H. (eds.) *English in the World: Teaching and Learning of Language and Literature*. Cambridge: Cambridge University Press, 11 – 30.

Kachru, B. B. 1986. The power and politics of English. *World Englishes*, 5: 121 – 140.

Kachru, B. B. 1994. Englishization and contact linguistics. *World Englishes*, 13: 135 – 154.

Kamwangamalu, N. M. 1989. Code-mixing and modernization. *World Englishes*, 8: 321 – 332.

Kamwangamalu, N. M. 1992. 'Mixer' and 'mixing': English across cultures. *World Englishes*, 11: 173 – 181.

Kamwangamalu, N. M. 1999. The state of codeswitching

research at the dawn of the new millennium (1): Focus on the global context. *South African Journal of Linguistics*, 17: 256 –277.

Kronrod, A. & Engel, O. 2001. Accessibility theory and referring expressions in newspaper headlines. *Journal of Pragmatics*, 33: 683 – 699.

Labov, W. 1972. *Sociolinguistic Patterns*. Philadelphia: University of Pennsylvania Press.

Law of the People's Republic of China on National General-purpose Language and Characters (中华人民共和国国家通用语言文字法, Zhonghuarenmingongheguo guojia tongyong yuyan wenzi fa). 2000.

Lemke, J. L. 1983. Thematic analysis: Systems, structures, and strategies. *Semiotic Inquiry*, 3: 159 –187.

Lemke, J. L. 1985. Ideology, intertextuality, and the notion of register. In Benson, J. D. & Greaves, W. S. (eds.) *Systemic Perspectives on Discourse*. Norwood, N. J.: Ablex. 275 –294.

Lemke, J. L. 1995. *Textual Politics: Discourse and Social Dynamics*. London: Taylor & Francis.

Lemke, J. L. 1998. Multiplying meaning: Visual and verbal semiotics in scientific text. In Martin, J. R. & Veel, R. (eds.) *Reading Science*. London: Routledge, 87 –113.

Lemke, J. L. 2002a. Ideology, intertextuality and the communication of science. In Fries, P. H., Cummings, M., Lockwood, D., & Spruiell, W. (eds.) *Relations and Functions within and around Language*. London and New York: Continuum, 32 – 55.

Lemke, J. L. 2002b. Travels in hypermodality. *Visual Communication*, 1: 299 –325.

Li, D. C. S. 1996. *Issues in Bilingualism and Biculturalism: A Hong Kong Case Study*. New York: Lang.

Li, D. C. S. 1997. Borrowed identity: Signaling involvement with a western name. *Journal of Pragmatics*, 28: 489 –513.

Li, D. C. S. 2001. L2 lexis in L1: Reluctance to translate out of concern for referential meaning. *Multilingua*, 20 (1): 1 – 26.

Li, D. C. S. 2002. Hong Kong parents' preference for English-medium education: Passive victims of imperialism or active agents of pragmatism. In Kirkpatrick, A. (ed.) *Englishes in Asia: Communication, Identity, Power & Education*. Melbourne: Language Australia Ltd, 29–62.

Li, D. C. S. (李楚成) 2003. Xianggang yueyu yu yingyu de yumazhuanhuan (香港粤语与英语的语码转换, 'Code mixing between Hong Kong Cantonese and English'). *Waiyu jiaoxue yu yanjiu* (外语教学与研究, 'Foreign Language Teaching and Research') (1): 13–19.

Li, J. W. (李经伟) 2002. Cong Sikedun de biaoji moshi kan yumazhuanhuan yanjiu de xin fazhan (从司科顿的标记模式看语码转换研究的新发展 'Scotton's Markedness Model and new development in code-aswitching studies'). *Jiefangjun waiguoyu xueyuan xuebao* (解放军外国语学院学报, 'Journal of PLA University of Foreign Languages') (2): 12–16.

Li, J. W. & Chen, L. P. (李经伟、陈立平) 2004. Duowei shijiao zhong de yumazhuanhuan yanjiu (多维视角中的语码转换研究, 'A multidimentional view of code-switching research'). *Waiyu jiaoxue yu yanjiu* (外语教学与研究, 'Foreign Language Teaching and Research') (5): 337–344.

Li, P. 1996. Spoken word recognition of code-switched words by Chinese-English bilinguals. *Journal of Memory and Language*, 35: 757–774.

Li, W. 1998. The 'why' and 'how' questions in the analysis of conversational code-switching. In Auer, P. (ed.) *Code-switching in Conversation: Language, Interaction and Identity*. London and New York: Routledge, 156–176.

Li, W. (ed.) 2000a. *The Bilingualism Reader*. London: Routledge.

Li, W. 2000b. Introduction to part I (Sociolinguistic dimensions of bilingualism). In Li, W. (ed.) *The Bilingualism Reader*. London: Routledge, 59–62.

Li, W. 2002. 'What do you want me to say?': On the conversation analysis approach to bilingual interaction. *Language in Society*, 31: 159–180.

Li, W. & Milroy, L. 1995. Conversational code-switching in a Chinese community in Britain: A sequential analysis.

Journal of Pragmatics, 23: 281 – 299.

Li, W., Milroy, L., & Pong, S. C. 1992. A two-step sociolinguistic analysis of code-switching and language choice: The example of a bilingual Chinese community in Britain. *International Journal of Applied Linguistics*, 2 (1): 63 – 86.

Li, Y. S. & Bai, D. (李元授、白丁) 2001. *Xinwen yuyanxue* (新闻语言学, 'News Linguistics'). Beijing: Beijing Xinhua Press.

Luke, K. K. 1984. Expedient and orientational language mixing in Hong Kong. *York Papers in Linguistics*, 11: 191 – 201.

Luke, K. K. 1998. Why two languages might be better than one: Motivations of language mixing in Hong Kong. In Pennington, M. C. (ed.) *Language in Hong Kong at Century's End*. Hong Kong: Hong Kong University Press, 145 –159.

Lü, D. R., Huang, G. W., & Wang, J. (吕黛蓉、黄国文、王瑾) 2003. Cong gongnengyuyanxue jiaodu kan yumazhuanhuan. (从功能语言学角度看语码转换, A Functional Linguistic approach to code-switching). *Waiyu yu waiyu jiaoxue* (外语与外语教学, 'Foreign Languges and Their Teaching') (12): 6 –10.

Mackey, W. F. 1962. The description of bilingualism. *Canadian Journal of Linguistics*, 7: 51 – 85.

Malinowski, B. 1923. The problem of meaning in primitive languages. Supplement I to Ogden, C. K. & Richards, I. A. (eds.) *The Meaning of Meaning*. New York: Harcourt Brace & World, 296 –336.

Martin, J. R. 1992. *English Text: System and Structure*. Amsterdam: Benjamins.

Martin, J. R. 1997. Analyzing genre: Functional parameters. In Christie, F. & Martin, J. R. (eds.) *Genres and Institutions: Social Processes in the Workplace and School*. London: Cassell.

Martin, J. R. 1999. Modeling context: A crooked path of progress in contextual linguistics. In Ghadessey, M. (ed.) *Text and Context in Functional Linguistics*. Amsterdam and

Philadelphia: Benjamins.

Martin, J. R. & Rose, D. 2003. *Working with Discourse: Meaning beyond the Clause*. London: Continuum.

Maschler, Y. 1994. Metalanguaging and discourse markers in bilingual conversation. *Language in Society*, 23: 325 –366.

Maschler, Y. 1998. On the transition from code-switching to a mixed code. In Auer, P. (ed.) *Code-switching in Conversation: Language, Interaction and Identity*. London and New York: Routledge, 125 –149.

Matthiessen, C. M. I. M. 1993. Registers in the round: Diversity in a unified theory of register analysis. In Ghadessy, M. (ed.) *Register Analysis: Theory and Practice*. London: Pinter, 221 – 292.

Matthiessen, C. M. I. M. 1995. *Lexicogrammatical Cartography: English Systems*. Tokyo: International Language Sciences Publishers.

McArthur, T. 2002. Editor's note to ' Reading, writing, listening and thinking in English'. *English Today*, 18 (2): 46.

Meeuwis, M. & Blommaert, J. 1998. A monolectual view of code-switching: Layered code-switching among Zairians in Belgium. In P. Auer (ed.) *Code-switching in Conversation: Language, Interaction and Identity*. London and New York: Routledge, 76 –98.

Mejía, A. M. de 2002. *Power, Prestige, and Bilingualism*. Clevedon: Multilingual Matters.

Milroy, L. & Li, W. 1995. A social network approach to code-switching: the example of a bilingual community in Britain. In Milroy, L. & Muysken, P. (eds.) *One Speaker, Two Languages*. Cambridge: Cambridge University Press, 136 – 157.

Milroy, L. & Muysken, P. (eds.) 1995a. *One Speaker, Two Languages*. Cambridge: Cambridge University Press.

Milroy, L. & Muysken, P. 1995b. Introduction: Code-switching and bilingualism research. In Milroy, L. & Muysken, P. (eds.) *One Speaker, Two Languages*. Cambridge: Cambridge University Press, 1 – 14.

Moyer, M. G. 1998. Bilingual conversation strategies in

Gibraltar. In Auer, P. (ed.) *Code-switching in Conversation: Language, Interaction and Identity*. London and New York: Routledge, 215 – 234.

Muysken, P. 1995. Code-switching and grammatical theory. In Milroy, L. & Muysken, P. (eds.) *One Speaker, Two Languages*. Cambridge: Cambridge University Press, 177 – 198.

Muysken, P. 2000. *Bilingual Speech: A Typology of Code-mixing*. Cambridge: Cambridge University Press.

Myers-Scotton, C. 1992. Comparing codeswitching and borrowing. *Journal of Multilingual and Multicultural Development*, 13: 19 – 39.

Myer-Scotton, C. 1993a. *Social Motivations for Code-switching*. Oxford: Oxford University Press.

Myers-Scotton, C. 1993b. *Duelling Languages: Grammatical Structure in Codeswitching*. Oxford: Clarendon Press.

Myers-Scotton, C. 1999. Explaining the role of norms and rationality in codeswitching. *Journal of Pragmatics*, 32: 1259 – 1271.

Myers-Scotton, C. 2000. Why bilingualism matters. *American Speech*, 75: 290 – 292.

Myers-Scotton, C. 2002. *Contact Linguistics: Bilingual Encounters and Grammatical Outcomes*. Oxford: Oxford University Press.

Myers-Scotton, C. & Jake, J. L. 1995. Matching lemmas in a bilingual language competence and production model: Evidence from intrasentential code-switching. *Linguistics*, 33: 981 – 1024.

Myers-Scotton, C. & Jake, J. L. 2000. Four types of morpheme: Evidence from aphasia, code switching, and second-language acquisition. *Linguistics*, 38: 1053 – 1100.

Newmark, P. 1981. *Approaches to Translation*. Oxford: Pergamon Press.

Nishimura, M. 1989. The topic-comment construction in Japanese-English code-switching. *World Englishes*, 8: 365 – 377.

Nishimura, M. 1995a. *Japanese/English Code-switching: Syntax*

and Pragmatics. New York: Lang.
Nishimura, M. 1995b. Varietal conditioning in Japanese/English code-switching. *Language Sciences*, 17: 123 – 145.
Ong, W. 1982. *Orality and Literacy*. London: Routledge.
Pfaff, C. W. 1979. Constraints on language mixing: Intrasentential code-switching and borrowing in Spanish/ English. *Language*, 55: 291 – 318.
Phillipson, R. 1992. *Linguistic Imperialism*. Oxford: Oxford University Press.
Phillipson, R. & Skutnabb-Kangas, T. 1996. English only worldwide or language ecology? *TESOL Quarterly*, 30: 429 – 452.
Poplack, S. 1980. Sometimes I'll start a sentence in Spanish Y TERMINO EN ESPAÑOL: Toward a typology of code-switching. *Linguistics*, 18: 581 – 618.
Poplack, S. 2001. Codeswitching (linguistics). In Smelser, N. & Baltes, P. (eds.) *International Encyclopedia of the Social and Behavioral Sciences*. New York: Elsevier, 2062 – 2065.
Poplack, S. & Meechan, M. 1995. Patterns of language mixture: Nominal structure in Wolof-French and Fongbe-French bilingual discourse. In Milroy, L. & Muysken, P. (eds.) *One Speaker, Two Languages*. Cambridge: Cambridge University Press, 199 –232.
Poplack, S. & Sankoff, D. 1984. Borrowing: The synchrony of integration. *Linguistics*, 22: 99 –135.
Poplack, S. & Sankoff, D. 1988. Code-switching. In Ammon, U., Dittmar, N., & Mattheier, K. J. (eds.) *Sociolinguistics: An International Handbook of the Science of Language and Society. Vol.* 2. Berlin: Walter de Gruyter, 1174 –1180.
Poplack, S., Sankoff, D., & Miller, C. 1988. The social correlates and linguistic processes of lexical borrowing and assimilation. *Linguistics*, 26: 47 –104.
Poplack, S., Wheeler, S., & Westwood, A. 1989. Distinguishing language contact phenomena: Evidence from Finnish-English bilingualism. World Englishes, 8: 389 –406.
Poynton, C. 1985. *Language and Gender: Making the Difference*. Geelong, Vic.: Deakin University Press.

Quirk, R. 1985. The English language in a global context. In Quirk, R. & Widdowson, H. (eds.) *English in the World: Teaching and Learning of Language and Literature*. Cambridge: Cambridge University Press, 1 – 10.

Richards, J., Platt, J., & Weber, H. (eds.) 1985. *Longman Dictionary of Applied Linguistics*. Harlow, Essex, England: Longman.

Ritchie, W. C. & Bhatia, T. K. 2004. Social and psychological factors in language mixing. In Bhatia, T. J. & Ritchie, W. C. (eds.) *The Handbook of Bilingualism*. Oxford: Blackwell, 336 –352.

Romaine, S. 1989. *Bilingualism*. Oxford: Blackwell.

Sachdev, I. & Bourhis, R. Y. 1990. Bilinguality and multilinguality. In Giles, H. & Robinson, P. (eds.) *Handbook of Language and Social Psychology*, 293 – 308.

Sankoff, D. & Poplack, S. 1981. A formal grammar for code-switching. *Papers in Linguistics: International Journal of Human Communication*, 14: 3 – 46.

Saraireh, M. A. T. 2002. Inconsistency in technical terminology: A problem for standardization in Arabic. *Babel* 47: 10 – 21.

Schiffrin. D. 1994. *Approaches to Discourse*. Oxford: Blackwell.

Scollon, R. 2000. Generic variability in news stories in Chinese and English: A contrastive discourse study of five days' newspapers. *Journal of Pragmatics*, 32: 761 – 791.

Scotton, C. M. 1976. Strategies of neutrality: Language choice in uncertain situations. *Language*, 52: 919 –941.

Scotton, C. M. 1988. Codeswitching as indexical of social negotiation. In Heller, M. (ed.) *Code-switching: Anthropological and Sociolinguistic Perspectives*. Berlin: Mouton de Gruyter, 151 – 186.

Shin, S. J. & Milroy, L. 2000. Conversational codeswitching among Korean-English bilingual children. *International Journal of Bilingualism*, 4: 351 – 383.

Sridhar, S. & Sridhar, K. 1980. The syntax and psycholinguistics of bilingual code-mixing. *Canadian Journal of Psychology*, 34: 407 –416.

State Language Work Committee. 1998. *Guanggao yuyan wenzi guanli zanxing guiding* (广告语言文字管理暂行规定, 'Temporary Specification of Language Use in Advertising').

Stroud, C. 1998. Perspectives on cultural variability of discourse and some implications for code-switching. In Auer, P. (ed.) *Code-switching in Conversation: Language, Interaction and Identity*. London and New York: Routledge, 321 – 348.

Stubbs, M. 1980. *Language and Literacy: The Sociolinguistics of Reading and Writing*. London: Routledge.

Tabouret-Keller, A. 1997. Language and identity, In Coulmas, F. (ed.) *The Handbook of Sociolinguistics*. Oxford: Blackwell, 315 –326.

Tannen, D. (ed.) 1982. *Spoken and Written Language: Exploring Orality and Literacy*. Norwood, N. J.: Ablex.

Taylor, J. 2002. China's English language push. ABC News Online. November 3th. http: //www. abc. net. au/correspondents/s717371. htm.

Thibault, P. J. 1987. An interview with Michael Halliday. In Steele, R. & Threadgold, T. (eds.) *Language Topics: Essays in Honour of M. Halliday*. Amsterdam: Benjamins, 601 – 627.

Thibault, P. J. 1989. Semiotic variation, social heteroglossia, intertextuality: Thematic and axiological meaning in spoken discourse. *Critical Studies*, 1: 181 – 209.

Thibault, P. J. 1991. *Social Semiotics as Praxis: Text, Social Meaning Making, and Nabokov's Ada*. Minneapolis: University of Minnesota Press.

Thomason, S. G. 2001. *Language Contact*. Edinburgh: Edinburgh University Press.

Thompson, G. 1996. *Introducing Functional Grammar*. London: Arnold.

Thompson, G. & Hunston, S. 2000. Evaluation: An introduction. In Hunston, S. & Thompson, G. (eds.) *Evaluation in Text*. Oxford: Oxford University Press, 1 – 27.

Threadgold, T. 1986. The semiotics of Vološinov, Halliday, and Eco. *American Journal of Semiotics*, 4: 107 –142.

Timm, L. A. 1975. Spanish-English code-switching: El Porqué y how-not-to. *Romance Philology*, 28: 473 - 482.

Ure, J. & Ellis, J. 1977. Register in descriptive linguistics and linguistic sociology. In Uribe-Villegas, O. (ed.) *Issues in Sociolinguistics*. The Hague: Mouton, 197 -243.

van Dijk, T. A. 1998. Opinions and ideologies in the press. In Bell, A. & Garrett, P. (eds.) *Approaches to Media Discourse*. Oxford: Blackwell, 21 - 63.

Wang, D. L. (王东莉) 1999. Waiyu diaocha de biyaoxing he kexingxing (外语调查的必要性和可行性, 'The necessity and feasibility of surveys on foreign languages'). *Yuyan wenzi yingyong* (语言文字应用, 'Applied Linguistics') (1): 11 - 13.

Wang, J. & Huang, G. W. (王瑾、黄国文) 2004a. Yumazhuanhuan zhi jiegou yanjiu shuping (语码转换之结构研究述评, 'A Review of the Studies on the Structural Dimensions of Code-switching'). *Waiguo yuyan wenxue* (外国语言文学, 'Foreign Languages and Literature') (2): 16 -24.

Wang, J. & Huang, G. W. (王瑾、黄国文) 2004b. Yupian jidiao yu baozhang yumazhuanhuan (语篇基调与报章语码转换, 'A tenor analysis of code-switching in newspaper discourses'). *Waiyu jiaoxue yu yanjiu* (外语教学与研究, 'Foreign Language Teaching and Research') (5): 331 - 336.

Wang, J., Huang, G. W., & Lü, D. R. (王瑾、黄国文、吕黛蓉) 2004. Cong huihuafenxi de jiaodu yanjiu yumazhuanhuan (从会话分析的角度研究语码转换, 'A Review of the Conversation Analytic Approach to Code-switching'). *Waiyu jiaoxue* (外语教学, 'Foreign Languages Teaching') (4): 1 - 6.

Wei, L. X. 2002. The bilingual mental lexicon and speech production process. *Brain and Language*, 81: 691 - 707.

Weinreich, U. 1953. *Languages in Contact*. The Hague: Mouton.

White, P. R. R. 2001a. An introductory tour through appraisal theory. Retrieved Mar. 21st, 2002, from http://www.grammatics.com/appraisal/.

White, P. R. R. 2001b. Appraisal: An Overview. Retrieved Mar. 21st, 2002, from http://www.grammatics.com/appraisal/.

World Association of Newspapers. 2003. *World Press Trends*. Retrieved Apr. 16th, 2004, fromhttp://www.wan-press.org/article2825.html.

Woolford, E. 1983. Bilingual code-switching and syntactic theory. *Linguistic Inquiry*, 14: 520–536.

Wu, D. 2000. Orality in Hong Kong print media. In Li, D. C. S., Lin, A., & Tsang, W. K. (eds.) *Language and Education in Post-colonial Hong Kong*. Hong Kong: Linguistic Society of Hong Kong, 81–94.

Wu, D. (吴东英) 2001. Zailun yingyu jieci dui xiandai hanyu cifa de yingxiang (再论英语借词对现代汉语词法的影响, 'The impact of English loanwords upon the morphology of Chinese'). *Dangdai yuyanxue* (当代语言学, 'Contemporary Linguistics') (3): 81–89.

Xu, D. M., Tao, H. Y. & Xie, T. W. (徐大明, 陶红印, 谢天蔚) 1997. *Dangdai shehui yuyanxue* (当代社会语言学, 'Current Trends in Sociolinguistics'). Beijing: China Social Sciences Press.

Yang, T. (杨挺) 1999. Zhiyong yuanwen —— xiandaihanyu wailaiyu yunyong zhong de yige xin qushi (直用原文——现代汉语外来语运用中的一个新趋势, 'Using the original directly: A new tendency of the adoption of foreign words in the modern Chinese'). *Zhongguo yuwen* (中国语文, 'The Chinese Language and Characters') (4): 263–266.

Yang, X. Z. (杨信彰) 2003. Yupian zhong de pingjia shouduan (语篇中的评价手段, 'Evaluative devices in texts'). *Waiyu yu waiyu jiaoxue* (外语与外语教学, 'Foreign Languages and Foreign Language Teaching') (1): 11–14.

Yang, Z. Q. (阳志清) 1992. Lun shumian yumazhuanhuan (论书面语码转换, 'On written code-switching'). *Xiandai waiyu* (现代外语, 'Modern Foreign Languages') (1): 1–6.

Yau, M. S. 1993. Functions of two codes in Hong Kong Chinese. *World Englishes*, 12: 25–33.

Ye, X. L. & Qin, X. B. (叶秀兰、秦秀白) 2004. Guangzhou diqu baokan guanggao de yinghan yumazhuanhuan ji qi chengyin (广州地区报刊广告的英汉语码转换及其成因, 'The code-switching in Guangzhou newspaper advertising discourse and its motivations'). *Huanan ligong daxue xuebao* (华南理工大学学报, 'Journal of South China University of Technology') (6): 13-20.

Yong, D. J. 1985. Some applications of systemic grammar to TEFL, or whatever became of register analysis? In Benson, J. D. & Greaves, W. S. (eds.) *Systemic Perspectives on Discourse*. Vol 2. Norwood, N. J.: Ablex, 282-294.

Yu, G. D. (于国栋) 2001. *Yinghan yumazhuanhuan de yuyongxue yanjiu* (英汉语码转换的语用学研究, 'The Chinese/English Codeswitching as Realization of Linguistic Adaptation'). Taiyuan: Shanxi Education Press.

Yunick, S. 1997. Genres, registers and sociolinguistics. *World Englishes*, 16: 321-336.

Zhang, D. L. (张德禄) 1998. Lun huayu jidiao de fanwei ji tixian (论话语基调的范围及体现, 'On the scope of tenor of discourse and its realization'). *Waiyu jiaoxue yu yanjiu* (外语教学与研究 'Foreign Languages Teaching and Research') (1): 8-14.

Zhang, D. L. (张德禄) 2002. Yulei yanjiu gailan (语类研究概览, 'A general survey of genre analysis'). *Waiguoyu* (外国语, 'Journal of Foreign Languages') (4): 13-22.

Zhang, M. F. (张美芳) 2002. I. T. shuyu hanyi wenti tantao (I. T. 术语汉译问题探讨, 'Issues on translating I. T. technical terms into Chinese'). *Shanghai keji fanyi* (上海科技翻译, 'Shanghai Journal of Translations for Science and Technology') (1): 42-43.

Zhu, Y. S. & Yan, S. Q. (朱永生、严世清) 2001. Xitong gongneng yuyanxue duowei sikao (《系统功能语言学多维思考》 'Reflections on Systemic Functional Linguistics'). Shanghai: Shanghai Foreign Language Education Press.

Appendices

Appendix I Some bilingual section titles

Appendix II Chow Sang Sang's advertisement [YEN 9/10/2003 B2]

Appendix III An advertisement in the IT section [NCN 29/10/2002 C55]

非同一般"闪"给你看

"铃……"下课铃响过，我抱起藏在桌子底下心爱的滑板，飞似地冲出了教室。踩着滑板在人流和车流中自在地穿梭，上坡、下坡，上台阶……想起一会就要跟小伙伴们闪个痛快，我不禁加快了速度。拉风的网眼衫、宽角裤在风中抖擞，挂在胸前的C300手机随我急驰的步伐上下起伏。她宛若一只可爱的精灵，小小的机身随节奏交替变换着三色波光背景灯，盈盈熠熠，绚烂耀眼。

皓子已经来了很久，发现了我胸前这闪烁多变的小玩意儿，不由分说地把玩起来，我知道他平日里就喜爱亮闪闪的东西，夜里时时发亮的荧光吊饰，镶嵌闪片和烤印着ET图案的T—shirt都是他的最爱。看着皓子垂涎倾心的神情，我乐不可支，哈哈，MOTO就是这么抢眼！我趁皓子不注意抢过我的手机，他加足马力，骑着单车在我身后追赶。我轻松地翻动滑板Kick—flip，接着冲上U型板的顶端，他紧跟着回应了我一个180度的急转弯。我们感觉到耳边风声忽忽掠过，尽情享受那飞一样的感觉。看着围过来的小伙伴们羡慕的眼光，按捺不住的冲动与渴望刺激着我继续挑战下一个极限。带着在滑板翻动的瞬间，胸前的C300手机忽然响起，它屏幕上明艳的光芒和按键间闪烁变换的色彩恰到好处的配合了我的动作，让我感觉此刻自己就是最闪的明星。

我们爱闪，因为我们不忍平庸，渴望张扬自我的机会，追求非同一般的生活感受；我们要闪因为我们热衷最FUN的运动，崇尚最IN的理念；我们会闪因为我们是滑板天王、单车至尊或是灌蓝高手；总之，我们身怀非凡闪光之处，我们是这闪亮年代赋予的骄傲——MOTO"闪客"族！

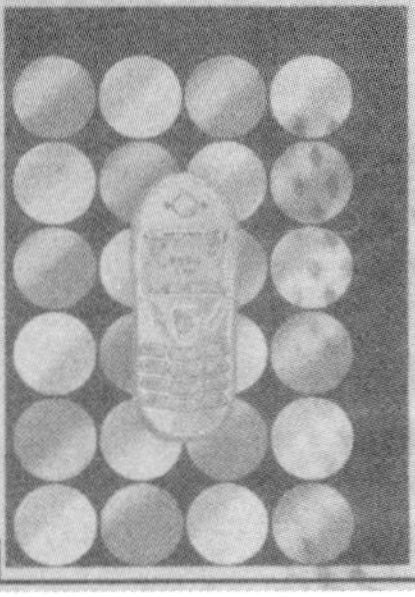

广告

Appendix IV The text ‘Packages have their words to “say”’ [YEN 1/11/2003 C1]

礼品篮

包装有话“说”

送礼物给女友或者朋友，最头疼是在于新意，想好了礼物，包装还是不能马虎。有的商家就专门为此设计出带包装的小礼物，给要送礼的朋友们省下不少心。

小礼物是名副其实的“小”，例如拼图、瓶塞、去水塞等，样式别出心裁。小礼物通常放在玻璃瓶或考纸皮罐里“密封”着，因为都是一些零碎的拼图、漩涡中的小手之类的设计，未拆封之前一般无法知道里面到底藏着什么，有一种保密的意味。

外包装相当简单——居室一些写着字句的招牌式的小卡片，把一些祝福或者表达的情感写在上面：“happy day!”、“I LOVE YOU”，又或者用一些抽象画来含蓄地表达。售价十几元到几十元都有，在年轻人当中相当受落。

图文/曾敏妍

Appendix V　Code-switched 'Top Villas' advertisement [YEN 1/10/2003 A11]

Appendix VI Code-switched ‘hospital’ advertisement [GZD 31/10/2002 A27]

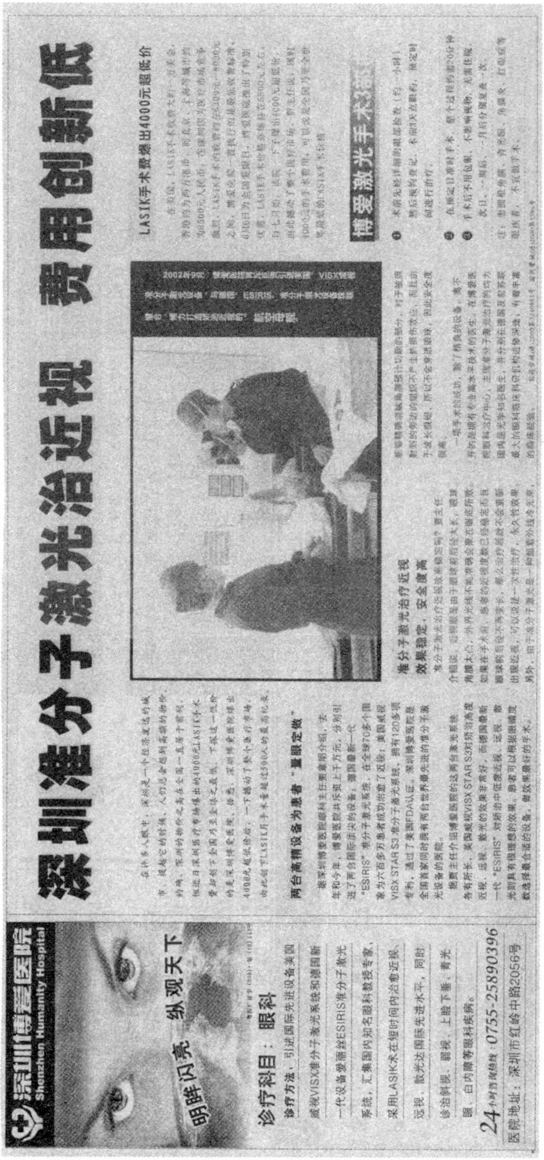